VIOLENT ACTS AND URBAN SPACE
IN CONTEMPORARY TEL AVIV

Jewish History, Life, and Culture
Michael Neiditch, Series Editor

VIOLENT ACTS AND URBAN SPACE IN CONTEMPORARY TEL AVIV

Revisioning Moments

TALI HATUKA

FOREWORD BY DIANE E. DAVIS

UNIVERSITY OF TEXAS PRESS

Austin

The Jewish History, Life, and Culture Series is supported by the late Milton T. Smith and the Moshana Foundation, and the Tocker Foundation.

This project was also supported by Marie Curie Outgoing International Fellowships (OIF, FP6), the Commission of the European Communities.

Requests for permission to reproduce material from this work should be sent to:
Permissions
University of Texas Press
P.O. Box 7819
Austin, TX 78713-7819
www.utexas.edu/utpress/about/bpermission.html

∞ The paper used in this book meets the minimum requirements of
ANSI/NISO Z39.48-1992 (R1997) (Permanence of Paper).

LIBRARY OF CONGRESS CATALOGING-IN-PUBLICATION DATA
Hatuka, Revital.
[Rig'e tikun. English]
Violent acts and urban space in contemporary Tel Aviv : revisioning moments /
Tali Hatuka ; foreword by Diane E. Davis.
p. cm. — (Jewish history, life, and culture)
Includes bibliographical references and index.
ISBN 978-0-292-72882-0
1. Tel Aviv (Israel)—Buildings, structures, etc. 2. Architecture—Israel—Tel Aviv.
3. Architecture and society—Israel—Tel Aviv. 4. Environmental policy—Israel—Tel
Aviv. 5. Architecture and state—Israel—Tel Aviv. 6. Violence—Political aspects—
Israel. 7. Public spaces—Social aspects—Israel—Tel Aviv. I. Title.
NA1478.T45H38 2010
720.95694'8—dc22
                                                                    2009035515

Originally published in Hebrew as *Revisionist Moments: Political Violence, Architecture, and Urban Space in Tel Aviv,* © Resling, 2008.

For Yoav

Contents

Foreword

Travelogues and promotional documents portray contemporary Tel Aviv as a sparkling oasis in a sand-encrusted region of the world, filled with history, culture, and visionary promise. From its modernist architecture to its origin as host to one of the world's most culturally vibrant and politically significant diasporas, Tel Aviv has much to commend. According to a city-authorized website, it was founded by

> a group of people with an extraordinary dream . . . [whose] vision trans-
> formed an area made of sand dunes into the first Hebrew city. They carried
> out their city plan without formalities, in an innovative style that differ-
> entiated it from the past. . . . Today it is a bustling, effervescent metropo-
> lis characterized by an environment encouraging openness, originality and
> freedom of thought.[1]

UNESCO's proclamation of Tel Aviv's White City as a World Heritage site adds to the city's special character, as does its clean and white beaches, warm sea, and hopping nightlife, leading to a similarly robust endorsement: "Put simply, Tel Aviv is where the action is in Israel."[2]

Tali Hatuka's magnificent new book inserts itself directly into these divergent sets of narratives, even as it links them to each other. *Violent Acts and Urban Space in Contemporary Tel Aviv* not only raises questions about what and whose vision persists in contemporary Tel Aviv, or whether the utopian ideals of the city's original founders—not to mention the tradition of planning "without formalities"—still continue to define the place. By addressing the city's historical, architectural, spatial, and urban dynamics, this book also reinforces the sense that Tel Aviv is still where the action is, going one step further to suggest that the latter derives from the former. Nonetheless, for Hatuka the inter-related dynamics of spontaneity, vision, and action, all deeply embedded in the history of Tel Aviv's founding as the first "Hebrew city," do not today translate into the benignly appealing urbanism evident on promotional websites so much as sustain the darker subtext of everyday life in the White City and its larger surrounds. Stated differently, *Violent Acts and Urban Space in Contemporary Tel Aviv* suggests that "the action" that most defines Tel Aviv is not that which is seen in the peaceful and life-affirming activities associated with beaches and nightclubs, but rather, that which is manifest in the outbursts of violent action and reaction that individually and cumulatively pit citizen against state in a vicious cycle of political contestation where episodic destruction of bodies and buildings is the likely outcome.

When I wrote *Urban Leviathan* almost fifteen years ago,[3] I worked in a disciplinary world where most urban scholars tended to use either a local *or* a national point of entry to understand planning, politics, and the built environment of capital cities. I further found that few scholars had explored the connections between local and national domains, or the ways that politics on the city level informed and were informed by politics on the national level. My efforts to expose these lacunae and bridge these domains led one back cover review by Ira Katznelson, himself a leading scholar of urban politics, to highlight the importance of "rethink[ing] the place of cities in relationship to national institutions and practices" while also making "the built environment central to our understanding of political and economic development." Few have accepted this challenge, and even fewer have sought to do so in the context of raging political conflict where the borders of national sovereignty remain under contention. Not Tali Hatuka. *Violent Acts and Urban Space in Contemporary Tel Aviv* jumps squarely into the fray, presents a no-holds-barred approach to the city and the local-national nexus that frames its urban development, and comes up triumphant as the leading interpretive source of material on Tel Aviv and its built-environmental significance in the Palestinian-Israeli conflict.

By identifying "violence and the struggle over resources, territory, and capital among groups as part of the city's history," and by linking certain aspects of this history and struggle to the founding of the city and the nation as well as to the social and spatial exclusion of Arab populations, Tali Hatuka lays a foundational argument for how and why Tel Aviv has become a notable site of power and conflict in the struggle between Israelis and Palestinians. Her claims set this book apart from conventional understandings of the Israeli national space, by virtue of the focus on Tel Aviv rather than Jerusalem, and will undoubtedly start a much larger debate over whether and why Tel Aviv may be just as important to the country's larger narrative identity as Jerusalem, despite the fact that the latter is now claimed as the site of Israel's capital. To be sure, Jerusalem has attributes that will always place it squarely in the midst of the conflict, both spatially and symbolically. Its physical situation within— and more recent expansion beyond—the green line, as well as longstanding efforts by multiple parties to claim Jerusalem as a capital city, will continue to make that holy city the lightning rod for the Palestinian-Israeli conflict. But such characteristics have allowed scholars, diplomats, and urban planning practitioners to "exceptionalize" Jerusalem as the main—if not a singularly emblematic—contested site of a larger political struggle, while treating the physical terrain of all other significant Israeli cities, including Tel Aviv, as more or less normalized in conflict terms.

Violent Acts and Urban Space in Contemporary Tel Aviv will put to rest this false dichotomy, giving us the methodological tools to find the source and meaning of nationalist conflicts in the everyday built environment of Tel Aviv, despite the surface appearances otherwise. In that sense, *Violent Acts and Urban Space in Contemporary Tel Aviv* actually offers a "spatially revisionist" account of the Palestinian-Israeli conflict, if you will, an account that is given life not just through the selection of Tel Aviv as the site of study, but also by the author's intra-urban spatial deconstruction of the city as a series of con-tested sites in which borders, neighborhoods, and other spaces define social inclusion and exclusion, ethnic conflict, and reconciliation (or its absence).

In its magisterial sweep, this book brings together a series of literatures, disciplines, and debates that are rarely combined in a single narrative. As an account of the built environment, space, and urban planning in a particu-lar city, *Violent Acts and Urban Space in Contemporary Tel Aviv* offers a new methodology for understanding national politics and its relationship to the Habermasian-conceived "everyday life world" of cities. Its framing is robust enough to inspire further methodological attention to the city-nation nexus, even though the book can stand on its own as a case study of a single city. As one of the few scholarly books focused on Tel Aviv, it gives a grounded sense of how this city's urban, political, and social history have laid the foundation for the social and spatial production of an "infrastructure" of violence; yet we also find within its pages a loftier epistemological aim: to link the social and spatial sciences together in ways that remind the reader that all power is embedded in control over space. And although many of the arguments made in this book will make architects and urban planners ask themselves difficult questions about the nature of their profession and the ways that city-building practices crafted to produce positive change may also reinforce a vicious cycle of destruction, there is plenty in this narrative to suggest that no one design or plan, or citizen response, is singularly responsible for the collectively produced traumatic practices and routines of violence that flourished in the urban environment of Tel Aviv.

Last but not least, this is a book that examines how and why violence becomes a central means of either challenging or reinforcing both national and local power dynamics. As such, it speaks to scholars of nation-building, state formation, and political resistance as much as to those concerned with urban order, city planning, and citizen participation. In these regards, the methodology and analytical framing are also instructive for many of us who are studying violence in other conflicts, whether in more "garden variety" settings like Mexico, where I tend to focus my sights, or in civil war settings like Iraq, where the problematic relationship between violence and nation-building is depressingly clear. Even so, there are few lessons here for those who think that the road to peace in Tel Aviv, Israel, or beyond can be built either through national and international diplomatic efforts or with the im-plementation of new urban plans. Rather, the subtext of this book seems to be that the entire cycle of construction and deconstruction, combined with the continual jockeying for national political power through struggles over the control of space, both have to stop. After reading *Violent Acts and Urban Space in Contemporary Tel Aviv* it is hard to avoid the conclusion that violence only begets violence, whether it comes from "above" or "below," and whether it is enacted through buildings or bodies. This is a book not for the faint of heart, or even just for the bold in spirit. It is for the emancipated of mind who recognize that conventional practices, assumptions, and appropriations of space in most modern urban and national environments rarely lead to posi-tive outcomes, particularly in intractable conflict settings. This is a book for those willing to consider a call to jettison old techniques and practices in the search for what might really constitute a "new" urbanism,[4] and who might join in collective scholarly pursuit of what exactly that might be.

DIANE E. DAVIS
Cambridge, Massachusetts
November 2008

Preface

Violence in Israel-Palestine is a daily reality, an ongoing struggle that expresses grief and causes grief, expresses pain and creates more pain. After the confrontations, we count the dead on both sides as if this were a measurement of sorrow, destruction, or anguish. Israelis and Palestinians always refer to key dates of wars—after 1967, before 1948. War dates, lines on maps, the green, the red, and the blue are all there in the individual and collective minds of both groups, concrete pain and abstract representations that fuel the engine of an unceasing war. But sad as it is, the reality of violence is one of the ways Israelis and Palestinians encounter each other, communicate, and modify space. Violence is a way of confronting each other to be able to respond to, amend, and revise the differing concepts of homeland.

In this conflicted reality, it seems rather paradoxical to be an Israeli architect and planner in a profession that promotes construction, buildings, and hopes. But in the Israeli context, being in this profession also carries the responsibility of examining the morality of environment defined by boundaries, inequalities, and injustice. Often, when I am asked what it means to be an architect or planner in this context, I am hesitant. How can one explain that, in spite of the ongoing conflict, urban reproduction continues as usual in Israel? How can one explain that many Palestinian workers participated in the construction of Israeli settlements in the West Bank? This paradox and other such contradictory forces of separation and integration between Israeli and Palestinian territories constantly redefines the 1967 borders, and also redefines the life of people in cities throughout Israel and Palestine. These paradoxes, studied in depth by scholars like Ariella Azoulay and Adi Ophir, Meron Benvenisti, Leila Farsakh, Lev Grinberg, Rashid Khalidi, Ilan Pappe, Juval Portugali, Edward Said, and others, refers to the *implicit relationships* of the two people—defined (in *Implicate Relations* by Juval Portugali) as *that which implies that the two nations contain each other, exist inside each other, and cannot evade the reality of coexistence*—is difficult to explain in simple terms to those who insist on seeing the situation in black and white.

Over the last decade, many scholarly articles and books in urban studies and planning have addressed the complex relationship between occupation and planning, between the separation wall and the cumulative grief and injustices inflicted by the Israelis on the Palestinians. These studies have underscored the reality of the political role of planning and architecture—suggesting how it is used and recruited to control the West Bank and Gaza. These significant studies by Jeff Halper, Eyal Weizman and Rafi Segal, Michael Sorkin, Haim Yacobi, and Oren Yiftachel, to name a few, help create awareness of the political complexity of architecture and planning in Israel, forcing many professionals to consider their actions and decisions more carefully. While most of these studies raise the issue of territorial occupation—what Israel as a nation is doing to the Palestinians—my intention is to try to understand what is happening in Israel, to us as a society on the streets of Tel Aviv, and to understand in particular how the acts of violence and the discourse about violence affect the reproduction of space. In a sense, then, this book is the unabridged answer to the question of what it means to be an architect and planner in Tel Aviv.

I can trace the beginnings of this search to my studies at the Technion, the Israel Institute of Technology, in Haifa in the early 1990s, where I gained professional skills but little understanding of the society in which we live or the context in which we operate. Perhaps this explains why the studies and the atmosphere were enthusiastic, detached from any political reality, keenly embracing postmodern architecture. We played with forms, influenced by Frank Gehry, Peter Eisenman, Bernard Tschumi, and others. It was fun, but it was empty. We realized this fact but lacked the tools to do something about it. Our teachers, raised in a modernist culture, crafted the Israeli landscape and were themselves happy to embrace postmodern architecture as a sort of salvation from modernism's rigidity. It took me several years of practice and many years of study abroad to give words to my thoughts. I have never doubted the significance of the profession or its role, but I began to question whether the field, as practiced in Israel, could make a positive contribution to society. Working in an architect's office in Tel Aviv in the mid-1990s, exposed to the daily suicide bombings in the city, on one hand, and the misery of the Palestinians, on the other, only accentuated my need to understand the whole situation "better." But the political and social element was missing in architectural practice and yet was present in full force in daily reality.

Back in the 1990s, two societies were battling daily, but the discourse was absent from professional life. This has changed in recent years, since scholars have reinforced the social and political dimensions of the profession, but we still have a long way to go to fully grasp the impact of the Israeli/Palestinian conflict on cities. With all the particularities of the case, this reality is not unique to Israel or Palestine. Conflicts, violence, and suicide bombings occur today in many places throughout the world. By understanding how violence shapes the process of urban reproduction, I hope we can understand the implications of the conflict's effect on our daily lives. By understanding this everyday environment, I hope we can reassess the role of urban professionals in these conflicted times.

Acknowledgments

Most of the ideas on the following pages are the fruits of my Ph.D. dissertation at the Technion Institute of Technology, Haifa, Israel. My first thanks goes to Professor Rachel Kallus, my Ph.D. advisor, for her guidance, support, and wisdom throughout our long journey. I would like to thank the Technion for funding this research throughout my Ph.D. studies and the Sapir Fund and Blaban Glass Research Fund in Israel. The completion of the book was only possible due to the support of the European Commission (EC) FP6 Marie Curie OIF program, which funded my research at MIT and allowed me to complete this book.

I am also appreciative of the support of the Department of Urban Studies and Planning at MIT, which hosted me for three and half years as a Fulbright Post-doctoral Fellow and as a Marie Curie Fellow. In particular, I am indebted to Professor Diane Davis for her intriguing ideas, her insights, and her amazing hospitality. Also, I want to thank Professor Lawrence Vale for his good advice and for inspiring me to address issues of social and spatial importance.

My deepest appreciation goes to Marilyn Levine, who has meticulously read, suggested better words, and proofread the manuscript.

Some of these chapters have appeared in earlier versions: Parts of Chapter 3 appeared in the *Journal of Architectural and Planning Research* 26/3 (2009): 198–212. Certain ideas articulated in this book were explored in articles I wrote with Professor Rachel Kallus: in the *Journal of Planning Perspectives*, volume 21 (January 2006): 23–44; the *Journal of Architectural and Planning Research* 24, no. 1 (2007): 23–41; and the *Journal of Architectural Education* 61, no. 4 (2008): 85–94.

From different archives in different countries, my research benefited from the help of many others. I thank the Zionist Archive in Jerusalem, the Archives of the Israel Defense Forces, the Public Record Office (U.K. National Archives), the Palestine Exploration Fund in London, and especially Felicity Cobbing, St. Anthony's Middle East Centre in Oxford, and, in particular, the wonderful staff of the Tel Aviv Municipal Archives, Ziona Raz, Neli Varzarevski, and Rivka Preshel-Gershon, for their great assistance and professionalism.

VIOLENT ACTS AND URBAN SPACE
IN CONTEMPORARY TEL AVIV

Political Violence and the City

Sunday, July 11, 2004, 7 a.m. An earsplitting noise rouses me from my bed. Ambulance sirens invade the room. I stand at the window and watch the crowd gathering, standing, running, looking lost in the commotion, shifting the landscape of the street. Policemen in grey and blue uniforms are running too, trying to disperse the crowd. The buzz of a helicopter adds to the chaos. A policeman is now closing off the street with red and white plastic tape; nearby some ambulances offer emergency assistance to the injured. I can only watch. The telephone rings, I pick up the receiver. It is my family, confirming that I am at home, that I am okay. Yes, I answer, it happened here at the end of the street. I hang up and turn on the radio. The announcer informs us that the temperature is rising; it is going to be very hot. He does not announce the events taking place outside my window; that will take a few more minutes. My mind wanders. I am thinking about the people who waited at the bus stop, standing in the blazing sunlight on Har-Zion Boulevard. A new noise joins the general tumult—some trucks are unloading paving stones. The City Council is renovating the pavement on our street, the result of a long negotiation between the neighborhood committee and the Council. The crooked pavement makes the dense everyday traffic in the area intolerable. The radio is now telling everyone to stay away from the area. I will stay at home today. I make myself coffee and go to my study, to write. The voices and sounds of war, death, street renovation, and everyday life are all mixed together in one continuous violent and clashing negotiation that modifies and designs our environment. And the architects? They make plans. And daily life? A non-stop negotiation of construction and destruction.

At this point the radio continued broadcasting from the site of this event. Words of war such as *violence, aggression, hostility, nationalism, bloodshed,* and *destruction* were voiced in concert with words of heartache such as *pain, fear, memory, scars, wounds,* and *death.* Broadcasters, eyewitnesses, government administrators, and police were all searching for the right words to describe the event and explain its meaning. But how can we begin to understand arenas of violence? Where do we start—with the personal scarred body[1] or with an unveiling of the ideology of the national body, the generator and political manipulator of violent events?[2] This tension between the personal and the national is familiar to Israelis and Palestinians alike. It is apparent in the private domain and in the public arena that it is not merely a locus where violent events take place but is a catalyst, a symbol. The violent events and the arena where they occur—the concrete and the cognitive sacred public spaces—are the departure points for discussion in this book. The intention is to try to understand the relationship between the occurrence of violence and the spaces where violence occurs.

Although most people are aware that the Israeli reality is fueled by violence, most of us have difficulty defining the violence, per se—partly because violence takes many different forms in modern society—that is, institutional violence, psychological violence, and physical violence. Therefore, let us start by clarifying the term. According to *The Concise Oxford Dictionary of Politics,* violence is the exercise of physical force so as to inflict injury on, or cause damage to, persons or property. This definition does not refer to psychological abuse or attack, does not include animals or objects that could be exposed to violence, and assumes a direct connection between attacker and attacked.[3] A more inclusive definition was suggested by sociologist Johan Galtung: that, in addition to direct violence, there are forms of structural violence by individuals or social institutions that use either physical or psychological force.[4] However, we need to ask, particularly in the political arena, under what circumstances are acts of violence morally justified? When is it legitimate for a country to oppress a population in the name of authority? When is resistance by the oppressed legitimate? In order to answer these questions, we need to acknowledge that currently the nation-state is the monopolizer of a "legitimate" use of power. When citizens challenge this legitimacy through their own acts of violence, the State immediately brands the violence as negative, evil, civil disobedience.

From within the wide range of definitions of violence, I choose to focus in this book on political violence in Israel as a form of contentious politics— contentious because the participants make claims that affect each other's interests,[5] politics because relations of participants to governments are at stake. Like other national struggles, the Israeli-Palestinian case is circular. The nation-state oppresses and occupies another nation's territory and violates its interests. Citizens, in turn, use political violence against the oppressor. The nation-state responds harshly, increasing urgency and fear among its citizens, creating social camaraderie among citizens, on the one hand, and economic sanctions and violent action against the oppressed nation, on the other. When public opinion advocates the notion of the "external collective enemy" it prevents political mediation, concession, and compromise, as noted by Lev Grinberg.[6] This state of affairs accelerates extreme emotions of hatred on both sides and encourages many to volunteer for resistance against the oppressor, and the whole cycle of violence re-commences.

As a result, this conflict shifts constantly between what Charles Tilly names as *coordinated destruction* and *broken negotiations*. *Coordinated destruction*[7] takes place when persons or organizations specializing in the deployment of coercive means undertake a program of damage to persons and/or objects. Examples include war, self-immolation, some kinds of terrorism, and genocide. *Broken negotiations*[8] are forms of collective action that aim to generate resistance or rivalry, to which one or more parties respond by actions that damage persons and/or property. Examples include demonstrations, government repression, and military coups. The two forms are connected, as it often happens that the threat of force exacerbates conflict. When these forms of violence are repeated, violence becomes a ritual.[9]

This ritualistic violence occurs not simply along one straight path but rather in a jagged, unpredictable trajectory of eruptions. As Hannah Arendt reminds us,[10] violence always has an element of arbitrariness, which is why it is unpredictable. Predictions of the future are no more than projections of present automatic processes and procedures.[11] Setting the violent (unexpected) act within its concrete socio-physical context illuminates the city's configuration as a complex, dynamic, changing entity. Thus, it is extremely difficult to calculate the consequences of the violent act on everyday life. But we know for sure that the trajectory of violence disrupts, invades, and intersects with the mundane trajectory of daily life and that this juxtaposition encourages us to see the city as a dynamic entity that adjusts itself according to social pressures, political ideology, and urban planning ideas.

To clarify this juxtaposition, we offer the term *revisioning moments*. This concept refers to actions of people exposed to violent acts. These actions can be understood to be a form of mediation or recovery from the violent events, actions that aim at repairing or improving space, whether physical or imagined. As we see with Germany's unification, for example, revisioning moments are applicable to the realm of the everyday and to the realm of the

Utopian (presenting Berlin as a global entity in unified Germany). The term also applies to actions following the attacks of September 11, which included "getting back to normal" and initiating the symbolic reconstruction of the Twin Towers. Harold Garfinkel discusses this phenomenon of revision immediately after a moment of crisis, showing that individuals read the reality in an interpretative process with the assumption that there is a "social order."[12] Furthermore, people construct a social order that normalizes that which was chaotic or accidental. From this perspective, revisioning moments follow the violent act and contribute to organizing it as a clear cognitive reality. That is to say that the violated order is reconstructed by revisioning moments that create an illusion of stability and agreement. Thus, revisioning moments are a way to codify the process of production in a city and a way to codify the daily rhythm of cities frequently exposed to violence.[13]

You could say the plot of this book is the confluence of violent acts and the spaces in which they occur. In this sense, there are three plot lines, three central sites in the city: Rabin Square (formerly Malchei Israel Square), the Shore, and the Neve Shaanan neighborhood. Within this framework, the lead characters in the plot are the State, the citizens, and professionals all of whom we use to interpret the socio-spatial psychology of Tel Aviv to understand the distinctive dynamic between violence and cities.

Planning and Architectural Perspectives on Urban Violence

The relationship between violence and the city is not new. The war as a particular typology of collective violence has always destroyed living places. Cities as commercial, social, and economic centers have always been agents of a specific power or regime and thus, by definition, a center of political control and a target in war. Since the sixteenth century,[14] the State has had a monopoly on violence, but this central control has not decreased the vulnerability of cities as targets. On the contrary, modernity has increased vulnerability, in particular since the nineteenth century, when cities developed as industrial and population centers.[15]

Today, scholars tend to see a connection between the weakened nation-state and increased contestation in cities.[16] Wars between armies are now rare events, replaced by new strategies, formal and informal, in the city that are embedded in technology and the global economy.[17] Although the events of September 11[18] symbolized for many this shift to city warfare, it is inappropriate to define this event that accelerated the U.S. war in Afghanistan and Iraq as a phenomenon of the twenty-first century. Rather, we witnessed a change in the form of violence and in its simultaneous effect on the local, national, and international scene. Our discussion follows this line of thought, seeing violent occurrences in Tel Aviv as continuous forms of contestation.

So what is the context of contemporary urban violence? Stephen Graham argues that the current epoch, which he calls "post-colonialism" or the "post-cold war," brought to an end the polarized political era and released long-restrained tensions among ethnic groups.[19] These tensions are nourished by geopolitical, cultural, and economic changes such as increasing urban alienation, the increased power of religious groups, the armies of city gangs, population growth, etc.,[20] all of which have created a social "ticking bomb" that expresses itself in violence, as in the 1992 riots in Los Angeles,[21] the riots in Paris suburbs in 2005,[22] and the October 2000 events in Israel.[23] But, as Arjun Appadurai reminds us, violence and "new" wars, nourished by global politics and waged in the everyday life of the neighborhood, are just another phase in the development of city life.[24] Unfortunately, violence and loss of lives often divert attention from the struggle, from the anger of the powerless and the needy,[25] and from measures taken by the State, including violations of human rights and the law.[26]

Violence infringes on urban order, or at least challenges it. How and what are the mechanisms for re-establishing order? Obviously, the army and the police force are the immediate resources for restoring social order; planning institutions are also recruited to impose spatial order. These institutions, essential to the existence of any society, are both pragmatic and tangential. Referring to this link between violence and space in the early 1990s, the architectural theoretician Mark Wigley wrote that it is so obvious that it is often ignored.[27] Today, this link, with our increased knowledge about control and surveillance of public spaces worldwide[28] and the debate about whether we now have increased security in cities or are creating cities of fear, is not ignored at all but is rather a focal point in professional discourse.[29]

In this discourse, we identify at least three perspectives, namely the physical, the behavioral, and the socio-political. The physical approach (at times deterministic), dating back to studies conducted after World War II,[30] emphasizes the power of the physical environment to influence social behavior. According to proponents of this approach who emphasize solutions for preventing violence, graffiti and spatial-physical decay are considered signs of violence. This relationship between physical space and society is acknowledged in the behavioral approach, but it is not identified as a departure point. Rather, what is emphasized is the impact of human behavior on the built environment.[31] Thirdly, the socio-political approach emphasizes the impact of politics, such as oppression and control, on space. This approach investigates questions of identity, power, and memory, presenting a more complex picture of the thematically linked relationship between violence and the city.[32]

In the Israeli context, the focus of the socio-spatial approach is on how architectural and planning practices are recruited by the State for the oppression and separation of populations in occupied territories.[33] However, these previous studies, examining the interrelationship of violence and the city, present a broad analysis but without the advantage of going deeply into the relationship of particular events in space. To do this, we have chosen to identify particular events in order to examine the socio-spatial changes generated by specific acts of violence in Tel Aviv during the 1990s.

Tel Aviv as an Arena of Power and Conflict

Violence and the struggle over resources, territory, and capital among groups is part of the city's history. However, understanding the contested forces operating as part of its historical development is an essential part of the narrative about violence and public space.

Located along the seashore in what was Palestine, the pre-state national Jewish renaissance was, since the beginning of the twentieth century, centered in the area of Jaffa rather than in the more traditional centers of Jerusalem, Tiberias, and Tzefat. Jaffa's conglomeration of ethnic and religious communities led to the establishment of autonomous Jewish neighborhoods apart from the Arab city's Moslem and Christian communities in the 1890s during the Ottoman Empire. This kind of development outside a city wall is characteristic of modern urbanization of medieval cities worldwide,[34] but in Jaffa the new development outside the wall signified the emergence of an autonomous entity (Map 0.1, Figure 0.1). As opposed to the new Jewish neighborhoods outside the wall in Jerusalem, the new Jewish neighborhood of Jaffa—Achuzat Bayit, later to become Tel Aviv—was conceived as a separate entity.

The establishment of Achuzat Bayit in 1909, constructed with the assistance of the international Zionist establishment, marked the real beginning of Tel Aviv.[35] From the outset, Achuzat Bayit was a new neighborhood that expressed its founders' political and cultural boundaries. Its construction of cultural difference was based on autonomous communal life and a new spatial order. The adoption of a novel physical and morphological order, in contrast to Jaffa's crowded streets, emphasized the neighborhood's boundaries. The new neighborhood was characterized by a grid of suburban streets divided

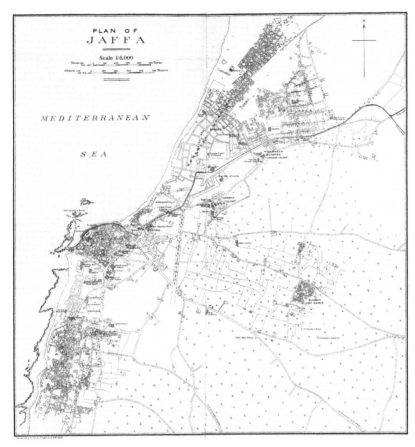

MAP O.I *Jaffa, 1918. The city of Jaffa with the new neighborhoods outside its walls. Upper right, Achuzat Bayit, later to become Tel Aviv. (Source: Department of Geography, Tel Aviv University)*

into spacious building lots, allowing for European-style detached residential buildings with pitched roofs and small gardens. These were new aesthetic ideas and social norms influenced by the Garden City Movement,[36] expressing the separation between work and living and the regulation of hygiene, light, and air. Although in terms of management and capital the neighborhood was still part of Jaffa, its spatial conceptualization allowed the community to separate itself, and thus delineate its identity, from the linear Jaffa's history.

Initially, Achuzat Bayit's cultural and architectural boundaries did not give rise to conflict, since it was managed like other peripheral neighbor-

FIGURE 0.1   *Aerial View, Jaffa and its neighborhood (Taken by the 304 German Air Force), 12/12/1917. (Tel Aviv City Council Historic Archive)*

hoods of Jaffa, and thus presented no threat to the city unity. However, this situation was changed with the British occupation of Palestine in 1917. The British perceived cities as important locations for deploying power technologies by means of which populations could be categorized and controlled. In this context, town planning became the mechanism by which aspirations toward cleanliness, civility, and modernity were realized, quite literally, "on the ground."[37] In an effort to control newly acquired territory, the new rule created surveys, reports, and maps, along with demolition and construction.[38] This aim to control population along with the spatial practices of demarcation eventually assisted the Jewish community in achieving autonomy from Jaffa, following the conflicts between the two ethnic communities during the riots of 1921.[39] Although the Scottish town planner, Patrick Geddes, reported in 1925 that "with all due respect to the ethnic distinctiveness and the civic individuality of Tel Aviv as a township, its geographic, social and fundamental economic situation is determined by its location in relation to northern Jaffa; . . . The old town and the modern township must increasingly work and grow together" (Map 0.2),[40] separation was inevitable. The parallel development of the two communities, increased tensions and violence between groups, and especially the Jewish demands for autonomy, contributed to the British Mandate's decision to separate Tel Aviv from Jaffa.[41]

Thus, Tel Aviv's evolution is first identified with moving Jewish neighborhoods outside the walls of Jaffa in the early 1900s and the unification of these neighborhoods under one presiding committee in 1913. On May 11, 1921, Tel Aviv was recognized as a separate township from Jaffa. However, only in 1934 did Tel Aviv receive municipal autonomy from the British Mandate authorities. The 1926 Geddes plan (and its approval in 1927, followed by the council's new amendment plan in 1938, Map 0.3) largely determined the character and

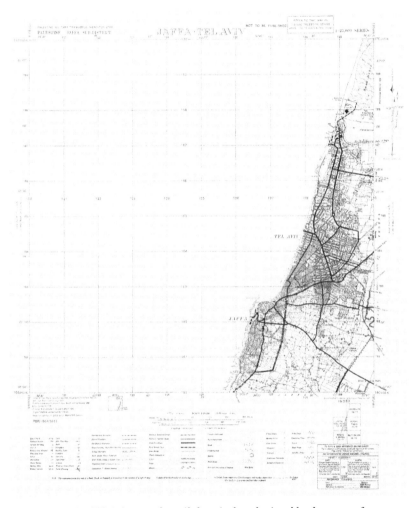

MAP 0.2   *Jaffa–Tel Aviv, 1943 (compiled, revised, and printed by the survey of Palestine). A map supporting Patrick Geddes's argument that Tel Aviv and Jaffa are geographically and socially inter-related. (Source: Department of Geography, Tel Aviv University)*

MAP 0.3   *Tel Aviv General Plan, 1930. The original Geddes plan is lost. This map, incorporating the plan layout, is dealing with solidification of the different components of the city into one municipal unit functioning as a big city. (Tel Aviv Municipal Archives)*

growth of the city, although the massive growth took place only after the 1948 war with the occupation of Arab lands and the annexation of Jaffa.

One can notice value changes by looking at the different plans that had been prepared for Tel Aviv over the years. The first comprehensive plan[42] — the Geddes Plan—dealt with the solidification of the different components of the city into one municipal unit functioning as a big city (to this day the Geddes plan is the official master plan for Tel Aviv).[43] Other plans, including the Horovitz Master Plan (prepared at the beginning of the 1950s, but never approved), dealt with density problems, traffic, and the operation of activities in space. Subsequent plans dealt with the importance of the city within the metropolis, the region, and the country as a whole. For instance, the Shimshony master plan (prepared at the beginning of the 1960s) defined the main business district of the city, regarding Tel Aviv as the center, the metropolis. The strategic Mazor plan (prepared at the beginning of the 1980s and accepted by the City Council in 1985) referred to the entire metropolis, defining it as the financial and cultural center of Israel. Redefining the relationships between land use and activities, the Mazor plan had significant influence on the development of the city center, the designation of specialized areas within it, and the revision of the relationship between residential and commercial areas.[44] Since early 2000 the Municipality of Tel-Aviv has been preparing a strategic plan for the city. Aiming at addressing all the city's facets—social fabric, economy, culture, leisure, land use, urban fabric, transport, and environment—in a participatory planning process, this plan allows short-term and long-term "Action Plans" in the Neoliberal context.[45] Thus it is clear the development of the city has been affected by ever-changing global concepts and local values that characterize each period in time.

Beyond understanding the physical growth of the city, one must understand the dynamic changes influencing the conflicts in Palestine (later to be renamed Israel). Since the early days of its establishment, Tel Aviv as a place was hierarchically located within the rest of Israel—within the "big place" (i.e., the State)[46]—and particularly in relation to Jerusalem. Indeed, the spatial borders of Jerusalem are directly related to both historical and contemporary conflicts (the 1948 war, the 1967 war, and the acts that followed, whose purpose was to establish Jerusalem as an *Israeli city*). But Jerusalem's birth and development has always been based on an enlisted mythology.[47] The mythical dimension of Jerusalem as a "city in conflict" intensifies the differences of the daily material existence in Tel Aviv. Furthermore, the status of Jerusalem, especially within a reality so loaded with political and ideological implications, has strengthened its abstractness against the concreteness of Tel Aviv's mundane life. "Tel Aviv is the opportunity to deal with the business of the

TABLE O.I   DEVELOPMENT OF CITY AREA DURING THE YEARS 1909–2006

Year	Area (Dunam)	Density (Person per Dunam)	Year	Area (Dunam)	Density (Person per Dunam)
1909	109	2.7	1950	42,420	7.9
1912	990	0.8	1951	48,500	7.1
1914	990	1.5	1962	49,600	7.9
1921	1,430	2.5	1980	50,440	6.6
1924	3,580	6.0	1983	50,553	6.5
1926	6,320	6.0	1995	51,423	6.8
1932	6,500	8.0	2001	51,423	7.0
1933	6,500	11.1	2003	51,423	7.1
1943	12,650	13.8	2004	51,423	7.1
1948	25,500	9.7	2005	51,423	7.2
1949	35,920	8.7	2006	51,423	7.4

Source: Tel Aviv Statistical Year Book, Tel Aviv-Yafo Municipality, 2007.

small place. This is exactly what it celebrates . . . the ultimate Israeli cosmos whose focus is the everyday—making a living, participating in cultural events, living in society, having fun."[48]

However, the conflicts of the 1990s disrupted Tel Aviv's daily life and made it the center of conflict. In 1991, during the Gulf War, Iraqi forces attacked Tel Aviv. So the war and suicide bombings, which became an everyday occurrence as a result of the Second Intifada,[49] turned the city into a war zone. Examples of these suicide bombings include one in 1996 on the Number 5 Bus, the 1997 suicide bombing at the Dizengoff Shopping Center, the 1998 suicide bombing at the Apropo Cafe, and the 2001 suicide bombing at the Dolphinarium Discotheque. This violence that was perpetrated on the city resonated nationwide. These attacks were most commonly followed by a rapid resumption of day-to-day routines, repair of the physical damage, and an increase in security measures, all in an attempt to erase the violence from the urban landscape. Significantly, the specific locations where these attacks occurred were minimized in order to establish these attacks as national-political conflict—creating imagined solidarity. At the same time, it became clear that this solidarity was, and still is, contested and debated by forces within the city and the state.[50]

To fully understand this argument, which is further developed throughout the book, it is important to address the relationship between the city and the state. First, one of the distinct characteristics of Israel is its relatively small national scale—both in terms of land and population. As of 2006, the number of citizens living in Tel Aviv was 384,400, with only 7,116,700 comprising the whole country. Another distinct characteristic is that, while Israel's central government plays an authoritarian role, this authority selectively gives municipalities an ability to influence some local decisions. At the same time, Tel Aviv's role as the powerful economic and cultural center of the region and the state has enabled the city to significantly contribute to the central government's decisions. As a result, Tel Aviv is in the position to modify and even initiate national policy, or operate parallel to it. For example, in the area of education, Tel Aviv is a full partner in the decisions made by the education ministry; it also has an influence on the development of master plans on national and regional scales. In other situations, Tel Aviv stands directly contradict national policy, as, for example, when Tel Aviv founded a center for foreign labor to provide legal and illegal foreign workers support—against the state's policy of deporting illegal immigrants. These powers in Israel's different arenas, which lead to both negotiations and conflicts, are the context in which we examine urban violence in this book.

Violence and Spatial Conflicts in Tel Aviv

Over the last years, we have witnessed the emergence of new historiographic perspectives of Tel Aviv, offering an understanding of the power struggle among the different groups in the city. These perspectives, expressed in scholarly works,[51] challenge the canonical image of Tel Aviv, placing the city in its contested social political reality and showing how the urban space cannot be separated from it. My aim is, however, to track the dynamic of the ongoing processes of urban production and the changes taking place in the city during violent events.

Focusing on space and time, this book presents three trajectories that together illustrate the powers, acts, and lives of the city.[52] To understand the mosaic of Tel Aviv, we look at violent acts as points of departure for examining the socio-spatial fabric of the city. In other words, the book offers an analysis of the construction and deconstruction of space through violence and a complex socio-physical portrait of Tel Aviv.[53] It does not aim to provide a comprehensive account of the Israeli-Palestinian conflict, nor a chronological thread of Tel Aviv history. Instead, it concentrates on how acts of violence change and affect the production of space and the discourse about space.

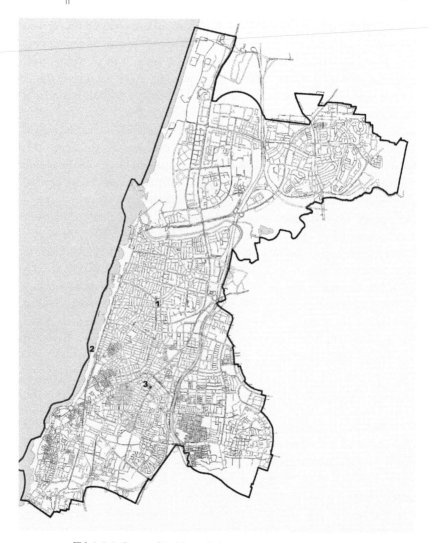

MAP 0.4   *Tel Aviv's Geographical Boundaries, 2008, and Sites under Analysis. 1. Rabin Square; 2. Dolphinarium Discothèque on the Beach; 3. The Central Bus Station in Neve Shaanan neighborhood. (Tel Aviv Municipal Archives)*

The first trajectory traces the evolution of Rabin Square (formerly Malchei Israel Square) as an arena of rituals and civic congregations (Map 0.4). Tracing the evolution requires establishing reference points to particular events that help us understand the complex relationship between political discourse and social process in Israeli society. This relationship was also the context of the assassination of Prime Minister Rabin, which took place in the square, November 4, 1995. The idea of revisioning moments helps us comprehend the voices and acts regarding the place immediately after the assassination.

The second trajectory focuses on the border zone between Tel Aviv and Jaffa, and on the ethnic and political conflicts that have taken place there since the 1920s until today. Here, we have an opportunity to understand the way the rhythm of space was affected by the conception of border and the economic interests of the city and the State. The violent history of this border zone pinpoints the significance of architecture and planning as practices that

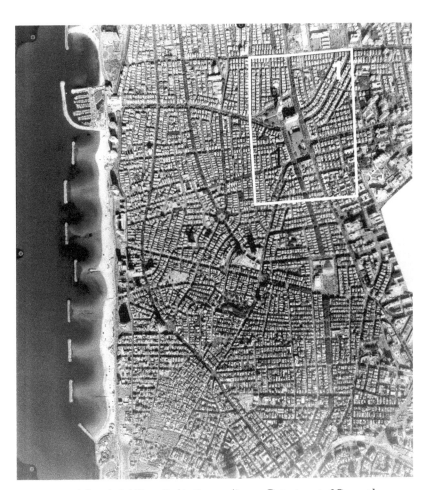

FIGURE 0.2 (A) *Aerial View, Rabin Square. (Source: Department of Geography, Tel Aviv University)*

FIGURE 0.2 (B) *Aerial View, Dolphinarium Discothèque on the Beach.*
(Source: Department of Geography, Tel Aviv University)

order space and restructure it. This connection of the city, violence, and architecture is looked at through a set of plans of the beach, in the context of the
suicide bombing of the Dolphinarium Discothèque on the beach in 2001.

The third trajectory traces the development of the Neve Shaanan neighborhood, which, developed in Tel Aviv's geographical periphery, is perceived
as the "backyard" of the city. This site illuminates the way violence is a catalyst
in the initiation of citizens' tactics and policy strategies to affect the socio-
spatial design of the neighborhood.

By tracing the process of the construction of space in Tel Aviv, the role and
effects of violent events throughout the city's history are made more visible.
Space has no voice, but by mapping the cultural and social struggles within

space we can tell the story of the reciprocal relationships between architec-tural and planning practices and violence, defining physical and symbolic boundaries, alienation, and conflicts among diverse groups.

The concluding chapter explains how order is restored by citizens and po-litical actors alike, who are re-making, re-visioning, and re-acting in response to violent acts. These negotiating forces, a portrait of a social struggle em-bedded in space, reveal the role of professionals (architects and planners) as mediators in the conflicted human drama of space. By examining the con-nection between violence and urban space, we stress the importance of urban planners and architects as active agents in the socio-spatial arena. This is a call to engage with the process of spatial production beyond the architectural or

FIGURE 0.2 (c)   *Aerial View, Central Bus Station in Neve Shaanan neighborhood.*
(Source: Department of Geography, Tel Aviv University)

urban design discourse about the object or the environment, per se. In other words, this critical mode aims not only at understanding the world but also at transforming it.

Finally, despite its focus on Tel Aviv, the analysis of the relationship between space and violence is applicable to other cities in Israel and Palestine, such as Jerusalem, Haifa, Netanya, and Hadera in Israel; Ramallah, Bethlehem, and Hebron in Palestine. All of these cities were, and still are, exposed to political violence. Each city has its own particularities and history that influence the relationship between space and violence. Still, it is beyond the scope of the book to detail these particularities, but I would like to argue that there are similarities in the way human beings respond to, interpret, and address violent events. Thus, aside from giving a detailed perspective on Tel Aviv, the book's goal is to address the way violence profoundly alters civil rituals, cultural identity, and the meaning of place in our cities. By explaining the way social discourse influences planning and architectural practices, across time, place, and social setting, I hope to illuminate the temporal dimension of space. If successful, such an approach will resonate within a broader geographical territory, stimulating dialogue about the relationship between space and violence.

Chapter 1

Violent Acts and
Revisioning Moments

W hat is the influence of the violent act on the place in which it occurs? How does violence influence perceptions of place? What changes, if any, does it generate? Is violence always an evil that must be eradicated? Addressing these questions will help us understand how violent political acts influence spatial production. Our hypothesis is that violence influences the production of space, but, unlike the Marxist approach that sees a sequence of struggles in a particular regime as a rite of passage to another form of regime, the following discussion illuminates how violent acts generate processes of revision in order to maintain order.

Because violence is visible and concrete, it is an essential device for social groups to be able to transform environments and send an ideological message to the public.[1] Thus, violence is not an isolated act but is part of the competitive relationship between groups and/or individuals.[2] Its meaning comes from its performative and creative qualities. First are the performative qualities, which are crucial to public impact; violence without an audience is socially meaningless. In this respect, the physical space where acts of violence occur is significant. Whether taking place in the backyard, a central space, or an army base, the location affects the visibility and meaning of the act for both the perpetrators and the victims. Space is not merely the context of the event; it also provides the medium, the drive, and the scale for the act itself.[3] In addition to the physical space, the media provide an imagined space of pain/entertainment and serve as mediator between the actual occurrence and the people located beyond the scene of violence.[4] This is why violence is not merely about physical injury and death; it is also a performance that sends messages to those not directly involved.[5] Thus, violent acts gain their effectiveness not so much from the physical act itself but from its staged power and public exposure.[6] Another characteristic of the violent act is its creative qualities; before it is performed, it must be imagined. From this perspective, violence is not just a method of solving conflicts about territory or resources; it is also a source of creativity, building and constructing worldviews, and legitimizing one group's truth over that of its rival. These qualities, creative and performative, assist in understanding violence not merely as a negative phenomenon but also, sometimes, as a generative one.[7]

Based on these qualities, we explain the following trajectory. Political violence attracts citizens living under a given regime, and by doing so, challenges the regime's authority. Then the regime and its citizens act to re-establish their violated space, which become revisioning moments. Looking more deeply at this trajectory, we further explore the relationship between regime, political violence, and revision.

Regime. Used interchangeably with the term *government* to denote an organized system of rule (e.g., aristocracy, monarchy, democracy) by government, agents, politicians, and citizens. The term is also sometimes used in place of *administration* to refer to a specific government office. *Regime* can also signify a broad framework of rules and norms that govern a particular issue, such as security, intellectual property, or the environment.[8] From the social perspective, *regime* implies repeated interactions between dominant key actors, institutions (e.g. army, political parties, religious institutions, etc.), and citizens constituting their membership. The powerful actors in a regime have relatively strong control over government. This system of social relationships is the place where rulers and citizens bargain about possible and effective means of making collective claims. Clearly, the characteristics defining the process of bargaining differ significantly from one regime to another.[9]

This process, where rulers and citizens bargain with each other, could accelerate violence, especially in non-democratic regimes. Whether or not this violence achieves its target, this process may contribute to reforming the regimes' mechanisms and institutions.

Recently, historians examining political violence have pointed out that violence is not a single act or a series of single acts. Hannah Arendt and others perceived violence as accidental, or as a temporary anomaly.[10] But contemporary scholars view violence as a social phenomenon, or, as Gyanendra Pandey defines it, routine violence[11] that is embedded in the political hierarchy of states and the groups within them. That is to say, violence is a tool that also assists in building hierarchies within the nation-state.[12]

Political violence. This state of continuous negotiation of social relationships makes it difficult to separate the term *regime* from other terms, such as *contention, contestation, power, force, strength,* and *authority.* As Hannah Arendt suggested, it is crucial to differentiate power from violence. These are not dissimilar terms, but opposites; violence appears when power is in jeopardy, but left to its own course, violence can destroy power; it is utterly incapable of creating it.[13] Thus, even though power and violence are distinct from one another, they usually appear together and are interrelated.

The phrase "political violence" has been used since the 1960s to refer to the implementation or threat of physical harm by groups involved in domestic political conflicts. Initially, it was an inclusive term for all disruptive forms of internal opposition to governments, including political terrorism, assassination, antigovernment riots and demonstrations, rebellions, and revolutionary warfare, also known as "civil violence." Later, usage was extended to include government acts of repression and violence against its own citizens, also known as "state violence."

As suggested by Charles Tilly, political violence involves social interactions that immediately inflict physical damage on persons and or/objects. It involves at least two perpetrators and is the outcome of coordination among people who perform the damaging act. Exposure of individuals to an experience of violence without being physically harmed makes political violence a quotidian experience. In the Israeli context, in particular since the 1990s, suicide bombing has become a form of violence that has frequently influenced the daily life of citizens countrywide. The frequency of this form of violence is an outcome of technological developments (i.e., production of tools, exposure in the media)[14] and increased social surveillance and control that have made it more applicable and effective than other forms of violence.[15] The body of the suicide bomber, unlike the tank or weapon, is not an identifiable threat, and thus its presence creates horror and surprise in the vulnerable public, contributing to the media's coverage of the act and its visual exposure.[16] Suicide bombings would not be so potent and successful were it not for the media, which mediates between the masses and the event.[17]

Revision. The violent act, at least from the perspective of the perpetrators, is a call for a change in worldview. Collective recognition of the violent act produces an opportunity for revision; after the violent act, citizens within a regime usually aspire to amend the concrete and discursive violated boundaries in order to reestablish the status quo. Moreover, the citizens and government cannot simply leave the post-violence state as is—they must reconstruct the social order to maintain their own power. In other words, violence and conflicts are mediated by cultural and social mechanisms that give these acts meanings. These acts are a means of communicating among social groups.[18] Whether spontaneous or planned, they aim at re-establishing the social order. Thus, violence causes disruption of the everyday, framing it in the collective memory. The collective memory is critical to the construction of the revisioning moment, which formulates new social meaning. In that sense, despite its dynamic and temporary features, the violent act is relocated and reorganized from its concrete place to an imaginable, organized interpretation. This assists in the construction of an illusory order, stability, and a shared narrative. The illusion of a community's stability, along with the need for safety, is further accentuated by the contemporary reality of terrorism. However, as Bauman says, "'community' is nowadays another name for paradise lost—but one to which we dearly hope to return, and so we feverishly seek routes that may bring us there."[19]

Similar to the violent act, the revisioning moment is a performance that needs its audience in order to acquire social meaning. That is why the revisioning moment often takes place in the space in which the violence occurs, an affinity that also contributes to its symbolic, sometimes mythic, meaning. In addition, like the violent act, the revisioning moment needs to be imagined and created; it is a war on the memory of truth, order, worldviews, and power. In that respect, the revisioning moment, like violence, is a resource for creating a worldview of one group's reinforcement of its rivals. Thus, violence and the revisioning moment are an interwoven, inseparable phenomenon. As such, violence and the revisioning moment should not be seen as autonomous points in time and space but as part of a chain of events.

The Ideology of the Revisioning Moment

Henri Lefebvre, in an earlier work, defined the "moment" as a re-presentation of a form that is rediscovered and re-invented.[20] In anthropological theories, the relationship between events and narratives as cultural-ritual symbols is addressed, but with limited reference to physical space itself.[21] In architecture, Bernard Tschumi suggests analyzing the relationship between the event (program, activity) and the object (building), claiming that architecture is a compound of space, movement, and program, which together define the physical, the symbolic, and the narrative. But how does the temporality of both violent and revisioning acts affect space? What are the parameters that influence the form of the revisioning moment?

The act of the revisioning moment takes multiple forms, influenced by the actors' ideologies and identities. If the state is the actor, social and physical boundaries are tightened, which consolidates the tension between "us" and "them." Alternatively, if citizens initiate a revisioning moment, then, in response to the violence, actions and symbols are spontaneously created, expressing grief and loss. Secondly, the revisioning moment is highly influenced by the interpretive perception of the violent act, an interpretation of the relationship between the perpetrators and the victims. If the state initiates the revisioning moment, then these moments are framed by the power relationships and thus concentrate on decreasing the power of the perpetrators. This action is often legitimized by citizens who perceive the violent act as a personal and collective attack. As such, even when diverse actors interpret violence differently, these interpretations rarely conflict, strengthening social consolidation and the determination of the collective to respond. Because of this interpretive consolidation, moral reflection about the reasons for the violent act is rarely embraced by those under attack. Thirdly, the revisioning moment is influenced by place, and in particular by the effect of the violent act on the imagined and concrete space, an effect that imbues the place with mythical and sacred characteristics. The power of the violent act lies in the fact that, in many aspects, it postpones daily routines or planned developments, if momentarily. But, as frequently happens, place cannot be reduced to a single event of violence, and so its meaning and use remain contested.

It must be noted that, while the revisioning moment is linked to the discourse on trauma,[22] which largely focuses on concepts derived from psychoanalysis and the work of Freud,[23] it is not synonymous with it. Recently, writers have stressed the difference between victims of traumatic historical events and others who have not directly experienced trauma but have been exposed to it through the media and often manipulate this collective memory for political reasons.[24] However, this discourse can be relevant to our discussion only if we extend the understanding of trauma from individual experience to ongoing collective social practices in the place where violence occurs. Thus, we focus on the implications of how trauma is encoded in the production of space and contributes to its development.

To further clarify the relationship between trauma and spatial revisioning moments, it is necessary to differentiate between the idea of *loss* and the idea of *absence*. Loss, as Dominique LaCapra defines it, is specific, relating to a particular event; absence is trans-historical, sometimes approaching myth.[25] When a trauma is acknowledged as loss, the urban context (as in post-war environments) can be dealt with, improving conditions or basic structural-social transformations. Where the trauma is perceived as absence, the urban context becomes a socio-political abstraction, an endless search for secular salvation or a calculated return to a "lost" unity. Thus, the revisioning moment can either involve *acting out* (perceiving trauma as absence) or *working through* (perceiving trauma as loss). Relating to Freud's "Mourning and Melancholia," Dominique LaCapra argues that mourning might be seen as a form of *working through* and melancholia as a form of *acting out*. Freud saw melancholia as an arrested process in which the depressed person, locked in compulsive repetition, is possessed by the past and remains identified with the lost object. Mourning offers the possibility of engaging trauma in a way that allows beginning again. Historical losses call for mourning—and possibly for critical and transformative socio-political practices. When absence is the *object* of mourning, mourning may become impossible, continually reverting to endless melancholy.

Because the revisioning moment uses traumatic memory for political purposes, it also serves as a tool that reshapes (i.e., changes or stabilizes) power relations among actors in a collective. But, although groups outside the collective hegemony may try to use the revisioning moment as a tool for change, they frequently do not have enough power to do so. Therefore, in most cases, violence and the revisions that follow merely reinforce the power of the dominant groups in society. Still, revisioning moments (like violence) are not predetermined or deterministic acts, but rather are social constructions of power by which new possibilities and events can occur.

Revisoning Moments and the Urban Discourse

The idea of revision is not essentially foreign to the architecture and planning discourse. It is embedded in the modernist philosophy, which was attacked for the Utopian failure to fulfill its social promise.[26] Despite this critical antagonism, we argue that the revisioning moment is endemic to the production of physical and social order. Furthermore, we contend that this idea bridges the gap between two binary concepts in architectural and planning discourse: the concrete everyday life and the Utopian vision.[27]

Since the modernist movement in architecture and planning in the 1960s, Utopia has been perceived as a failure and was dismissed from the professional discourse. The key reason for its dismissal is its dialectic resonance, which, on the one hand, creates a reformative imaginable space, and, on the other, frames space through control and order.[28] However, we should not dismiss the idea of reform so easily. Architecture and planning practices are based on the relationship between revision and space. So, too, the revisioning moment, emerging from the violent act, calls for revision and reform. These concepts of revision and re-visioning are essential to the professional practice of modifying space—a modification that is a repetitive and reversible process derived from the human need to visualize space.

The revisioning moment emerges from the violent act and can be perceived as a call for reform. It is a social tool that assists in processing and modifying place (discursively and culturally). This repetitive and reversible process derives from the human need to visualize the future. Nevertheless, unlike models of Utopia, the revisioning moment offers a dynamic model in which the individual plays a significant role in fostering change. Thus, the value of the concept of the revisioning moments, first, lies in shifting the discussion from an analysis of architectural objects or environment to an analysis of events that affect the social-physical processes of the built environment. Second, it is a tool for understanding the personal and collective dimension of political violence and the way it influences daily life. Third, it is an exploration of the dynamic of time-space,[29] which encourages further study of the unexpected influences on the fundamental values of a society.

In sum, below are the key assumptions of revisioning moments:

(1) Space is a social frame where different powers work to establish and maintain order. This order is based on the relationships established among key actors, including the government, the army, political parties, religious institutions, capital owners, etc. This order is in constant flux, as it is based on repetitive actions among groups and individuals within the regime.

(2) Political violence as a social practice and as a source of worldviews challenges this order and power. The effect of the violent act stems from its performative characteristics and its impact on people who have not attended the event or been physically injured.

(3) As responses to the violent act, spontaneous and planned revisioning moments emerge. Their aim is to re-establish the social order—a natural human response to the need for social order. In addition, both the violent act and the revisioning moment have similar features (performative, creative), and both are catalysts for change.

Yet what is the value of conceptualizing the revisioning moment when the city is constantly changing? The answer lies in the way these moments help us address the temporal dimension of daily life and to understand the unexpected influences of these moments on the values of society, the meaning of place, and the rhythm of life. In the Israeli context, addressing these moments is a means of bypassing the binary reading of the Israeli-Palestinian space and expanding the way groups are being perceived, negotiate, intersect, and act.

Chapter 2

Absence, Urban Space, and Civil Participation in Rabin Square

THE ASSASSINATION OF PRIME MINISTER RABIN, NOVEMBER 4, 1995

M alchei Israel Square was constructed in the 1960s as a void surrounded and defined by six-story buildings. The dimensions of the Square are approximately 260 meters north to south, and about 160 meters east to west (see Figures 2.1, 2.2). On the northern edge of the Square stands City Hall, twelve stories high. Constructed on the former Portalis orchard in the Arab village of Summeil, the Square was initially demarcated in Geddes's plan (approved in 1927), which called for the construction of a city hospital, but the site was used instead as a public garden and a zoo until the 1950s. Architectural designs for the Square were presented over two decades in three different competitions. For the first competition in 1947,[1] competitors were asked to suggest continuous façades to define both the Square and the private development at the site. Four years later, in 1951, a competition focusing on the plaza itself was announced. In 1957, the third competition for the City Hall building was announced. The winning design created physical and social relationships between the municipal building and the open plaza. Although this was a joint effort by three different architectural offices, the space projects unity of design (see Figures 2.3, 2.4). According to its architect (Avraham Yaski), the design of the Square did not aim at beauty or special features. As Yaski said, the meaning of the Square went beyond aesthetics—it was intended as an urban-social instrument.[2]

Four features characterize this urban space: the continuous repeated elevations, unique among Tel Aviv's urban fabric of detached buildings; the comparatively large scale in relation to other urban spaces in Tel Aviv and in Israel in general; the unique relationship between City Hall and the Square, connecting the civic institution with its citizens; and, lastly, the strict regulation that prevents any construction that would restrict public access to the Square

FIGURE 2.1   *Rabin/Malchei Israel Square—aerial view. Note City Hall on the northern edge of the Square, with its balcony and formal steps bridging the street and retaining the continuity of the plaza with the building. 1. City Hall. 2. Balcony. 3. Plaza. 4. Holocaust Memorial. 5. Public Garden. 6. Shopping mall and residential tower complex. (Tel Aviv Municipal Archives)*

as well as prohibiting all commercial advertising and prohibited commerce at the site.[3]

The four features create an open public space that is deserted for most of the year, though the borders bustle with activity. Day and night, the neighboring arcades are filled with people sitting in the coffee shops, visiting restaurants and kiosks, and waiting at bus stops. The empty plaza stands in stark contrast with the lively space around it. At the same time, the need for a civic arena has endowed the Square with status as an ideological focus at both local and national levels. Locally, this was due to the vice-mayor's suggestion of installing facilities in the plaza for the national elections and allowing lectures

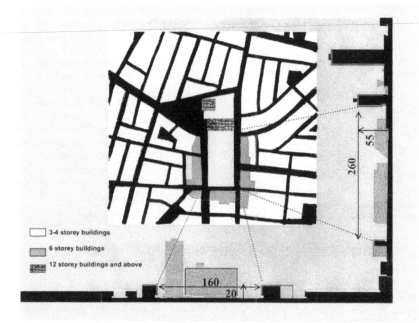

FIGURE 2.2   *Rabin Square, section the scale of the City Hall as compared with the typical three- or four-story residential buildings. (Tel Aviv Municipal Archives)*

and debates on controversial subjects.[4] After the occupation of the West Bank and Gaza in 1967, disputes raged over Israel's collective identity.[5] The public form of the disputes in the Square transformed it into an arena of contestation. The political upheaval between the two major competing parties of 1977 further contributed to the use of the Square by polarized factions, competing for party ideologies and political power.[6]

A rally in the Square on September 25, 1982, contributed to turning the space into a political arena. Named the "Protest of the 400,000,"[7] this event—immediately ingrained in the collective memory—called for a national investigation of the Sabra and Shatila massacres,[8] withdrawal of Israeli forces from Lebanon, and the resignation of the government. Organized by the Labor Party and the "Peace Now" movement, the protest alerted citizens to their role in democratic decision-making and their right to refuse to participate in policies that went against their conscience (see Figures 2.5, 2.6). This and many other events contributed to the collective representation of the Square. Above all, it became an arena for orderly demonstrations of various power hierarchies (national, communal, and private) in Israel.[9]

This social order was challenged on November 4, 1995, when Prime Minister Yitzhak Rabin was assassinated during the "Yes to Peace, No to Violence" Rally in support of the Oslo Accords.[10] Leading up to the event, thousands of youngsters in the Square were waving banners and calling for peace, with organizers constantly updating the crowd about the masses that were still pouring in. After the assembly, the Prime Minister went down the service stairs and was shot in the back by a young religious Jew.

Rabin was rushed to the hospital, and his death was announced at 11:14 p.m. His assassination by a Jew totally disrupted the internal order, violating every written and unwritten Jewish code. Suddenly, the constructed separation between the Israelis (internal, "protected") and the Palestinians and the rest of the world (external, "violators") had collapsed.

This event disrupted the linear (and rather peaceful) evolution of the

FIGURE 2.3 *Paving asphalt, Malchei Israel Square, 1958. (Photo: Willi Folender, Tel Aviv Municipal Archives)*

FIGURE 2.4   *Rabin Square, façade. (Photo: Author)*

Square as an arena for ceremonies and congregations in Israel. We use the word *disrupted* to emphasize that the assassination altered the image of the Square as a civil space for "all" groups. This perception of the Square as a plural place is anchored in the Western concept of cities in which the urban square is an ideal public space, but it ignores the fact that many European squares were historically also used as arenas of public punishment and symbolic violence.[11] Indeed, public execution as a spectacle was part of daily life in medieval Europe, a dark, repressed chapter in the history of today's public squares.

Until the moment of assassination, the history of the square in Tel Aviv was not stained. This is different from other sites in the city where traces of political violence defined their history. It is true that, prior to the establishment of the state, Palestinians resided in the areas adjacent to the square, but the arena itself and the site were bought by the city council in the 1930s; in addition, assemblies held on this site enhanced its identity as a civil space for the Jewish community, and later as a national collective. Furthermore, assassinations and political murders took place prior to and after the establishment of the state, as in the cases of Haim Arlosoroff (Tel Aviv, 1933), Israel Kastner (Tel Aviv, 1957), Emil Greenzweig (Jerusalem, 1983), and Rehavam Zevi (Jerusalem, 2001). All of these events took place in mundane situations: on

FIGURE 2.5   *The Square as a public and political forum. City Hall terrace becomes a stage for speakers, celebrities, and high-ranking supporters. Speeches alternate with musical performances, the audience responds loudly and enthusiastically, and every event concludes with the singing of the national anthem. In the photograph is Prime Minister Golda Meir, 1975. (Photo: Milner Moshe, 13.11.1975, Government Press Office)*

FIGURE 2.6   *Protesting the Lebanon War, 1982. (Photo: Jacob Saar, Government Press Office)*

the way to work, near the entrances to homes, along the beach. Despite the reverberation of these events in the public discourse, none of them is associated with a particular site, a site of national and social significance. Thus, the particularity of the event of the assassination of Yitzhak Rabin is its occurrence in a public square, an event that profoundly altered the representation of the place.

The assassination is our reference point in time and space for examining the complex relationships between the construction of the place, the citizens, and the multiple revisioning moments that emerged from it. A subsequent section of this chapter, titled "Ideology," introduces an interdisciplinary framework that examines the Square as a place of rituals and public assemblies. It includes references to particular moments in the history of the Square and allows an examination of the socio-political history of the Jewish community. In particular, it examines the relationship between architecture and civil participation by looking specifically at the formal attributes of the Square, its development as a public urban space, its national symbolic meaning, and its civic role. The analysis will show that the form of public assembly and the physical space in which it occurs are indivisible, revealing architecture's unique contribution to the shaping of citizenship. Another section, "Memory," addresses the tensions arising from the assassination and their effect on the development of space. It details the spatial practices in the space since that event and reveals the ongoing conflicts over the design and meaning of the Square. Specifically, this section introduces reactions to a planned change in the Square (the proposal for new underground parking) and explains how this exacerbates the discrepancies between the temporal and everyday life of the Square (as advocated by the City Council and citizens), on the one hand, and its role as a democratic and national memorial space (as advocated by the State and other groups), on the other.

IDEOLOGY
Urban Space and Civil Participation

A political assassination of a prime minister takes place in a public square—a violent act at an organized peace rally, creating chaos, panic, and anxiety, and filling the concrete space of the plaza with grief. A personal tragedy, a national loss, a social crisis—all phrases used to describe this moment. But what does this event mean to Tel Aviv's citizens? How does the social meaning of the Square affect the meaning of the act itself? Understanding this violent act in the national history of Israel and Tel Aviv begins in the early 1930s with an analysis of both the space and the way ideologies are publicly practiced in Israeli society. Addressing these issues through analysis of civil assemblies reveals how architectural place-making has contributed to the public discourse.

These formal patterns have been accentuated since the 1990s, when the Palestinian Intifada and the ensuing fear of violent attacks justified increased surveillance. Thus, public spaces in Tel Aviv are often modified by barriers and security guards affecting their use and meaning. Therefore, paradoxically, although civic participation often calls for political or social change by negotiating the existing order, in fact, they are frequently static social rituals. Still, this ritualizing or institutionalizing of protests in the Square does not imply environmental determinism, or insinuate that it would be hopeless to foster social change in public spaces, but rather emphasizes the relationship between the Square's urban form and its use for civil gatherings and the tension between Tel Aviv and the Square's secular meanings, as opposed to the religious identity of Jerusalem.

Urban Squares and Civil Congregations

Architectural theory and practice define the urban square as a public space demarcated by buildings. Scholars elaborate and explore this definition from at least three perspectives: the *formal*, the *psycho-visual*, and the *socio-spatial*. The formal perspective defines a square as a geometric space with distinct architectural features, typologies, and tectonic and morphological attributes, as depicted in plans, façades, and sections, expressing scale and architectural language.[12] The psycho-visual perspective explores how public squares and spaces are used and perceived by individuals or collectives in the space.[13] Lastly, researchers and practitioners see squares as a spatial-cultural phenomenon,[14] envisioning them as public arenas dominated by power relations. To these architectural theories we add anthropological theories exploring social congregations as ritual performances,[15] events at which participants follow a repetitive set of actions with known aims and symbolic meanings. This is true for formal religious ceremonies and also for some secular and civic festivals, protests, and assemblies.[16] Though civic events unlike religious rituals, connect participants during a discrete time period. The secular ceremony or assembly is intended to increase social solidarity and reinforce an existing cultural-ideological regime.[17] Especially since the beginning of the twentieth century, challenges to the social order have given rise to meetings at which politicians court the masses; spaces for such assemblies are created in order to strengthen the illusion of social order and unity.[18] Thus, these anthropological theories see assemblies as a particular type of ceremony in which the square functions as a public forum for voicing disagreements.[19]

A key element of public forums is their *symbolic meaning*. Civic squares are key spaces for placing the individual in a meaningful social hierarchy.[20] In these spaces, architectural aesthetics are often recruited to emphasize symbolic meaning by integrating vistas and perspectives that promulgate the power relationships implicit in the square, as did the theater and the agora of Athens.[21] Richard Sennett points to two visual rules dominating in the Greek theater, namely, exposure of the speaker to the audience and the standard spatial configuration between the speaker and the audience as observers. The agora, on the other hand, was an open space with few visual barriers, permitting a fluid transition between private and public, with the stoa allowing people to be engaged, even at a distance, in the event taking place. The spatial form of the agora includes both active participants and passive observers, similar to the spatial forms of contemporary protests taking place in public squares all over the world that include both marchers and accidental observers (i.e., waving, cheering, and standing).

This relationship during contemporary assemblies is carefully planned. The formal space has a major role in defining this relationship, as in the example of a speaker standing in a center of a circular space, projecting a message of being part of the crowd, as opposed to a speaker standing on a high podium at the edge of a rectangular space, evoking distinct hierarchy and theatricality. Sometimes the desired setting of the participants follows the physical setting of space, but more often it is modified with additional means, such as with an installation of a stage, microphones, flags, and posters, reinforcing the visuals and textual symbols of the event.

To intensify the symbolic use of the civic square for assemblies, many events are scheduled at night, when lighting can add a dramatic impact. This aestheticizing was evident during the Nazi regime, which relied on carefully contrived architectural orchestration and lighting, as in the 1934 Zeppelin Field event masterminded by the architect Albert Speer. Speer directed a battery of 130 anti-aircraft searchlights in the night sky to create his famous "cathedral of light." By developing the sublime, argues Leach,[22] in Nazi Germany the architecture set the scene for an aesthetic celebration of the violence that underpinned fascist thinking, thereby enlisting architectural aesthetics to serve political power and increase the tensions between ideologies and ethics.

Another key element of the public forum is *crowd configuration*, generally taken to mean an assembly of people. For example, in the 1960s, crowd theories suggested that groups merge into a collective consciousness,[23] here addressed from a spatial perspective. Generally speaking, the scale and geometry of a space designed specifically for the masses supports both the presence and the absences of crowds. In a *present crowd*, when mass congregations take place, features of the space such as scale and power geometries between the regime and citizens intensify the presence and the imagined unity of the group. However, when the space is unpopulated—in an *absent crowd*—the scale and power geometries of the space alone project monumentality. In other words, even when the crowd is absent, this absence echoes its potential presence.

Furthermore, crowd configuration depends on the space's physical attributes, surveillance, and enforced order. This is intensified by the use of light, spatial proportions, and building masses often defined by laws of symmetry and perspective, along with rules, laws, and social codes that govern space, all of which affect participants' movements and performances. One example is the Mothers of Plaza de Mayo in Argentina, marching in circles around the monument in the plaza, performing a repetitive ritual that redefines access to, and the appearance of, urban space. This act reclaims the space and thus modifies its cultural meaning.[24] Similarly, Israeli "Women in Black" temporarily appropriate "informal public spaces" throughout Israel every Friday afternoon.[25] These relatively small groups decide their own spatial configuration and performance acts. In the case of large assemblies, the powers (i.e., political parties, institutions) often choose to maintain control and order by actually collaborating with activists through a careful selection of spaces of a certain size, scale, and orientation.

One of the key elements that define contemporary protest is the relationship between socio-spatial order and surveillance. By the term *order*, I mean two interrelated order systems: the order of the assembly and the order of the space. The order of the assembly and its ritual performance components (marching, gathering, singing, etc.), clothing, and schedule (timing and length of the event) represent the way the participants see themselves, either as supporters or protesters against social order, all within the culture of their society. We suggest this order has a dual role: it is a mechanism for constructing meaning and for interpreting social reality and a device for negotiating between the state and the citizen. The order of the assembly takes place within the arrangement of a physical space, which includes the setting's topography, boundaries, traffic movements, and buildings uses. The latter (buildings uses) is crucial to the space's identity; for example, government buildings defining a plaza differ significantly from commercial or residential buildings. The space's setting and design, defined by architects and authorities, is a representation of the civic identity of the society. Some of these characteristics are modified temporally to fit the order of the assembly, with barriers, blocked routes, and adjusted traffic rules to control the order of the crowd's movement. In addition, police attempt to maintain this order through different means of surveillance, such as cameras and secret agents in a crowd to identify any form of violence that might occur. In many of the assemblies, there is direct coordination between the organizers (activists or political powers) and the police. This type of surveillance, similar to Jeremy Bentham's Panopticon concept, is the means through which an observer can watch the participants without the participants knowing they are being watched, in effect creating an invisible omniscience.[26] Surveillance is also empowered by modern technology and is clearly the most effective means to achieve what Foucault has named "docile bodies," citizens targeted by power control.[27] However, one must be careful when using these terms, as surveillance and enforced order *can* be challenged through socio-political agencies, as in the case of the Mothers of Plaza de Mayo operating under a military coup. The order's significance, of both assembly and space, is that it serves as a means of control, but it can also be a means of liberation and mediation. Only through knowledge of the social order of a regime and its designated spaces can one resist it, by protesting or suggesting an alternative.

The three elements—symbolic meaning, crowd configuration, and order and surveillance—are the lenses through which the concrete and abstract meaning of the Square is examined.

A Gathering at a Site on the Outskirts of the City

On October 8, 1945, Tel Aviv's Jewish community gathered on the unbuilt site of Malchei Israel Square to protest the White Paper of 1939, a British proposal to create one state to be governed by both people, in proportion to their numbers in the population, by 1949. The proposal also limited Jewish immigration.[28] A period photograph shows hundreds of people crowded into the site, yet it is unmarked on the 1945 map. The crowd faces an open truck adorned with flags on which a figure stands, apparently making a speech. Other figures surround the truck, facing the crowd. Dressed in white, groups of people hold banners, one of which clearly reads, "Shoulder to shoulder against British policy." The spatial location of the gathering looks flat and exposed, an unregulated city edge, with no particular attributes. It has a rectangular shape but is architecturally undefined, with no clear borders, access, or hierarchical definition. The gathering activates the place, but the crowd configuration does not alter its spatial identity. This organized protest by the Jewish community against British domination demanded that the country's gates be opened to concentration camp survivors coming from Europe. A municipal newsletter estimated the number of participants in the crowd to be more than 50,000, within a city population of 166,660. It reported that the meeting in Malchei Israel Square came after a parade through the city.[29] Analysis of this public gathering's characteristics and its spatial location, as of other Jewish gatherings in the 30s and 40s, sheds light on the civil practices of the Jewish community during the British Mandate prior to the development of the space as a square.

The area on the edge of the city border, near the Portalis orchard in the Arab village of Summeil, was designated as a square in the city plan of 1927, based on the 1925 Geddes report.[30] Pressed by the British, the Tel Aviv municipality, the only autonomous Jewish city under the British Mandate, had invited the Scottish biologist-planner Patrick Geddes to report on the condition of the city. His six-month survey, presented in a thorough report, became the basis for a plan that was approved by the British Mandate in 1927, amended in 1938, and is, to this day, the official master plan of the city.[31] The site was acquired in the late 1920s from Ibrahim Shuka Effendi Harbitali[32] by the Tel Aviv municipality, a sale of Arab land to a Jewish community that was quite common in the context of the autonomy granted to Tel Aviv by the British Mandate. Following the transaction, the orchard was perceived by the Jewish community to be a conflicted border region whose economic potential had not been fulfilled.

The cartographic and textual (mainly newspaper) representations of the area at the time demonstrate the gap between the Jewish community's concept of space, emphasizing the prospective role of the place, and the British cartography that portrays the space's current identity and use. Thus, the Jewish map defines the area as a geometric square, following the official town plan based on Geddes's report (Map 2.1). On the other hand, the British map makes no reference to the Square, instead showing the existing Arab village of Summeil. A decade later, a British map from 1945 (Map 2.2)[33] indicates the zoo and the public garden but makes no reference to the Square. Additional support for this gap appears in the local Jewish publications and newspapers that discuss the space's public role. It appears that this role had been well-known to the citizens of Tel Aviv, contributing to the interrelationship between the city's emerging society and its locale, and reinforcing the institutional and ideological role of the Square as a civic meeting place. This gap in the space's representations emphasizes the tension between the

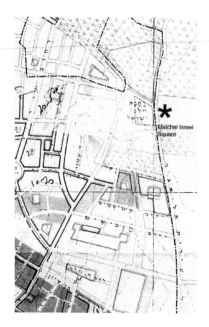

MAP 2.1 *The Square area, from Tel Aviv and environs, 1935 (Extract). A Jewish map defining the geometry of the square, following the official town plan based on the Geddes Report. The area marked "Malchei Israel Square" is an empty site adjacent to the Arab village of Summeil on the northern edge of the city. (Tel Aviv Municipal Archives)*

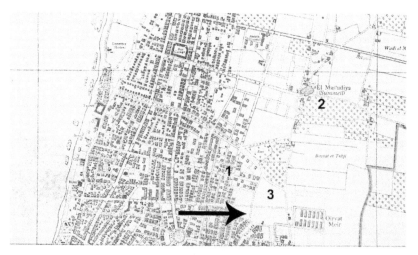

MAP 2.2 *Tel Aviv–Jaffa, 1945, British Survey of Palestine (Extract). On the map, the site of the Square is indicated as part of the Arab village of Summeil at the edges of Tel Aviv City. 1. Tel Aviv City 2. Summeil 3. The site of the Square. (Tel Aviv Municipal Archives)*

conceived space (as defined by the British), the abstract domain of scientists, planners, and technocratic sub-dividers, and the perceived space as defined by the community.[34] Thus, although the place was not yet defined in terms of urban form, its symbolic meaning was apparent to the community through other representations.

The order of assembly as practiced in the 30s and 40s, a dynamic socio-spatial phenomenon, was repeated in other parts of the city (Figures 2.7, 2.8, 2.9).[35] The site of Malchei Israel Square was significant, but it was not exclusive for public gatherings. The absence of a defined public civic space in the city allowed for flexible and imaginative forms of civil participation. Each assembly had its own order, banners, and flags. Moreover, the Jewish collective identity was not yet based on denial of, or resistance to, a Palestinian state. Rather, it focused on strengthening the national claims of the Jewish people. As an earlier assembly in 1939 is described, "in front of the huge parade that numbered 70,000 people and stretched for 10 kilometers, marched the various organizations."[36] Marching as a precedent to the gathering itself was also a way of engaging viewers and attracting more participants for the event. The number of people, often mentioned in the newspapers of the period, was significant both in terms of gaining credit for the claims of the Jewish community, externally (with the British government) and also internally (in the community itself). This latter fact is of particular significance, as it gave form to the fragmented, heterogeneous Jewish society comprised of different groups—orthodox, national-religious, secular, and workers.[37] These groups were neither politically nor socially hostile to one another, adhering to a rational public discourse over the "struggle for a homeland."[38] Rallies like the one on October 8, 1945, promoted the shared belief that each group could develop an individual agenda that would contribute to the common goal of national struggle. With the retreat of the British forces in 1947, the occupation of Jaffa and the establishment of the State of Israel in 1948, there was a radical shift in the configuration of society: from a city that included 66,310 non-Jews residing in Jaffa and 660 in Tel Aviv, it became the joint city of Tel Aviv–Jaffa, with only 5,000 non-Jews left by 1950.

After the war, the Jewish community's main effort was directed toward immediate concerns such as housing new immigrants and establishing state institutions. However, major efforts were put into the reconstitution of the fractured society to achieve one state entity.[39] Parallel to these social processes, and as part of the establishment of national institutions, the definitions of both assemblies and space were altered.

FIGURE 2.7   *A protest march against the British "White Paper" policy in Tel Aviv's "Ben Yehuda" street, 27/05/1939. (Photo: Pinn Hans, Government Press Office)*

FIGURE 2.8   *Women's organizations taking part in the protest march against the British "White Paper" policy in Tel Aviv, 27/05/1939. (Photo: Pinn Hans, Government Press Office)*

FIGURE 2.9 *A mass demonstration against the British "White Paper" policy, outside the "Habima" theater in Tel Aviv, 18/08/1946. (Photo: Pinn Hans, Government Press Office)*

Gathering in the Municipal Square

The late 1940s and, in particular, 1948 marked the beginning of a new era. It differentiated between Tel Aviv as the cultural and economical center of the State and Jerusalem as its national core with the relocation of power entities such as the Knesset (Parliament), the Supreme Court, and government offices. As early as 1945, Yaacov Ben Sera, Tel Aviv's city engineer, had proposed that Malchei Israel Square, already designated in the Geddes scheme, become the civic heart of the city. He argued that the city's development had transformed the site into a central node, dictating that City Hall, originally located in a southern venue central to "little Tel Aviv," be relocated. His concept included the removal of the zoo and other recreational institutions to allow a new civic representation of the Square (see Figure 2.10).[40] The decision to construct a monumental municipal building appealed to the mayor, who initiated an architectural competition. This process resulted in a redefinition of the attributes of the space.

The architectural framing of the Square stretched over two decades through the mechanism of three different design competitions, all of which contributed to the reshaping of the Square's urban form and symbolic role. The first competition in 1947 called for an urban plan to reconstruct the streets

FIGURE 2.10   *The City Hall and the Zoo, 1970s. (Photo: Willi Folender, Tel Aviv Municipal Archives)*

and define the plaza's boundaries, to be implemented by private developers.[41] Competitors were asked to design a continuous façade and designate the heights of the buildings surrounding the Square, the streets, sidewalks, etc. As a result of this competition, the spatial urban setting was redefined, along with the role and size of the plaza, in response to crowd configuration. As envisioned by the city engineer in 1947, the space was to have "no vegetation, be paved, and be able to accommodate crowds of up to 80,000 people."[42]

Four years later, in 1951, Abraham Yaski and Shlomo Pozner won the competition, focusing on the design of the plaza itself. Yaski and Pozner designed the plaza as an arena for public meetings, adding vegetation at the south end (see Figure 2.11a). However, it wasn't until 1957 that another competition to design City Hall reconfigured the relationship between the building and the Square (Figures 2.11b, 2.12). The competitors were required to design a building to face the plaza that would "be of at least the same height as the

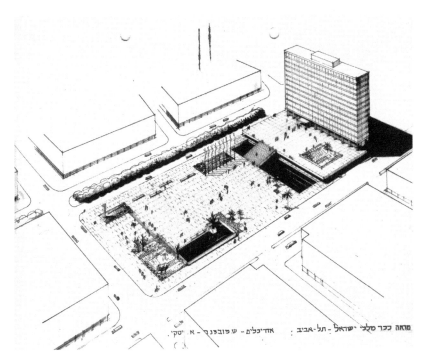

מאה ככר סלבי ישראל - תל-אביב : אדיכלים - ש פובזנר - א. יסקי.

FIGURE 2.11 (A)   *The second (1951) architectural competition—designing the plaza as a leisure site for local residents and as an arena for public meetings. (Drawing by architects Abraham Yaski and Schlomo Pozner from 1966, Tel Aviv Historical Archive)*

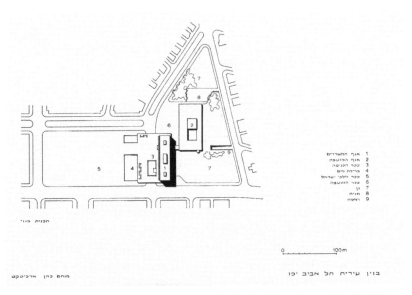

אגף המשרדים	1
אגף המזועפה	2
ככר הכניסה	3
בריכת מים	4
ככר זלקי׳ ישראל	5
ככר התועפה	6
ןן	7
חניה	8
רמפה	9

0 _____ 100 m

תכנית בנוי

בנין עירית תל אביב יפו

מחם כהן ארכיטקט

FIGURE 2.11 (B)   *The City Hall competition (1957), the design of a municipal building facing the plaza. (Drawing: Architect Menahem Cohen, Author's Collection)*

FIGURE 2.12 *The City Hall under construction, 1964. (Photo: Willi Folender, Tel Aviv Municipal Archives)*

buildings surrounding the plaza."[43] The winning entry, by architect Menahem Cohen, marked a dramatic change in the Square's spatial and architectural identity. Unlike the majority of the entries that suggested a complex of low-rise buildings at the northern edge of the Square, Cohen proposed a single high-rise building that would create a hierarchal relationship with the Square and enhance its urban symbolic significance.

Although the Square was designed by three different architectural firms and constructed in three stages, its tectonic elements and materials remained consistent throughout the process. The architectural language was highly influenced by post-war modernism, and in particular by Kenzo Tange's winning entry in the 1952 design competition for Tokyo's Metropolitan Government Offices.[44] Similar to Tange's proposal, the dominant feature of the space was the twelve-story City Hall building, supported by pillars of reinforced concrete with a concrete and glass exterior, ten stories above ground featuring a repetitive array of windows facing the plaza. Broad steps lead to the terrace that spans the street and, with a pool of water, bounds the north side of the plaza. These steps were an attempt to connect City Hall directly to the plaza; while not interrupting the street movement, these steps create a direct connection between the citizens and the municipality. One level above the plaza, the foyer was used for exhibitions and as a locus for general information. Culminating in a wide terrace that extends along the southern side of the building, these steps were also planned as the main ceremonial access to the building, but are mainly used today as a platform for speakers during public gatherings. The plaza itself, with only a small area of greenery and pool of water, is paved with gray and white granulite in a repeating geometric pattern. Along its western edge are posts for hanging banners, loudspeakers, and light fixtures. The six-story buildings around the Square lack the decorative detail and balconies that typify most residential buildings in Tel Aviv; rather, the street levels of these buildings form a continuous arcade that bustles day and night with people in shops, restaurants, and cafés, in sharp contrast to the vast emptiness of the Square itself (Figure 2.13). This disparity between residential and commercial activity and the ceremonial space is intensified by municipal regulations prohibiting all billboards in the Square, so that visual order is maintained and the Square's institutional dimension is emphasized.[45]

The contrast between the intense informal activity of the arcades around the Square and the formality of the plaza itself triggered public debate as early as the 1970s.[46] Proposals to establish cafes and additional green areas in the Square were denied by the municipality on the grounds that "a Square presenting the City Hall cannot include coffee houses." The symbolic dimension of the Square was further reinforced with the decision to install a monument commemorating the Holocaust. This decision modified the municipal status of the plaza to a national Square and furthered the argument against its quotidian meaning. As stressed by the city engineer, "the Square and the City Hall Building should together symbolize dignity and municipal authority . . . I don't think a 'Levantine moment' such as a café is suitable if a national monument (i.e., a monument commemorating the Holocaust) is installed. How would it fit with a café?"[47]

The Holocaust monument, larger than anticipated by the municipality, was designed by the artist Yigal Tumarkin, who won the competition. To give the Square a national identity, he specified that the monument symbolize Jewish history. As he says, it serves as a "small temple and a place for reflection by visitors to the city."[48] This is also clearly expressed in the words of Abba Kovner, a poet and a partisan who fought with the resistance in the

FIGURE 2.13 *Edges of the Square. The ground floors of the residential buildings form a continuous commercial arcade, contrasting with the vastness of the plaza. (Photo: Author)*

Vilna Ghetto in World War II: "The Square is surrounded by main roads. Men, women and children, old and young, cross it every day. What we ask is to add to the plaza, in the center of the first Hebrew city, a place to pause and remember."[49] Tumarkin's winning entry, selected by a jury dominated by architects, was an inverted pyramid. This abstract sculpture in rusted metal suits the modernistic lines of the Square (Figures 2.14, 2.15). In Tumarkin's own words, the monument expresses the weight of a prison, with the narrow base of the pyramid expanding and opening to the sky, sun, and light.[50]

The design generated much public dispute that went all the way to the Supreme Court.[51] The argument against the memorial focused on two main issues. Some council members claimed that a monument commemorating the Holocaust might be detrimental to the atmosphere of the Square as an everyday space.[52] The second issue was the symbolic nature of the work itself, which the public felt was not an appropriate symbol of the Holocaust.[53] However, in 1974, despite public protest, the City Council approved the monument's construction.[54] These architectural attributes of the Square, with their contested evolution, created a hybrid space, one which combines Sennett's two typologies—of the "agora," an open space lined with commercial activity, and a "theater," with its rectangular geometry that establishes an elevated hierarchy (raised terrace) between the crowd and the speaker/performer. This hybrid space and its geographic centrality, along with the need for an arena for public debate over the Israeli-contested reality, contributed to the evolution of the Square as an arena for political assemblies.

With the architectural and urban design competitions of the 1950s–1970s, the Square became an arena for municipal events, such as public concerts, folk singing, secular celebrations, religious festivals such as Purim and Hanukah, national holidays such as Independence Day, and commercial events with cultural goals, such as the National Book Fair (Figure 2.16). A photo taken in 1977 shows the newly adjusted order of gathering in the Square. Crowd configuration and symbolic hierarchy are achieved by urban and architectural definitions. Thousands of people sit in the Square on a summer evening, listening to a public concert (Figure 2.17). The seating is arranged as in a theater. At the southern end of the Square close to the Holocaust Memorial, people stand loosely gathered. The floodlighted City Hall façade forms a backdrop to the musicians' small stage. Unlike the early parades in which each group carried its own banner, here municipal and national banners and flags hang on the City Hall façade, enhancing the sense of a unified community. Residential buildings define the boundaries of the huge Square with their windows looking onto it, reinforcing the unification of personal lives and the formal-national attributes and roles of the Square.

FIGURE 2.14   *Holocaust and Revival Monument under construction in 1975. (Photo: Willi Folender, Tel Aviv Historical Archive)*

FIGURE 2.15 *City Hall (center) and Holocaust and Revival Monument (left), 2007.* *(Photo: Author)*

The Square as Ideology

This sense of national unity began cracking in the 1970s. The occupation of the Palestinian territories following the 1967 (Six-Day) War and the rise of the Palestinian national identity increased internal disputes over Israel's own collective identity. The Square became the forum for public protest, an arena for expressing political diversity and argument. These public disputes further increased in 1977, with the political upheaval and the Labor party loss in the national election. These events demarcate the Square's status as a national arena for disputes. Four key issues made the Square a locus for political protest: first was the legal decision, initiated by the vice-mayor, to increase the political use of the Square during the pre-election period, resulting in the installation of facilities such as a temporary stage and speaker-phones for national election campaigns, allowing for discussions, lectures, and debates about controversial issues;[55] second were the Square's open space and scale, as well as its construction as a national symbol; third, Tel Aviv, as the geographic center of the state and the most populated city in the area, made it easier for participants to arrive from all over the country; fourth, unlike public spaces

FIGURE 2.16   *Amusement Park, Purim Festival, March 1962. (Photo: Willi Folender, Tel Aviv Historical Archive)*

in Jerusalem, the Square represented, and still represents, the secular and civic core of the state.

Since the early 1980s, crowd configuration and assembly order were established as a repetitive form. Examples are the assemblies of the competing parties held in June 1981, prior to the national elections. The Labor Party's meeting was described by a local newspaper as consisting of "more than 200,000 people from all over the country. . . . Over 1,200 trucks and buses transported hundreds of people, arriving from distant settlements to participate in the event."[56] The newspaper reported the Likud Party rally, held a day later, in the same terms: "130,000 enthusiastic people raised their hands and sang . . . Menahem Begin (the Likud leader) spoke for two hours to the hundreds of thousands of people who came to the Square in buses from all

FIGURE 2.17   *Concert in the Square, 1977, the plaza as theater. (Photograph: Yosef Lior, Tel Aviv Municipal Archives)*

over the country."[57] Both demonstrations resulted in traffic jams and a strong police presence.

One of the most famous demonstrations in the Square of this period, deeply engraved in the Israeli collective memory, is the so-called "protest of the 400,000."[58] This number exceeded the population of the 325,700 living in Tel Aviv, out of a total population of 4,148,500 in Israel. The protest was held in the Square on September 25, 1982, to demand a state investigation into the Sabra and Shatila massacres. It urged the withdrawal of the army from Lebanon and the resignation of the government. Organized by the Labor Party and the Peace Now Movement, this assembly emphasized the Israelis' awareness of their role in democratic decision-making and their refusal to participate in government policy that went against personal conscience. The photo of this demonstration shows people standing on the Square at night waving signs in support of their demands (see Figure 2.6).

Thus, we see that, instead of being an organic and lived experience, the public rally had been transformed into a test of power, competing to see which side could assemble the greatest number of people in the Square. As Zeli Reshef, a Peace Now leader and one of the 400,000 Protest rally's organizers, said, "What is the political power of the Square? It is perceived as a place of power due to its size. Pictures of the crowd taken from the roofs convey that power."[59] The architectural geometry of Malchei Israel Square, its accommodation of vast audiences, its proximity to City Hall, its location in Tel Aviv, and the frequency and importance of these gatherings transformed it into the focus of political rituals.

Since the 1980s, public gatherings at the site have become carefully crafted performances with repeated rituals. The crowd usually gathers on Saturday evening after the Sabbath. Flags and banners are waved; the crowd moves arms and bodies in support of the speakers. The City Hall terrace has become a stage for speakers, celebrities, and high-ranking supporters. Speeches alternate with musical performances, the audience responds loudly and enthusiastically, and every event concludes with the singing of the national anthem. Images of the event are transmitted live to millions of television viewers, and the demonstrations are often synchronized with the end of the weekend evening news, also becoming the next morning's leading item. As a result, political events become television stage settings with aerial views of the masses.

Because of the increased tension between rival groups within Israeli society, the escalating Palestinian Intifada in the 1990s, and the growing involvement of the media at the assemblies, there has been an increase in surveillance in the Square (Figure 2.18). On days of assemblies, entrances to City Hall and to most of the restaurants and shops in the arcades surrounding the Square

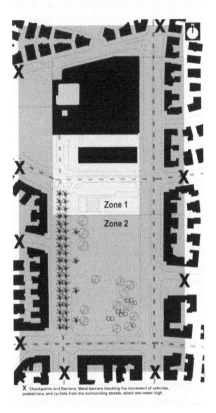

X Checkpoints and Barriers: Metal barriers blocking the movement of vehicles, pedestrians, and cyclists from the surrounding streets, about one meter high.

FIGURE 2.18   *Surveillance and Control during Civil Protests. Zone 1— Impermeable Checkpoint. Heavily guarded by policemen, barriers defining a sterile zone that includes the area of the balcony and the alley at the back of the City Hall building; Zone 2—Permeable Checkpoint (X). Metal barriers guarded by two or three policemen looking for suspicious individuals: checking IDs, contents of bags, and asking about weapons; only pedestrians are allowed to pass (vehicles and cyclists are not allowed). Surveillance Foot Patrol: Teams (usually of two or three policemen) with flashlights surveying the backyards of the residential buildings in the area. Surveillance in the Crowd: Policemen in civilian clothing strolling through the crowd; All Zones— Surveillance Watchers: Policemen located on the first and second perimeter of residential and public building roofs. (Drawing by author)*

are blocked by police at temporary checkpoints, which define new boundaries for the Square, turning it into a "sterile zone." The increased media attention provides additional surveillance, controlling events simultaneously from above and on the ground. Ironically, as opposed to the fenced boundaries, the inner space of the Square is unrestricted, allowing freedom of movement and departure via any of the barriers. This contributes to an illusion of democracy and safety, blurring the fact that the crowd's boundaries are strictly controlled, surveyed, and searched.

The Characteristics of Civil Assemblies in the Square

It is clear, then, that the history of both space and assemblies demonstrates that the space's symbolic meaning evolved prior to the formal design of the Square in the 1960s (Figure 2.19). Still, the architectural design created definite spatial boundaries and architectural attributes that dramatically changed

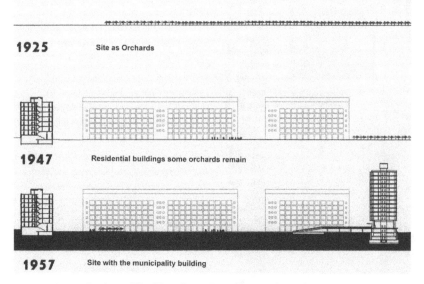

FIGURE 2.19   *Sections of Site Transformations. (Dates refer to planning proposal; drawing by author)*

the vistas and perspectives of power relationships in the Square. In particular, the design transformed the way in which the gaze of the crowd is controlled. The leaders stand on an elevated podium, high above the crowd, on the northern edge of a Square intensified by physical barriers unlike the open accessibility in 1945. Furthermore, distinct from the assemblies in the 40s, the rectangular space of the Square, with City Hall and its balcony, creates a hierarchical relationship between the speakers and the audience. This is amplified by the use of lighting, in particular both in and on the City Hall building, non-existent in the 1930s and 1940s, which, again, contributes to the theatricality of the event. Thus does the design of the Square transform the individual into an anonymous participant, particularly when an assembly takes place. The scale and physical features of the Square, the illuminated City Hall, and the size of the plaza all project power and monumentality that function as a constant reminder of a crowd that is absent from the city's daily life.

Socially, since the 1982 protest, different groups have identified Malchei Israel Square as *their* arena to reinforce their social and national identities. In the 1980s and 1990s, assemblies in the Square illustrated the fragmentation of national unity. Protests there expressed the divided opinions of isolated sectors of the Israeli society, with no outlets for communication. Unlike the situation in the 1930s, current sectors do not acknowledge each other's legitimacy. Even today, meetings in the Square do not represent social diversity as much as a congregation in which the different groups protest against each other, rather than against a common antagonist. Furthermore, tensions between the various groups using the Square have increased, underlining their differences. Moreover, gatherings of orthodox Jews and other right-wing groups in Jerusalem's Zion Square emphasized the rivalry between the two cities and their positions in the national arena. This antagonism is also associated with Tel Aviv's role as the cultural and business center, against Jerusalem's historic and symbolic role. The 1948 war and, especially, the 1967 war reinforced Jerusalem's status as Israel's capital.[60] Since 1967, Jerusalem's origins and urban development have derived from an enlisted mythology, a mystical dimension that has intensified, especially in contrast to the quotidian existence of Tel Aviv.[61] The concreteness and the physical setting of Malchei Israel Square, along with its centrality, nationally and within the city, have all reinforced a perception of it as an arena of contested civil participation.

Thus, the current form of protest in the square is a repeated ritual that exists through intentionality (design or structure) and practice (enactment). As noted by anthropologist Don Handelman, all public events began sometime and somewhere, regardless of whether their existence is attributed to tradition or invention. In instances of invention, the public event's intentionality may be created whole, and therefore its design and form will have temporal priority over its enactment. As shown, the forms of both space and the rituals in the Square are expressions of negotiations that construct order, making the logic of how they are put together crucial to how they work and to that which their designs enable them to accomplish.[62] Although the socio-psychological perception of the space and its use for public gatherings precedes its formal and architectural development, it is the latter that is responsible for the space's symbolic features, the order and scale, and the logic of the design of civic assemblies. But as Handelman reminds us, the Square may continue to be modified, as these ritual "forms" or "structures" are never fixed once and forever, even though people may refer to these as settled and set.[63]

The ritual order was in use during the most dramatic event in the Square, fixed forever in the national (and international) consciousness—the assassination of Prime Minister Rabin on November 4, 1995, after a rally in support of the Oslo Accords.

As usual, this rally commenced at 7 p.m. with musical performances. Thousands of youngsters came to the Square carrying Hebrew, English, and Arabic banners calling for peace. The organizers constantly updated the audience about the masses en route to the event. Hundreds of balloons were released after the speeches. As Prime Minister Rabin descended the service stairs below City Hall's terrace, he was shot by a young Jewish extremist.

One significant outcome of the assassination was that it triggered a collective recognition of the violent act, creating an opportunity for revision. Thus, after the event, Israeli society addressed violated codes and boundaries, aspiring to amend social order and re-establish the status quo. Like the violent assassination—a performance that needed an audience—the immediate revisions that took place in the Square, immediately renamed Rabin Square, were publicly performed and viewed. These revisions, resources for creating and constructing a view of one group's enforcement of its truth over that of its rivals, become the focus of the following.

MEMORY
Everyday Life versus Traumatic Practices

> *Rabin Square is definitely a symbol for the Israeli nation. This is where a Prime Minister was murdered. People come to this place from all over the world. I certainly think that, just as the Knesset [the Israeli Parliament] passed a law to establish the Rabin Israel Research Center and another to commemorate the anniversary of the Prime Minister's assassination, it is appropriate to legislate another law to preserve the Square as it was on the day of the murder, for everyone.*[64]

These words of Yoram Meuhas (representative of the Yitzhak Rabin Center), in a memo to Israel's Interior and Environment Committee from 2001, embody the resistance to the development plan of Rabin Square, initiated by Tel Aviv's city council. Meuhas proposed legislation that would help to establish the relationship between the space (the Square) and the collective trauma ("for everyone"), representing one sentiment among many that arose immediately after the assassination. At the same time as the name of the Square was changed, a memorial was constructed and memorial gatherings took place, all of which affected the Square's cultural associations. The new plan and the debate that followed only aroused further and deeper questions about the relationship between the collective trauma, the place, and its users. Who is the collective ("everyone")? Who is included? Who is left out? Who participates in making decisions about the place? How does the meaning of the violent act influence this process?

In contested urban situations, where population concentration is incremental and war and conflict play roles in shaping the environment, violent events affect the daily lives of people in cities all over the world. Spatial practices in the Square since the assassination, and the planned development initiated by Tel Aviv's City Council, support the argument that, although the production of post-traumatic space tends to be enlisted by national discourse, it is also challenged by design practices that confront the trauma of defining a new place that symbolizes a natural process of change, as well as by recognizing that chaos exists in the everyday. In this fashion, the focus is on the implications of how trauma is encoded in the production of space and contributes to the phenomenon of what we call *Urban Absence*.

Urban Absence

To further define *Urban Absence*, it is necessary to reiterate the differences between loss and absence. Loss is particular, immediate, and relating to a specific time and event, whereas absence is trans-historical, mythical, and intensifying over time.[65] When a trauma is accepted as loss, the urban context (as in post-war environments) can be dealt with in various ways, such as by improving conditions of basic structural-social city conditions. If the trauma is perceived as absence, urbanity becomes a socio-political problem, an endless search by inhabitants for a return to a sense of unity of both place and community. This situation trivializes and, at times, eliminates everyday practices at the trauma site, and thus simplifies the place's past and ongoing history.[66] This elimination *suspends* the past (history of place), the present (everyday practices), and the future (interventions or plans to modify space), merging the moment (of trauma) with the meaning of the place. This suspension is an *Urban Absence*.

   Urban Absence, maintained by the community, plays a central role in the production of symbolic representations of the event and the place. These practices are *acting-out* practices that transform the trauma from loss to absence. *Acting out*, in this instance, refers to the work of Dominick LaCapra[67] that distinguishes, in non-binary terms, between acting out and working through an interrelated response to loss or historic trauma. As mentioned in the previous chapter, LaCapra argues that mourning can be seen as a form of *working through* and melancholia as a form of *acting out*. Again, historical losses necessitate mourning—and possibly critical and transformative socio-political practices also. When absence is the cause of mourning, the mourning may become impossible, returning one continually to endless melancholy. However, the key problem with *acting out* the *Urban Absence* is that it contradicts the basic principle of democracy, which must allow for differences, antagonism, and conflicted voices.

Trauma Practices in Rabin Square: Stitching Together the Myth

The assassination of Prime Minister Rabin by a right-wing Jewish student was perceived as a violation of every written and unwritten Jewish code concerning mutual support, totally disrupting the internal order. Immediately after the assassination, all efforts were concentrated on reestablishing a sense of democratic/unified community.

As a culmination of social and political dispute, Yitzhak Rabin's assassination evoked post-traumatic practices nationwide, thus contributing to the production of a space that embodied reflective relationships between the assassination, the Square, and the collective—a stitching together of a perceived spatial dimension. The first action was the spontaneous response of the "candle children,"[68] young people who gathered in the Square in the days immediately after the assassination, weeping, singing, lighting memorial candles, and transforming the space into a temporary national graveyard (Figure 2.20). The mass of demonstrators was replaced by throngs of mourners, flags became candles, and slogans were replaced by songs. Thus, the mourners' actions did not challenge the local narrative or create spatial change, but rather created a collective identification that is reaffirmed annually in memorial ceremonies similar in size and content to the rally on the night of the assassination.[69]

Apart from these practices, some long-term changes have also followed, as in the changing of the name to Rabin Square and the erection of a memorial (Figure 2.22 a, b). Located on the site of the assassination near the side staircase leading to City Hall, the monument has become a tourist attraction. The memorial as a manifestation of the moment is an act of magnification— a symbol that has imbued the space with sanctity. In this context, the City Council decided to erase political graffiti (Figure 2.21) from the wall next to the staircase (inscribed immediately after the assassination), though a small section of the graffiti has been retained behind a glass frame.[70] The erasure and the framing both convey the conflict and announce that this is a sterile zone.[71] Although, at first glance, the Rabin memorial looks homogeneous, it is in fact a divided, disputed site embodying different memories; removing the graffiti and erecting the headstone nearby were attempts to "freeze" the trauma, inadvertently contributing to the construction of *absence*.

All these efforts were intended to heal and repair the deep divisions in Israeli society and to re-create an illusion of order, i.e., to strengthen the hetero-

FIGURE 2.20   *4/11/95. Taken immediately after the assassination, when people came spontaneously to the Square, lit candles, and grieved. Spatially, people gather in small groups throughout the space, creating a sense of intimacy. (Zvika Israeli, Government Press Office)*

topian[72] status of the space as a national archive. Since the assassination, no critical questions have been asked, questions such as: What are the connections between the physical dimensions of the site and the nature of the gatherings? What is the relationship between the mass gatherings and the spatial geometry of the space? The subordination of the space to the trauma focuses exclusively on the memory of the assassination and on the victim,[73] thereby ignoring the space itself. Hence, the City Council's idea of constructing a parking lot beneath the Square was perceived as blasphemous, totally inappropriate to the contemporary collective discourse (Figures 2.23, 2.24). Resistance to the planned parking lot represents the wish to maintain *Urban Absence.*

Urban Absence versus Lived Space

On March 3, 2002, the Tel Aviv City Council called for an open forum concerning future plans for Rabin Square. The following discussion outlines different approaches to the plan and to the role of the Square (see Table 2.1). These approaches—the *pragmatic, symbolic, sacred,* and *contextual*—were defined based on the speakers' conceptualization of the event, place, users,

2.21.A

2.21.B

values, and their attitudes toward change in the space. It is important to note that these approaches are not definite categories but rather analytic tools relating both to concrete and discursive space for place-making after a traumatic event.

The forum opened with the city engineer's plan, presenting the Square from two perspectives, as a space catering to the needs of the local community and as a national monument. His presentation took a *pragmatic* approach towards the space as part of the larger process of urban re-development in the area. He perceived the Square as a unique national monument and, at the same time, as a significant presence in the urban fabric, which permitted examination of the Square's multiple roles and identities. As the city engineer noted:

> When we speak of the activities in the Square, of its character . . . the nation's Square, where national events take place, there are at least three important functions that the Square serves. It is the Square of the City Hall, serving Tel Aviv's citizens. We also see the Square as the largest open space in the area, and there is the actual urban void, a space with meaning and a unique character, a pause in the urban fabric and a significant urban unit.[74]

Representing the Council, the city engineer viewed the assassination as a moment in a series of events that regularly occur at the site. In essence, the proposal to construct a parking lot beneath the Square would necessitate re-evaluation of its everyday use. This approach opposed the Square's geometry (i.e., the relationship between City Hall and the plaza), which should also be seen in the context of the ongoing post-modernist urban discourse that began in the 1960s.[75] As Zafrir, one of the architects involved in the project, said:

> When we established the state, the intimate meanings of the city were irrelevant for us. We were occupied with modern design. . . . Local architecture was irrelevant because it was created by others [i.e., the Palestinians]. That was also a period when design gave the "proper" solution to traffic problems. Plans of the time created urban axes 30 and 40 meters wide at the most sensitive points in the city, to allow free flow of traffic. This is an approach that, I hope, has now been sidelined.[76]

The concept of the Square as an everyday place legitimizes the construction of the parking lot, advocated not only by the city engineer but also by the citi-

(Opposite) FIGURE 2.21 (A, B) *Graffiti in the Square after the assassination, 7/11/1995. (Photographs: Israel Sun, Tel Aviv Municipal Archives)*

2.22.A

2.22.B

zens. The main difference between the citizens' and the engineer's perspective is how they each perceived the space. The citizens viewed the plaza itself as the space, suggesting changes, as Shimshi says, "to create some kind of layout . . . that will encourage people to come every day, all day, even when no dramatic events occur."[77] This approach was also expressed by the journalist Doron Rosenblum (2000), who wrote:

> Grow up from the "Square rituals" that ultimately cause more harm than use. . . . We must detach ourselves not only from the rituals, but also from the Square itself . . . we need to plough up—yes, plough up—this brutal Square, open it like a place hit by a meteorite . . . to construct an underground parking lot, to relate to the human dimension and not to the demonstrations of the masses. It is time to stop demonstrating normalcy and to start acting normal.[78]

As opposed to the *pragmatic* approach of those who advocate the lived experience, there are others who wish to conserve the *absence*. One dominant opinion proposes a *symbolic* approach, suggesting reinforcement of the Square's presence as an international symbol. This approach was conspicuous in the competition organized by the Engineers' and Architects' Association, the Rabin Square International Forum for Peace. The competition, open to all architects and planners, created identification between peace, the Square, and trauma. In addition, by opening up the competition to the world, the Association reaffirmed the site's universal importance and meaning. The competition results, published on many architectural Internet sites, were released on the anniversary of Rabin's assassination. The Association also initiated a petition protesting the Council's intentions to construct the parking lot without an open public discussion. The petition included the following statements:

> Rabin Square is a public and historical asset, a place where an important national event occurred. Since the Prime Minister's assassination, the square has become an international center for all peace lovers. To our amazement, the City Council and the planning department intend to destroy the Square and commercialize it.[79]

(Opposite) FIGURE 2.22 (A, B) *Memorial for Yitzhak Rabin, 2003. Basalt memorial designed by architect Claude Grundman-Brightman installed on November 1, 1996, near the service stairs where Prime Minister Rabin was shot. Its location on the pavement along one of the main routes in the city (Ibn Gvirol Street) integrates the memorial in the inhabitants' everyday life. (Photo [A]: author; Photo [B]: Yosef Lior; Tel Aviv Municipal Archives, 1997)*

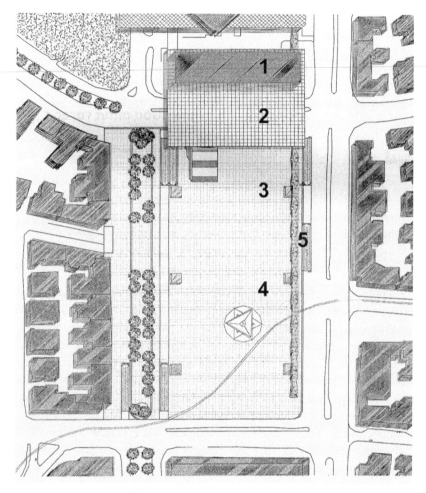

FIGURE 2.23 *Suggested Plan (Presentation A—prepared for the Local Committee 28.3.01, Farhi-Zafrir Architects). 1. City Hall. 2. Balcony. 3. Plaza. 4. Holocaust Memorial. 5. Parking lot exits.*

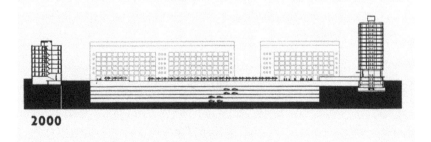

FIGURE 2.24 *Suggested section (Drawing by author)*

TABLE 2.1   APPROACHES TO A PLANNED CHANGE IN PLACE AFTER A TRAUMA

Approaches to a Planned Change in Place after a Trauma	Pragmatic	Symbolic	Sacred	Contextual
Conceptualization of the event	Views the event as part of the ongoing history of the place.	As a discrete event, representing the universal quest for peace.	As a deep wound, associated with this particular tragedy.	As one of the key political events within the collective memory of a national society.
Conceptualization of the place	*Everyday* The place is one zone in the city, not defined by the trauma.	*Idealistic* The place becomes a symbolic idea generated by the event.	*Static* The place merges with the event, no longer susceptible to outside influences.	*Proportional* The place is compared to other spaces with similar uses in the state.
Conceptualization of users	Focus includes everyone, especially local inhabitants.	Focus is on national as well as international users.	Focus is on national users as one unified collective.	Focus is on national users only.
Key value/concern	Identifies with the human scale and everyday activities.	Identifies with the universal symbol associated with the event.	Identifies with the preservation of the human legacy associated with the traumatic event.	Identifies with multiple spatial representations from the past.
Attitude toward spatial change	Concrete Advocates the primacy of the lived experience.	Symbolic Advocates a worldwide transference of the symbol.	Institutional Advocates ritual practices in memory of the event.	Contextual Advocates relative change according to use and context.

All this led to intervention by Cabinet members and discussions in the Interior Committee of the Knesset about "exposing" the municipality's plan for the Square. The plaza, as proposed by those who favor the *symbolic* approach, is conceived as a forum for public and national events, reducing the Square to an everyday meeting place and thereby establishing it as a national/international symbol. This would also remove the Square from municipal jurisdiction and transform it into a trans-historical symbol. To quote Kabel: "The Square, to my mind, was expropriated long ago from the Tel Aviv Council . . . it is a symbol . . . because it is where the prime minister was assassinated."[80] It should be emphasized that supporters of this attitude do not reject the option of architectural intervention in the space as long as the *urban absence* is magnified and/or sustained.

Another group, the Rabin Heritage Center Representatives' Group, advocates leaving the place in its current state. Yoram Meuhas, Director of the Rabin Center, demands that the Square be conserved. As he says,

> In the Rabin Heritage Center we want the Square to be preserved in its current character and to function as a place for pilgrimage and mass participants' commemorative ceremonies to Yitzhak Rabin's memory, and under no circumstances should it change the character of the place by adding buildings, cafés or stands. As for transforming the Square into a parking lot, we fear it will damage the character of the plaza and would prevent us from performing annual ceremonies.[81]

Unlike the *pragmatic* approach of the city engineer, the Rabin Center group views the murder as a social act that creates total identification between event and place, maintaining the character of the plaza as a place for commemorative assemblies. The supporters of this approach criticize the erasure of the "graffiti" as expressions of mourning, regarding it as sacred. Painting over the graffiti or changing the plaza character would "erase" the traumatic event, and "place" would be profaned.

The *contextual* approach views the assassination as a moment in the ongoing narrative of the plaza and the national history as a whole. The moment is not seen as a singular event but is rather linked to other events and places. As a city councilor stated: "this Square is important . . . because it is in the heart of the city. . . . We all remember Rabin's assassination, but I also remember the discussions about peace."[82] Advocates of this approach value the place according to its unique expansive physical scale in Israel, the political significance of the events taking place, its contribution to the practice of civil participation in Israel, and its emotional value. For the advocates of this approach, these meanings are interrelated and have implications on the national level. As Council member Michael Roea said, referring to the national value of the space:

> For me, Rabin Square is the democratic Square of the state of Israel . . . the heart of the Israeli state and society. . . . A tragedy occurred in Malchei Israel Square. A Prime Minister was murdered there. This event can only strengthen participation in democratic acts, and in the need to defend democracy.[83]

Again, for those who support the *contextual* approach, the scale of the Square as unique must be viewed in relation to Israeli society as a whole rather than to a particular political group. Because of this, the building of a parking lot in the space threatens democracy, even though the proposal does not modify the physical dimensions of the Square or alter the activities within it. As Nissim Calderon noted:

> If the Square is ruined, I must say that this would modify the culture of protest, because there is no other place . . . like it, neither in Haifa nor in Jerusalem. Protest is extremely important, a valuable asset. That is why . . . I personally support plans for rehabilitation, for dealing with problems and dilemmas . . . but I am not for perpetuating exciting places or holy stones.[84]

Thus, the supporters of this approach do not object to architectural intervention in the Square, but are cautious about broader changes that will modify its national status.

Urban Absence and the Future of the Square

The case of Rabin Square shows that diverse approaches to place-making can emerge from collective awareness of a traumatic event. Supporters of the *pragmatic* approach regard the moment as a productive opportunity. The plaza is identified not with the murder, but with an ongoing process of events (both human and physical). This sensitivity to, and awareness of, the traumatic moment maintains routines and calls on the citizens to re-normalize. Conversely, the supporters of the *symbolic* approach see the plaza as an international symbol of peace, a symbol whose meaning transcends place, thus transforming the place of the moment into an idealistic space. This is an ideology that distances its citizens from the everyday and views the site as an urban locus for monuments, memorials, and slogans.

Supporters of the *sacred* approach emphasize the distortion created by the moment and comprehend it as a trauma that cannot be grasped beyond its location. They do not distinguish the place from the narrative (i.e., the location of the assassination) or include its immediate environment. Both place and narrative are perceived as frames that cannot be changed or negotiated. This approach supports such practices as collective mourning and memorial ceremonies. The *contextual* approach regards the moment as connected to other events and places, rather than as autonomous. Accordingly, the meaning of the assassination derives from its social context. Although they differ, there is a strong resemblance here between the sacred and symbolic approaches, both of which advocate *urban absence* by re-creating a single memory for the place.

Those who favor the *contextual* approach see a threat to democracy if the plan is implemented. However, they do not ask whose democracy. Speakers for the municipality discuss the non-participation of certain groups (e.g., Israeli Arabs, Palestinians, foreign workers). This aspect of the debate arouses doubts concerning the integrity of a system that does not allow critical challenges to the current perception of the Square, but only reinforces the existing order by perceiving the Square as the gathering place for the Jewish collective. Thus, although the expressions "the democratic square" and "the people's place" are frequently heard, not all "the people" are included. It is also important to admit, as Butler says, that the public sphere is "constituted in part by what cannot be said and what cannot be shown. The limits of the sayable, the limits of what can appear, circumscribe the domain in which political speech operates and certain kinds of subjects appear as viable actors."[85] In other words, opening up the discursive boundaries of the Square and promoting free and unrestricted public debate are crucial to Israeli democracy.

Everyday Life, Trauma Practices and Architecture

Lefebvre's theory[86] concerning the relationship between everyday life and modernity discusses the ability of the everyday "spontaneous conscience" to resist the oppressions of quotidian existence. Ignoring the monotonies and tyrannies of daily living, De Certeau[87] stressed the individual's capacity to manipulate situations and create realms of autonomous action as networks of anti-discipline. Giddens[88] perceived everyday activities as a potential challenge to the modern nation-state. Accordingly, skilled manipulators daily construct a liberating social order through originality and creativity. Personal action is thus perceived as a means for cultural and social redefinition for effecting change.

This potential of everyday practices to challenge the modern nation-state via the lived space is questionable in cases of collective trauma, when both the social order and personal action become incomplete and insecure.[89] This psychoanalytic theory assumes that both the state and its subjects merely pretend to be secure. An event can be described as traumatic if it exposes or challenges this pretense.[90] However, traumatic events, though overwhelming, can also be revealing. They challenge the commonly accepted norms by which we lead our lives, and this awareness often presents opportunities for change and social revision. In other words, trauma is also a revisioning moment in that it often gives rise to change or re-visualization of a specific element. The phenomenon of changing direction and/or revision immediately after a crisis makes the individual re-interpret reality in light of a social order. This social order helps to normalize and organize the interpretation, evaluation, and encoding of sensory stimuli, however chaotic or accidental an event may be. Seen thus, the conflict over memory and post-traumatic practices contributes to organizing traumatic moments into a cognitive reality, a bounded security. However, when the locus is a public urban space that accommodates contradictory practices, a conflict occurs, thus evoking the struggle over *absence*.

What is the role of architecture in these processes? Architectural production in a post-traumatic situation accentuates the power differences between groups. By planning for the future, it challenges contemporary everyday life infected by trauma and calls for transformation. This analysis of the *pragmatic, symbolic, sacred,* and *contextual* approaches is not concerned merely with the concrete construction of place but also with how it is integral to the cultural, national, and political discourse of space. These complex relations among place, architecture, and nation-state are infinitely repetitive and reversible. Furthermore, the concept of revision through architecture/planning practices is inherent in the production of the cultural space. This aspect of professional practice makes it the mediator in contested arenas, integrating spatial production with political discourse. This role is often ignored by professionals who are not fully aware of their contribution to the process of place-making and their influence on the interrelationships between traumatic event and place. Though we do not know when the parking lot in Rabin Square will be constructed, the process of place-making has challenged *Urban Absence*, and some of the monolithic national perceptions of the Square have been reduced accordingly.

With the Square as an expression of socio-national construction, we can understand Israel's creation of mechanisms for civil participation in Rabin Square, which distinguish Israeli citizens from other residents in the state. In contrast to the Square's significance as a meeting point for Israeli citizens, the scarred site of the shoreline signifies the meeting point and struggle between two people prior to the 1948 war and Jaffa occupation. The history of the shoreline, despite its representation as a site of daily life—with people relaxing in cafes and walking along the beach—is actually saturated with political violence. This space represents the meeting and separation discourse between two ethnic groups, later to become nations, and allows discussion on two significant key terms—*Boundaries* and *Order*—both in the process of nation-building of two groups and in the architectural/planning practice. Here the concept *revisioning moments* is not discussed in the context of a single event but rather a continuous chain of violent events with reference to the suicide bombing in 2001. This event becomes a reference point from which to look at other violent events that, in turn, contributed to spatial revisions along the shoreline in the process of modifying boundaries and spatial order.

Chapter 3

Borders, Urban Order, and State-City Relationships along the Shoreline

THE SUICIDE BOMBING AT THE DOLPHINARIUM DISCOTHÈQUE, JUNE 1, 2001

Jewish demands for autonomy in the early 1920s contributed to the British Mandate's decision to separate Tel Aviv from Jaffa.[1] This decision, officially recognizing Tel Aviv as a separate entity, demarcated the Menshiyeh Quarter between Jaffa and Tel Aviv as a buffer zone with the Hassan Beq Mosque in the center (Map 3.1).[2] The establishment of this mosque in 1916 grew out of the decision of the military governor, Hassan Beq, to further develop Jaffa. At the beginning, the Arab community in Jaffa boycotted the mosque because of the forced labor and annexation of property that accounted for its construction. With the end of the Ottoman Empire, the community began using it, transforming it into an active community center.

The location and design of the mosque signifies its uniqueness and differences and also emphasizes its proximity to main axes and the communal intention of strengthening its accessibility. During the war of 1948, the mosque functioned as a strategic point in the conflict (Figures 3.1, 3.2, 3.3). When Menshiyeh was occupied by the Israel Defense Forces and with the transfer of the properties of the Palestinian community to the military governor, the mosque was cut off from the Muslim population of Jaffa, becoming a symbol of the exile of the Palestinian community.

The scarred and deserted area was changed by the planning and development initiatives of the 1960s, aimed at increasing the land and economic value of the Menshiyeh Quarter, and in 1967 the mosque reverted to the Palestinian Board of Trustees, whose limited means, together with the condition of the mosque, convinced them to lease the site to the Edgar Construction Company. The lease of the mosque (excluding the minaret and the hall below it) was limited to forty-nine years and included permission to use it for commercial purposes.[3] The plan, submitted by the architect Arie Elhanani, included

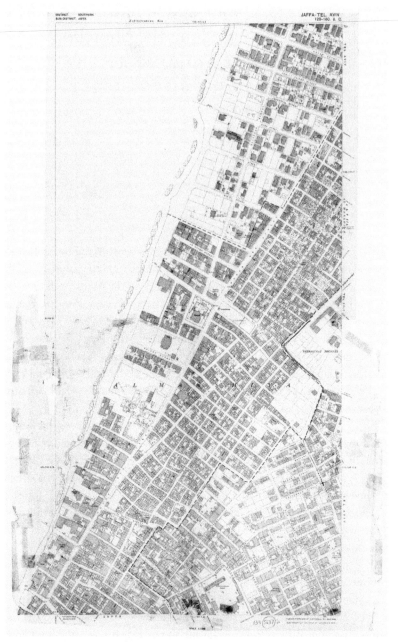

MAP 3.1   *Jaffa–Tel Aviv, 1936, British Survey of Palestine (Extract). Menshiyeh Village, as an extension of Jaffa bordering on Tel Aviv. (Source: Department of Geography, Tel Aviv University)*

FIGURE 3.1   *Hassan Beq Mosque during the 1948 war. (Photo: Collection of David Elazar, Israel Defense Forces Archives)*

FIGURE 3.2   *Hassan Beq Mosque, 1941. (Photo: Chava Dotan, Tel Aviv Municipal Archives)*

FIGURE 3.3 *Military forces at the mosque, before occupation, 8/4/1948. (Photo: Israel Defense Forces Archives)*

commercial and service use, but the capitalistic evaluation of the project, an insult to Palestinians and Israelis alike, aroused much debate, and the plan was rejected. The perception of the mosque as a "protected space" gave rise to another initiative in the 1980s to transform it into a Muslim-Jewish cultural center for meetings between Muslims and Jews of the city.[4] These plans were also rejected, and the work of restoration and renovation of the mosque commenced in the mid-1980s. This was a first step in strengthening the spatial and communal life of the Palestinian community in Jaffa.

Today, the spatial reality of the area is eclectic. In front of the mosque is the Dolphinarium complex for leisure activities; to the north there are residential neighborhoods, to the south a complex of high-rise office buildings, and to the east lies Gan Hakovshim ("The Occupiers' Park"), with a memorial to the Jewish battle in the 1948 war (Figure 3.4). The proximity of the south-facing memorial (towards Jaffa) with the gate of the mosque (facing north) exemplifies the realities and narratives of the two communities and the parallel discourse (real and imaginary) between them.

This spatial context is the site of the suicide bombing on June 1, 2001, when hundreds of youngsters were queuing to enter the Dolphinarium Discothèque.[5] This violent act is a reference point in time and space for examining the complex relationships between the spatial context (i.e., the seashore and the Jaffa–Tel Aviv borders) and the social context (Palestinians, Israelis, Jews, Christians, Muslims, orthodox, secular, labor immigrants) of the area. The discussion first addresses the question of *Borders* as an ideological socio-cultural construct by which communities define and defend their territory. It focuses specifically on the border zone between Tel Aviv and Jaffa, the Menshiyeh Quarter, and relationships between Israelis and Palestinians since the early twentieth century. It examines how borders are architecturally conceived and perceived through analysis of three border typologies—the *door,* the *bridge,* and the *gateway*—inviting a new discussion of architecture as a border-making practice. By examining border-making from architectural and urban perspectives, we clarify the relationships between conflict (destruction), architecture (construction), and everyday life in Tel Aviv and Jaffa in today's nationalist world.

The second section, *Order,* discusses cooperation between the state, the city, and the capital as well as the role of architecture in mediating between these forces and citizens. The aim of this cooperative action was aimed at developing the shoreline with the intent of clearly defining districts, landmarks,

FIGURE 3.4   *The Occupiers' Garden with the memorial to the Jewish battle in the 1948 war. (Photo: Author)*

and nodes. The common goal of the architectural and planning projects, addressed in this chapter, is the conceptualization of the shoreline as a linear continuum from southern Jaffa to northern Tel Aviv. Differing from the concept of *Boundaries*, this concept of order is seen as a pragmatic tool, less politically loaded.

The multiple interventions and projects along the shoreline make it impossible to present a chronological trajectory of its development because of these shared, though often conflicted, ideas and projects (see Map 3.2). Thus, by introducing these complementary concepts of order and boundaries, both chapters address the development of the seashore as early as the 1930s until the present day and become a prism through which we view the event of Friday evening, June 1, 2001.

The event, an attack on a Jewish disco located in front of a mosque, exacerbated a tense situation, exposing the complex mosaic of the local population. On the following day, a Jewish crowd gathered in front of the mosque, throwing stones and calling for revenge.[6]

The severity of the violent event thus created a temporary meeting point on the site for the two rival groups, the Israelis and the Palestinians. This situation of social exposure, the group's visibility to each other as well as to the municipality and the state, could have become an opportunity for change and revision, a situation that might have offered novel possibilities. But has it? Unfortunately it has not. Instead of creating a moment of recognition and acknowledgment, it created a situation by which the different groups became more alienated, and at the same time, the relationships between state, city, and capital became more cohesive, enhancing the process of place-making.

BOUNDARIES: *The Role of Planning and Architecture in Constructing Urban Borders*

In absolute terms, in the twenty-first century more collective violence has been visited on the world than at any previous time.[7] When violence occurs it differs in form, coordination, and prominence. How do we set about examining the suicide bombing in 2001? Should we see it as just another event, as part of the ongoing violent ritual between Israelis and Palestinians? The socio-spatial context of this event, rooted in the unstable geopolitical situation of undefined national borders, cannot be reduced merely to "another" violent act in the national struggle. We can assess it as part of an ongoing spatial struggle over borders and territory.

The concept of border as a spatial formation of power relations implies control over resources and the framing of movement.[8] The modernist project

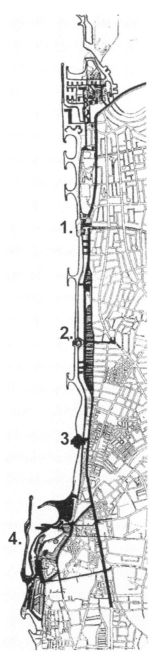

MAP 3.2 *Projects and developments along the shoreline. 1. Atarim Square (Machlul).*
2. Gruenblatt Plan Area (estimation). 3. Dolphinarium Plan (Menshiyeh). 4. Jaffa.
(Source: Tel Aviv Municipal Archives)

of creating state borders, intrinsic to the modern nation-state's struggle over territory,[9] generates order, both internally within the nation and externally between nations. However, the border also plays a significant cultural-ideological role in which geo-policy and culture intersect to establish a national identity.[10] Thus, the border influences all spheres of everyday life at different scales and levels, from the private home to the national arena, by defining the pattern and direction of movement[11] to establish connections and intersections. These patterns of movement are vulnerable to manipulation by the state and other institutions, through maps and other documentation, actual physical demarcation, signage, and usage. In many cities with multi-ethnic compositions, including Tel Aviv and Jaffa, borders have been contested, dynamically constructed, and reconstructed. However, unlike other places, the border between Tel Aviv and Jaffa is affected by the unstable geo-political situation of their undefined national borders. Hence, although defined as a concrete physical place and connected to architectural practice and everyday lived experience, the border between Tel Aviv and Jaffa is altered according to political events at the national level.

The discourse about borders in architecture and urban planning relates to the border in its *perceived* dimension. This envisions border space "as directly *lived* through its associated images and symbols, and hence the space of 'inhabitants' and 'users'."[12] This compound of physical space and symbolic use of its objects is evident in Lynch's analysis of the physical expression of borders and how they demarcate and organize space.[13] In this sense, spatial objects, such as buildings and walls, are products of architectural construction of both physical and imaginary borders. Lynch shows[14] how these borders (i.e., *edges, paths,* etc.) divide and separate a city, while at the same time they assist in constructing an image of place. Other theoretical approaches regard borders as socially imposed phenomena and emphasize the role concrete demarcation plays in voluntary and involuntary ethnic segregation.[15] Borders along streets, railway tracks, parks, and other urban landmarks set boundaries beyond which residents of one part of the city cannot or do not pass. Here, planners and architects play a major role, establishing these perceptual boundaries and how they affect difference, identity, and mobility.[16] There are many examples of these practices, such as fencing public parks to redefine the privatization of urban space as part of capitalist ideology,[17] walling a neighborhood,[18] or treating a building like a fortress.[19] From this perspective, the border is an ideological representation and a cultural category by which social groups define themselves and the world to construct spatial power relations. Urban borders are thus dynamic spatial productions, conditioned not by their design but by architecture that expresses the complex struggles of contesting forces for space and territory.

Discussions of *perceived* urban borders tend to overlook the *conceived* dimension and the contribution of architecture, especially with regard to the geo-political terrain of the nation-state. These discussions do not acknowledge the unique role of planning practices in supporting local-national ideology or their effect on the everyday lived experience at border zones. As noted by Lefebvre, conceived space is the abstract domain of "scientists, planners, urbanists, technocratic sub-dividers, and social engineers . . . all [of] whom identify what is lived and what is perceived with what is conceived."[20] One of the few works acknowledging the role of the conceived in the demarcation of borders, by the architect Rem Koolhaas,[21] discusses the Berlin Wall as an architectural object. It notes the Wall's *graphic* demonstration of efficient power of division, exclusion, and enclosure of space. The Berlin Wall, according to Koolhaas, suggested that architecture's beauty is proportional to its horror and cannot be disconnected from the political discourse of borders. Architectural measures to produce and preserve spatial control express rules, language, and behavioral norms, materializing ideologies to manipulate ways that people experience the world.

Thus, we focus on the urban border as a conceived phenomenon—an architectural expression of political ideology. To explore the unique role of architecture in local border-making, especially in the urban milieu, three border typologies are proposed: the door, the bridge, and the gateway.[22] These are presented as a means of discussing architecture as a border-making practice. Each of these borders implies a boundary—a separation intended to classify unbounded space and assist in its division and its connection. This view concurs with George Simmel's observation that things must be first separated in order to be joined together. "Practically as well as logically, it would be meaningless to connect that which has not been separated."[23] Thus, a door is not a separation but a possibility for an ongoing interchange. According to Simmel, the door actually suggests that separation and connection are two sides of precisely the same act,[24] simultaneously embodying the completely different intentions of entering and exiting. In contrast to the door, the bridge symbolizes the extension of a more volitional sphere over space. It connects the finite (one end) with the finite (the other end) regardless of direction. In addition to Simmel's typologies, we suggest a third hybrid typology—the gateway, similar to the bridge in that it is visible and has aesthetic value, and, like the door, has directional connotations (see Table 3.1). Also like the door, the gateway signifies flow while, at the same time, it physically and perceptu-

TABLE 3.1 BORDER SITUATIONS

Door	*Bridge*	*Gateway*
Daily value	Aesthetic value: visible	Aesthetic value: visible
Separation between inner and outer	Connecting finite with finite	Framing
Framing direction of entrance	Undirected movement	Framing direction of entrance and exit
Everyday practice		*Rite of passage*

ally frames the direction of entering or leaving as a rite of passage. Of these three typologies, the door is the most open, spatially and conceptually, and the gateway is the most rigid.

Conceptualizing these border typologies will assist us in analyzing the specific urban context of Tel Aviv and Jaffa. The focus on these cities illustrates how architectural practices and national aspirations intermingle in the construction of urban borders. Obviously, this is not unique to Tel Aviv and Jaffa; similar situations occur in cities all over the world. Nonetheless, a discussion of Tel Aviv and Jaffa, spanning a period of development of three urban schemes, can add to our understanding of the violence taking place on June 1, 2001, and the violence occurring there since the early twentieth century.

Menshiyeh: Conceiving Border as Door

> *It should be explained that one quarter of Jaffa, known as Menshiyeh, projects, as it were, into Tel Aviv; or, expressed more historically, Tel Aviv has extended around this quarter of Jaffa. (Mills, 1934)[25]*

The separation discourse and actual division of space, initiated in the early 1920s under British rule, indicated a new spatial relationship between Arabs and Jews in Jaffa/Tel Aviv. However, despite very different shapes, scale, materials, and nature of the urban fabric, the spatial continuity of residential buildings encouraged movement and ongoing exchanges between the two communities. Despite the fenced border between the two cities, the Menshiyeh boundary zone has been conceptualized, and actually functions, as a metaphorical door. This affected daily life, allowing simultaneous connection and separation, with an infinite number of possibilities for movement and passage. Moreover, even during conflicts (and perhaps because of them), the border has become not so much a dividing wall as a locus of negotiation between communities and cultures.

Menshiyeh was first developed as a fishing village on the coast and as an extension of Jaffa, bordering Tel Aviv (Figures 3.5, 3.6). The Tel Aviv City News[26] described Menshiyeh as an Arab neighborhood embedded in Jewish areas of the city so that it was hard to distinguish between the two cities. This is apparent on aerial maps of the period[27] in which the physical border between Menshiyeh and Tel Aviv is fragmented and the two neighborhoods coalesce. However, although the two neighborhoods are geographically indivisible, researchers[28] emphasize their architectonic differences and highlight their distinct formal attributes (Map 3.3). Built at the end of the nineteenth and the beginning of the twentieth centuries, Menshiyeh follows the planning principles of a traditional village, reflecting the economic, social, and cultural systems of its place and time. The basic building unit, a multi-functional residential space where all activities take place, is a cube constructed from local natural materials—stone and sand.[29] In contrast to this continuous urban vernacular, the new urban fabric of Tel Aviv followed the development scheme of Geddes. Influenced by the modernism induced by the Zionist ideology,[30] Tel Aviv's new residential architecture adopted the International Style,[31] its formal appearance influenced by both the Bauhaus and Le Corbusier, although actual implementation was driven by economic constraints and administrative bureaucracy.[32]

Although maps of the period show a continuous urban fabric, in reality socio-cultural differences between the cities made the border situation much more complex. The Jewish community's attitude towards Menshiyeh was ambiguous, seeing it, on the one hand, as providing shelter for new immigrants, especially those unable to afford the rising rents of Tel Aviv, and, on the other hand, as an enemy zone—the land of the "other." Perceived by the founders of Tel Aviv as "primitive," Menshiyeh was presented in Tel Aviv's modernization discourse as "somewhere else," reinforcing its status as a temporary solution to Tel Aviv's lack of housing. The Tel Aviv Council notes that "Menshiyeh is just a few seconds away from the corner of Allenby [the center of Tel Aviv at the time] and is surrounded on three sides by Tel Aviv's streets. The owners of the land and the houses, however, are mostly Arabs."[33] Menshiyeh is thus a transit station for Jews arriving from Asia and Africa; as the newspaper noted, "Who are the Jews in Menshiyeh? Newcomers, Jews from Arab countries, to whom the lifestyle and the environment are more familiar than the Hebrew settlement."[34]

This ambivalent border between Tel Aviv and Menshiyeh embodied the simultaneous acceptance and rejection, connection and separation, apparent

FIGURE 3.5 *Jaffa from the north, December 1917. South Palestine. (Photograph: Captain Arthur Rhodes, reproduced by permission of Palestine Exploration Fund, London)*

FIGURE 3.6 *Jaffa from the rocks, showing Andromeda's Rock. December 2, 1917. (Photograph: Captain Arthur Rhodes, reproduced by permission of Palestine Exploration Fund, London)*

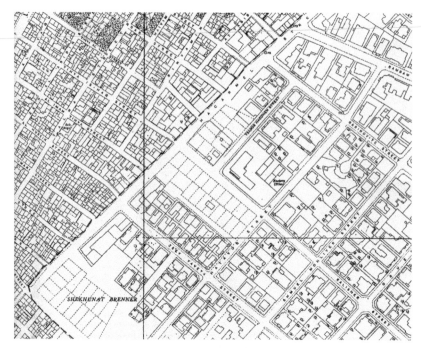

MAP 3.3 *Menshiyeh, urban block typology (Extract). Left: Menshiyeh. Right: Tel Aviv. (Jaffa, 1938, survey of Palestine, 1:2500, Tel Aviv Municipal Archives)*

in everyday life in the 1930s (Figure 3.7). A British report,[35] detailing the events of 1936, described Menshiyeh as vulnerable and susceptible to violent events. It refers to the Jewish protest that resulted in harassment of Arabs working in Tel Aviv. When rumors that Arabs had been killed spread through Menshiyeh and Jaffa, violent and destructive events ensued,[36] after which many Jews fled from Menshiyeh to Tel Aviv. However, the housing shortage in Tel Aviv and lower rents in Menshiyeh soon compelled the low-income and poor Jewish families to move back to Menshiyeh.[37]

The occurrences of 1936 were the Jewish community's justification for a call to revise the border between the two cities,[38] even though the Peel Commission (1937) declared decisively that Jaffa and Tel Aviv were a single geographical unit. It also commented on the hostility between the two communities. Although efforts were made to clarify the border line, no agreement was reached.[39] The British suggested constructing a buffer-fence, to include a road that would reinforce the border and allow British control if violent events recurred.[40] The limitations of this suggestion indicated that the British perceived the problem as "unsolvable." The Woodhead Committee, discussing the issue a year later, suggested demolishing a row of houses between the two neighborhoods, making a wide road, and constructing a wall with gates to be used for army movements if necessary.[41]

Parallel to the British separation discourse and the actual spatial and administrative separation, mutual relationships between the two communities still existed. The Menshiyeh quarter operated as a dynamic border zone that was "not physical but socio-spatial"[42] and, rather than dividing the cities, it allowed ongoing relationships. However, this dialectic attitude towards Menshiyeh changed irrevocably with the 1948 War and the occupation of Jaffa.

Menshiyeh: Conceiving Border as Bridge

Tel Aviv and Jaffa are separated from each other. Tel Aviv thrives and Jaffa stands still. Reconstruction of Menshiyeh will allow bridging the area between the cities . . . the idea of constructing a Tel Aviv center between the two cities, and the movement of population to the south will completely change the status of Jaffa. (Niv and Raifer, 1965)[43]

FIGURE 3.7   *British soldiers guarding a barbed wire barrier on the Jaffa border during the curfew imposed on Tel Aviv, 3/3/1947. (Photo: Kluger Zoltan, Government Press Office)*

From the end of the British Mandate and the establishment of the State of Israel in 1948, power shifts are evident in the Menshiyeh of the 1960s. It underwent forced movements of populations following the annexation of Jaffa to Tel Aviv and the unilateral arrangements made by the state regarding the land and property of absentee Palestinians. This is marked, both symbolically and physically, by the formal decision to turn Menshiyeh from a *backdoor* area of the city into a national and municipal *bridge*. That bridge, initially conceived as an imported element linking the two urban entities, in fact supported the arguments for separation. As an ambitious architectural project, it actually encouraged discontinuity, transforming residential neighborhoods into a business area that programmatically and practically separated two ethnic groups. This redefinition of the border and the role of Menshiyeh in constructing a national and municipal bridge must be understood in relationship to four conflicts: between the two communities, between the city and the state, between the city and its citizens, and among the professional planners and architects.

The first conflict erupted immediately following the United Nations' decision on November 29, 1947, to divide the country between its two communities. The separation plan saw Jaffa as an isolated Arab enclave. In the ensuing war, the Jaffa–Tel Aviv border became a battlefront, which resulted in the Jewish occupation of Jaffa, which, for the Jews, was perceived as an "end to a serious threat to the safety of the Jewish State."[44] For the Palestinians, the occupation and the consequences of the 1948 war are still perceived as *Al Nakba*—a national as well as a personal tragedy (Figure 3.8).[45] Although Menshiyeh had suffered heavy physical damage, parts of the village were still standing and were inhabited by Jewish immigrants, thus implementing the state's housing policy of utilizing abandoned Arab structures as temporary shelters for needy Jewish populations (Figures 3.9, 3.10).

The second conflict, an outcome of the occupation, was the struggle between the city and the state concerning Tel Aviv's municipal control over Jaffa.[46] On October 5, 1949, the annexation of Jaffa was approved by the government, and the combined city was named Jaffa–Tel Aviv. The annexation created a new situation, compelling the municipality to take upon itself national tasks. Objections were quick to arise. The municipality, threatened by a financial burden that would endanger Tel Aviv's lifestyle, refused to accept the unification. As Mayor Rokach explained, "Tel Aviv has developed areas according to a town-planning scheme. On the other hand, Jaffa is densely built-up, but has no proper infrastructure."[47] The Minister of Interior's response was that "if we follow this line of thinking, we will have to close the country's doors to newcomers. Since Jaffa is poor and Tel Aviv is rich—and

FIGURE 3.8 (A)   *Inhabitants leaving. (Photo: Collection of David Elazar, Israel Defense Forces Archives)*

FIGURE 3.8 (B)   *The British in Menshiyeh after the Occupation. (Photo: Collection of David Elazar, Israel Defense Forces Archives)*

FIGURE 3.9   *The Post War Urban Fabric, Menshiyeh, aerial view, 1955. (Tel Aviv Municipal Archives)*

(Opposite) FIGURE 3.10   *A. Menshiyeh, 1961; B. Menshiyeh, 1962. (Photos: Willi Folender, Tel Aviv Historical Archive)*

IO.A

IO.B

this is the situation—then the feelings of friendship and responsibility obligate rich Tel Aviv, in this time of crisis, to support poor Jaffa."[48] Another objection was that Jaffa "came first" in the city's name (i.e., Jaffa–Tel Aviv).[49] However, despite all objections, a government committee declared Jaffa a natural continuation of Tel Aviv, a financial and cultural basis for the annexation plan.[50] The mayor immediately called for "re-planning Jaffa right from its foundations," proposing Tel Aviv as a model for a new aesthetic tradition.[51] To achieve this end, as part of the new partnership between city and state, the "City Project" for "a new heart for Tel Aviv–Jaffa" in Menshiyeh was conceptualized. It materialized as a town planning competition to redesign Menshiyeh for the Tel Aviv–Jaffa Central Area Redevelopment Project.[52]

So, together with Jaffa, Menshiyeh underwent two interconnected processes in the early 1960s. On the one hand, it was systematically neglected— an attempt to cause a population transfer that would force urban redevelopment. On the other hand, the goal was to develop Tel Aviv as an alternative tourist attraction to the more traditional centers. Essentially, Jaffa was to be transformed from a hostile Arab town into an "Old City," integral to Tel Aviv and its heritage. The plan's commercial prospects were clear, as described by the City spokesman: "The development of Menshiyeh has first priority in the development plans of the City Council, due to its economic potential as the largest commercial center in proximity to the beach."[53]

Thus, the conceptualization of Menshiyeh as a bridge—as the commercial heart of the city—necessitated evacuating the population to refine its land use.[54] Menshiyeh was described in the competition booklet as "a peripheral district of Tel Aviv . . . [in which] the existing buildings are either obsolete or so old that they are only fit to be demolished or rebuilt."[55] The ongoing neglect of the area by the municipality also accelerated its abandonment. Residents wrote to the Mayor[56] and members of the City Council,[57] voicing suspicions about the professed aim of "cooperation with goodwill" in the redefinition of the area as a bridge (Figures 3.11, 3.12).[58]

However, the international competition to mark Menshiyeh as a bridge took place despite objections, and 152 entries were submitted by architects worldwide.[59] The first prize was given to Alexander Branca and Gerd Feuser from Germany, "for presenting an idea of fundamental importance to Tel Aviv . . . broadening the sea front, and constructing a lagoon, divided from the mainland but linked effectively with a new city center" (Figure 3.13).[60] This and other proposals expressed the high modernism of the international agenda. In the context of Tel Aviv, it proposed a cutting-edge image for the nation-state. However, the real purpose of this endeavor was to legitimize de-

MANSHIAH PROJECT
TEL-AVIV, ISRAEL
AS DELIMITED FOR STUDY

GOVERNMENT OWNED
PRIVATELY OWNED

FIGURE 3.11   *Menshiyeh Project, Real Estate Study, 1961. (Tel Aviv Municipal Archives)*

molishing the existing continuity of the Arab fabric, replacing it with isolated objects, utilizing new technology in line with the economic and ideological interests of the new Jewish state.[61]

It is important to note that, in spite of the first prize award, the project was given to three young architects: Niv, Raifer, and Mizrahi, under the super-

FIGURE 3.12   *Menshiyeh, Tel Aviv, 7/2/1964. (Photo: Collection of Ba'machane;*
Photographer: Miki Asted; Israel Defense Forces Archives)

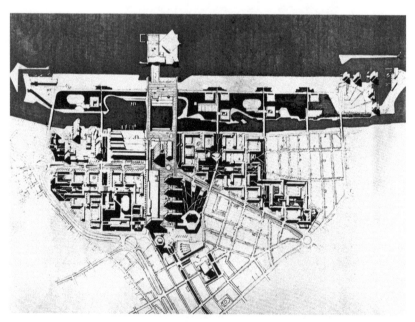

FIGURE 3.13   *First prize, the Menshiyeh Competition. (Tel Aviv Municipal Archives)*

vision of the more experienced architects, Sharon and Perleshtain. This was allowed because the jury[62] saw the prizewinners' design as schematic, to be further developed by local architects more familiar with the urban context. The process included studying all the winning plans and submitting a new layout. The new group envisioned the area as a potential municipal-national center that would assist in solving Tel Aviv's basic infrastructure and movement problems and improve poor neighborhoods, establishing physical links between the two cities.[63]

Further complications of conceiving the project as a bridge arose from subsequent conflict between the architects who won the competition and the local planners who drew up the city's master plan. For example, Zion Hashimshoni, who had been responsible for the 1960s master plan, favored a national modernist perspective. He called for looking at Menshiyeh not as a commercial bridge but as an integrated neighborhood within the city.[64] Two other planners also articulated their objection to the bridge concept. Aharon Horovitz, who had been in charge of the 1950s master plan, and Yaakov Ben Sira, who had been the city engineer from 1929 to 1950, criticized the bridge's capitalistic implications with its dismissal of community.[65] In a letter to the Menshiyeh community,[66] Horovitz wrote that the area was designated for a park and not for commercial development. The other planner, Ben Sira, called the plan "immature,"[67] attacking its development policy, warning against an "American capitalist agenda." This, he argued, would cause a gentrification process but would not solve the problems of the poor neighborhoods.[68]

Thus, the program for a business center, or bridge, and main motor route along the sea was never implemented. Opposition delayed the preparation of Menshiyeh's master plan and negated the necessity of the whole project. As a city engineer in the 1960s argued, ". . . the Menshiyeh plan is not viable in light of the new reality."[69] However, despite opposition, the mayor ordered the preparation of a detailed plan[70] that featured high-rise office buildings and hotel development. Yet, despite its partial realization, the Menshiyeh Project (Figure 3.14) created the visual and physical barriers between Jaffa and Tel Aviv. The architecture reinforced the fortuitous border with out-of-scale buildings, thereby separating the city from the waterfront. As a result of the new master plan in the 1980s,[71] the concept of the two entities connected through a commercial bridge was discarded in favor of regenerating adjacent neighborhoods to catalyze a regular flow between the privileged north of the city and its poor in the south.

FIGURE 3.14   *"City Project," 2003. (Photo: Author)*

Menshiyeh: Border as Gateway

The plan was suggested in order to connect by urban means the new Tel Aviv and its modern area of Menshiyeh to the delicate fabric of old Jaffa, and to create a functional unified continuity. (Bogod and Pigardo, 1992)[72]

In the end, the planning policies and the accelerated privatization processes of the 1980s resulted in the fragmented and eclectic Menshiyeh of the 1990s. Out of this situation, in the 1990s a new architectural border-making concept emerged in the form of a gateway. The "Jaffa Gate" project, still being conceptualized today, was influenced by three major issues. First, new power relations between the private sector and the national-municipal economy are required as part of the new capitalist logic of economic circulation; the poor city is continuing to initiate cooperation between private investors and national-municipal development companies. As opposed to the rationales of the 1960s, the 1990s plans are the result of private developers looking for profitable investments and the municipality's eagerness for urban development. Second, a shift in professional discourse among architects challenged the functional approach of modernism.[73] Repudiating utopian views and rethinking the linking of "social" and "architectural" space, these designers searched for other ways to conceive the city. They emphasized physical space, existing circumstances, and the local historical context,[74] paralleling architecture's search for place and its focus on critical regionalism[75] and the genius loci,[76] perceiving space as an archeological site constructed from layers of history and memory.[77] This architecture, rejecting the political modernist agenda, reverted to the formal-aesthetic, thereby opening the door to capitalist values.[78]

The third change derives from the Palestinian/Israeli dispute, the peace process of the 1990s, and the subsequent attacks on civilian centers, culminating in a series of violent activities in October 2000.[79] The world's economy and political processes in the early 1990s led Israel's leaders to support economic growth in real estate development, for which metropolitan Tel Aviv has been the center. Thus, while in the 1930s, Jaffa and Tel Aviv were perceived as binary entities, and in the 1960s as a unified entity, by the 1990s, they had become fragmented communities structured according to economic logic. Furthermore, despite bright prospects, the violent events affecting the cities' everyday experiences have altered the nature of their economic development. The question is, how do these changes affect border-making, and in what ways is the production of space influenced by national conflicts?

The current proposal, evolving from the 1990s partnership between the city and the private sector, offers Menshiyeh the architectural concept of a tourist gateway, an entry to the city. The Jaffa Gate Project embodies the desire to reframe the area, as a place/passage that marks the entrance to Jaffa's Mediterranean culture. In contrast to earlier beach plans, Bogod and Pigardo's scheme of 1992 was based on a commercial development of restaurants, shops, a fishing center, and hotels, all perceived as an expansion of Jaffa's tourist area (Figure 3.15). However, in the end, the City Council decided to establish, with minimal investment, a temporary promenade in the area. The result is a simple layout of railings, plantings, and sitting areas. Yet regardless of its scale, this modest promenade has changed the area irrevocably, increasing the Jaffa–Tel Aviv connection by inviting constant use of the area by Arab and Jewish families alike.

Yet this was not the end of the story: amid construction of the temporary promenade, an unexpected event occurred. During the process of installing a sewage line, the Ottoman Sea Wall of Jaffa was exposed, attracting the attention of two local architects, Eyal Ziv and Eitan Eden. They contacted Atarim, the company in charge of the development, suggesting that the wall be preserved as part of the promenade. Their detailed proposal illustrated how the project could contribute both culturally and historically to the city.[80] Work in the area was stopped, and the two architects were asked to suggest an alterna-

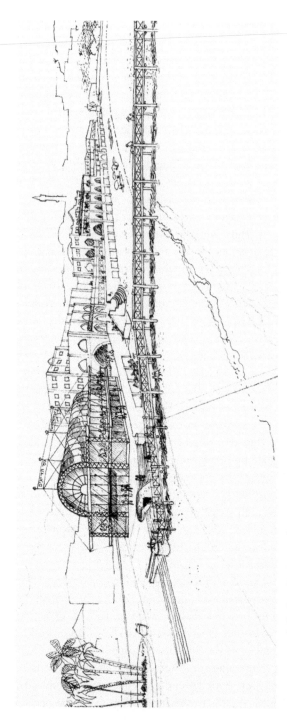

FIGURE 3.15 *Jaffa Gate Project, architects Bogod and Pigardo. (Author's collection)*

FIGURE 3.16   *Jaffa Promenade, 2003. (Photo: Author)*

tive to Bogod and Pigardo's plan. This remnant of the Ottoman Wall, initially destroyed at the end of the nineteenth century, was now the project's main generator, focusing the plan on preservation of the wall[81] (Figure 3.16).

As these recent projects demonstrate, the discourse of the 1990s is very critical of the modernist attempts of the 1930s and 1960s to erase the Arab landscape by assuming the place has no memory. The 1990s initiated a new search for identity, in contrast with the prevailing policies of blurring and forgetting. By exchanging the concept of a bridge with that of a gateway, the municipality can reconstruct the very fabric it demolished only three decades earlier. This has resulted in projects attuned mainly to the commercial market, to promote tourism. As the architects of the Menshiyeh Gateway say, "these are mostly ruins, and in some places there are dilapidated buildings and huts remaining from the original village. The old structures will be combined with the new buildings. The original scale of the village will be reconstructed, using Mediterranean materials and colors, all in the picturesque narrow alleys and the various squares."[82] This nostalgic approach is even more extreme at the Jaffa Promenade, where the imaginary borders of the analogical wall are invented. These projects demonstrate how the national awareness of border, discursive or real, is adapted to the everyday. This "normalization" may adopt a different spatial and morphological attitude from that of the 1960s, but it serves a similar function in its ideological support of the production of borders.

Borders and Architectural Practice

Architecture and planning play a key role in the conceptualization and management of borders by employing the formal language of the regime, loaded with cultural associations. Architectural and planning practice in Menshiyeh has furthered the Jewish community's attempts to differentiate itself. However, despite Arab and Jewish differences and conflicts in the 1930s, Tel Aviv and Jaffa were interconnected through the mutual practices of everyday life. The attempt to erase Menshiyeh during the 1948 War in order to create symbolic national and municipal borders raises complex questions. How were the local communities affected by these demolitions? How did they assist in the creation of actual and/or imagined space? And, essentially, is it actually possible to erase borders at all?

In the 1960s, the erasure had allowed the state a "redefinition of place" in which scale and lifestyle were completely modified. But this attempt to reproduce the space has, in our time, unstitched the fragile relationships between the two communities/cities. If Menshiyeh of the 1930s functioned as a door, connecting two communities linked to each other and to the sea, in the 1960s it became a "separating" bridge. This architectural vision, conceptualized with no reference to the inhabitants or to the actuality of the place, was bound to fail. In the 1990s the awareness of a real and discursive border, as in the 1930s, emerged through the practice of daily existence. Nevertheless, adoption of the language and vocabulary of "Old Jaffa" is ideologically based on national narratives of identity and meaning, similar to those of the 1960s.

Menshiyeh demonstrates that architectural border-making, by erecting boundaries, affects the tension between communities, as well as between the inhabitants and the establishment. It is enacted, by choice (as in the case of Ahuzat Bayit) and by force (as in the population transfer following the 1948 War). By reconstructing an imagined domain, Menshiyeh was lost to the Arab community, becoming part of "Greater Tel Aviv" for the Jewish community. This process is, of course, not unique to Tel Aviv/Jaffa. Here, as elsewhere, architectural conceptualization is based on professional knowledge and ideologies that are relative, subjective, and changing. It involves an abstract spatial representation that is, as Lefebvre reminds us, the dominant mode of production of any society, affecting both lived and perceived spaces.[83]

The dichotomy between the abstract vision of the profession and the conflicted lived space is clearly evident in the case of Menshiyeh. However, we do not argue that the profession should *not* engage in revisioning thinking. On the contrary, revisioning thinking has often helped to create discursive and physical shifts in conflicted situations by visualizing new spaces. In Lefebvre's terms, the conceived space plays a key role in changing both the lived and the perceived spaces. In fact, as demonstrated in Menshiyeh, each of the border-making typologies—door, bridge, and gateway—has contributed to the re-thinking and re-visualization of the place. What we argue is that, in the pro-cess of design, architects and planners should be more aware of their role in border-making. Often, in order to stabilize conflicted situations, they must challenge others' and their own ideological assumptions within the process of design, attempting to produce spatial "doors" that allow mutuality on both sides of a border. The practice must never predicate a static power-relation geometry that forms a separation, but always be on the alert for the infinite opportunities of exchange and modification.

This discussion of border-making and of architectural practice that creates various border typologies, the door, the bridge, and the gateway, helps us to grasp the imagined and concrete borders of the suicide bombing at the Dol-phinarium Discothèque facing the Hassan Beq Mosque on the other side of the street. However, one cannot address the concept of boundaries without addressing the concept of spatial order, a key idea in architecture and plan-ning. In fact, boundaries often represent a particular type of order. Further-more, both boundaries and order are influenced by the relationships between capital and the state. The next chapter addresses how the fragile socio-spatial order of Menshiyeh, violated by the bombings, was embedded in ongoing capitalist, economic forces of the state and the city.

ORDER
State-City Relationships and Their Effect on Urban Order

Before discussing the violent act as an expression of Israeli and Palestinian struggle, we must acknowledge that the beach, a leisure area, is a space con-tested by city, state, and citizens alike. Although, having clear structural boundaries and functional organization, the beach is extra-territorial, a place where the body can temporarily escape socio-spatial limitations.[84] For the individual, the beach provides an escape from day-to-day social and cultural routines. It permits non-conformity, uninhibited dress codes, and sexual per-missiveness that are not tolerated in other parts of the city. The beach is often organized spatially, being culturally and climatically modified for specific ritu-als according to the position of the sun and the direction of the wind. Personal belongings such as towels, games, and sunshades demarcate territories and express the politics of the body in space. From this lack of rigidity, this free-dom of expression, derive the beach's economic potential and real estate value. Many cities, such as Barcelona or Los Angeles, have transformed their industrial waterfronts into commercial leisure areas. But, as examples from other places show, seashore development is integral to the political construct of the city, especially in the socio-economy of the nation-state. Here the beach's economic potential is often confronted by conflicting local, national, and international forces, turning its development into an arena of struggle, not only against old forms of domination but also against new patterns of control.

The coastline of Israel lies along the western edge of both the city and the state, making it a conflicted place of interests, powers, and ideologies. As both a municipal and a national asset, it is continuously revised according to the needs and desires of state and city alike. As in other coastal cities elsewhere, Tel Aviv's seashore development exemplifies current changes in the production of urban space, and demonstrates the role of architecture in the context of late capitalism. However, in the midst of the Israeli-Palestinian conflict, urban production in Tel Aviv is severely affected, although, ironically enough, the violent events accelerate the city's urban production. The violent act in this context must be addressed from a socio-historical perspective by focusing on three periods of shoreline development in Tel Aviv and critically considering the architectural production of the urban space. The following section discusses the role of architecture in ordering space and society, examining its function as mediator between state, city, and citizens.

Urban Production and Architecture as Spheres of Mediation

The production of modern urban space through professional practice in the service of capitalism is widely acknowledged.[85] Capitalism has also been acknowledged as a leading force in urban production, especially in the context of late capitalism, the long post-war wave of rapid growth in the international capitalist economy, and its radical powers of globalization.[86] Capitalism produces landscapes appropriate to its own dynamic, only to have them destroyed and rebuilt to accommodate further accumulation.[87] To maintain capitalist order, the state uses experts—planners and architects—who legitimize the use of spatial resources. Thus, as argued by Harvey,[88] leading architects and social experts, such as Le Corbusier, Wiener, and Keynes, acquire social power to the degree that their expertise becomes a vital material force. These relationships between spatial order and capital establish architecture not as a mere process of esthetic manipulations, but also as a means of grounding capitalism in material realities.

Despite attempts to undermine itself and regard the state as a collective national space,[89] the city continues to flourish as the center of capitalist accumulation.[90] In the complex relationships between city and state, each manipulates the other to its own advantage. The city enlists the state to further its economic development, while the state uses the city to construct its national image. Peter Marcuse and Ronald Van Kempen argue that "while the market is a major determinant of city form and spatial differences within cities, it is not itself an actor."[91] As they point out, "market forces are the drivers (or struggle for the driver's seat) and provide the fuel, but the engine, the steering wheel, and the accelerator are those of the state."[92] Thus, while it is clear that architecture mediates between space and capital production, the modern state as a mobilizing force must not be underestimated.

Within this triangle of city, state, and capital production, citizens are often perceived as the raw material with which the nation is constructed and also as the mass consumer of capital production. The complex relationships between state, city, and citizenship, especially in the contexts of capitalism, globalization, and increased cultural heterogeneity, have made architecture an axis of consumption and commodification. By giving form to ideas, architecture could initiate new levels of spatial understanding and thus motivate possible exchanges between different bodies engaged in spatial production. As a professional practice that takes upon itself to make the invisible visible and transform resources into concrete realities, architecture has become a contested sphere of representation of the physical and the imaginable.[93] Architecture could become a mediator, not merely between state and capital, but also between multiple participants and powers. Its formal manipulation of ideas could give voice to the voiceless, since the power exerted by architecture is created via social relationships. It does not merely envision a future but is a social process of shared spatial construction, opening the route to collaboration and reciprocity. Being constructive and creative, architecture could be seen as a means of social change, mobilization, and mutual exchange, not as a mere repressive, economic, or legislative artifact.

Contested Forces along Tel Aviv Shoreline

Architectural mediation is particularly relevant in Israel, where intricate city-state relationships are the result of the complex and multi-layered hierarchies of internal colonization.[94] Regardless of the Zionist anti-urban movement, cities in Israel, even before the establishment of the state, were cores of a bourgeoisie based on a capitalist economy, while the development of the (rural) periphery was left to the "pioneers" who embodied the ethos and moral leadership of the new state. This tradition of cooperation between capitalism and the city[95] was accompanied by a crucial ideological shift when the socialist principles of the Zionist pioneers were subordinated to the ethnic melting pot of the state.[96] In return for a tacit laissez-faire, the bourgeoisie provided financial and moral support for Zionist "nation-building." This unwritten agreement allowed for the institutionalization of a mutually agreed upon division of labor between the state and the owners of capital, obviously with spatial and architectural consequences. While the urban centers were grappling with definitions of the city based on real estate transactions, peripheral towns and villages were being defined as communal spaces, thus creating a sense of national unity and public participation.

Tel Aviv stretches along the shore, but its early development as an urban center is not directly linked to the sea. Its early expansion to the north and the east was due to land availability. As ordered later by the Geddes plan,[97] many areas along the beach were designated for industries that would cause environmental pollution. Although the sea was considered an ecological resource that would allow sea breezes to penetrate the city, this did not motivate seashore development, though it did influence layout and orientation of the streets. This lack of official ordering is probably what gave the beach its sense of freedom, which, in the 1920s, made it a vernacular space for popular leisure activities like bathing and strolling. As noted by Azaryahu, "the beach was detached from national revival and not fettered by the Zionist ideology,"[98] thus not enlisted, as other resources were, into national state-building.

However, the beach did present a great economic potential which, since the 1920s, has motivated shoreline development over three time periods, and during three different socio-political orders. The first was in the 1930s, before the establishment of the state. During the British Mandate, Tel Aviv enjoyed autonomous status. Its Jewish municipality aimed at organizing the urban space with the assistance of the moneyed community and the support of the British regime. The second period was in the 1960s, a decade after the establishment of the state, and was based on official state cooperation. This administrative cooperation was manifested in national-municipal companies, which created spatial order in line with the modernist project of progress and development. The third period, during the 1990s, was a period of accelerated globalization and transnational forces. Within its limited flexibility vis-à-vis the state, the municipality has tried to encourage the architectural practices that create a new spatial vision called the "World City." Although the state was powerful in this process, it was the municipality that masterminded the development, assisted by private developers, and frequently opposed by local groups. What is interesting is how architecture has created order and has functioned as mediator in each of these periods, and particularly its mediating role after violent acts. This is evident in three plans made for the Tel Aviv shoreline: The Gruenblatt Plan (1930s), Atarim Square (1960s), and the Dolphinarium (1990s) (see Map 3.2).

The Gruenblatt Plan: A Beach Resort

To turn Tel Aviv into a second Nice would undeniably be a project worth considering. It should be remembered, however, that in Nice architects had to do the best they could in an admittedly difficult situation, and there was never any question of material amenities being destroyed in order to create artificial ones.[99]

The Gruenblatt plan to develop the seashore as a tourist resort was promoted by Meir Dizengoff, Tel Aviv's mayor, in the 1930s. Disagreements about the plan arose because the city inhabitants assumed it to be a popular leisure area, while the City Council recognized its economic potential. Although the plan was never realized, its initiation and the struggle over it exemplify how it was used as a sphere of mediation between the city and its citizens. Its study assists us to understand that the production of urban space results from socio-political order and its representation through architecture.

As stated earlier, Tel Aviv under the British Mandate was able to function as an autonomous entity, with much latitude for constructing its socio-spatial order.[100] In fact, the Tel Aviv municipality operated virtually independently, with its own administration and its own town planning committee. Regardless of the autonomy, the Jewish community adopted British planning standards and norms, and mobilized the development of space according to its own interests. Under British rule, Tel Aviv was able to define its development and establish its hegemony as the Jewish economic and cultural center of nascent Israel.

Despite the leisure and fun activities of the Tel Aviv beach, and its relativity short length, suggestions to turn it into a resort[101] or at least to improve and organize it[102] were initiated as early as the 1920s. But the economic potential of the beach was only fully realized in the 1930s, and the City Council initiated an architectural competition in 1933 for this purpose.[103] However, none of the proposals submitted won,[104] and an alternative plan was commissioned by the Mayor from the Jewish engineer Gruenblatt.

Initially, Gruenblatt's plan was rejected by the British, who demanded that Tel Aviv planners also include European experts, but it was ultimately submitted for review in 1933 and approved in 1936.[105] It included extending the shore by constructing sea walls and adding tourist areas with four- to five-story buildings. The land use program consisted of hotels, clubs, and galleries around a central public garden, to be implemented by a private share company, which promised 15 percent of the site (after development) to the City.[106] This scheme was based on the Geddes plan, approved in 1927, but changed the scale and designation of the area, so that it was considered a tourist resort with European urban block typology. The shoreline was divided into three sections: the southern area bordering Jaffa (sandy beach), the central area (sea-reclamation), and the northern area (sandy beach). This division, taking into account the existing city limits, deconstructed the shore into socio-physical fragments. The northern area was designated for citizens, the central area for tourists, and the southern area defined Tel Aviv's border with Jaffa, so that the plan framed not only beach facilities and activities but also the relationships between private and public property along the beach, as well as between communities and their spatial representation.

An important feature of the plan was its attempt to replace the traditional layout of Jaffa and Menshiyeh village along the beach with a European-colonial urban grid of wide streets and squares, completely negating the existing urban pattern. This, and the inclusion of European expertise, accelerated British approval of the plan. For the Jewish city founders, the adapted colonial planning approach achieved three goals simultaneously: a western image, a promotion of the marketing of the beach in Europe, and the encouragement of foreign investment; the support of the colonial regime; and another level of spatial separation from Jaffa and the Arab community.

The plan's dual approach, as an economic venture and as a popular leisure resource for city dwellers, was the key issue in the struggle over its suggested spatial order. Architecture was the negotiator between the city council and the citizens. One of the main arguments of the citizens against the plan was that the beach would no longer be accessible to them, as two-thirds of it would become a tourist quarter.[107] The plan was also attacked as a speculation that would compete with landlords and businessmen in other parts of the city.[108] The City Council, on the other hand, claimed that the project would contribute to the economy by creating jobs and increasing consumption and that the city would benefit from the architectural changes along the beach, which would affect real estate development.[109] Above all, it was claimed that the plan would improve "hygiene for both tourists and citizens."[110]

Negotiations around the plan and its physical-economic implications resulted in its rejection, although, as stated by the municipal engineer, "The Gruenblatt plan is only one possible solution, better than nothing, since it is dangerous not to organize the beach."[111] The problem was clearly the attempt to maintain order, define private-public relations, and safeguard the shore-

FIGURE 3.17   *View of the Tel Aviv beach, 1935. (Photo: Kluger Zoltan, Government Press Office*

line.[112] Thus the implementation consisted of an elevated promenade to cancel barriers between the city and the beach and to open the view to the sea.[113] This promenade, funded by the municipality with a British loan, "recognized" the sea as an open public space. As opposed to the Gruenblatt Plan, which incorporated a new urban block, the new plan offered small-scale places for sitting and strolling. Photographs of the beach in the 1930s and 1940s, after the construction of the promenade, show lively cafes and clubs, indicating the daily role of the beach (see Figure 3.17).

However, like the Gruenblatt Plan, the new layout was strongly connected to socio-economic order and also employed capitalist tactics. Although offering an alternative physical solution that made it more acceptable to the citizens, it also divided the shoreline into linear strips of beach, promenade, streets, and buildings (hotels, clubs) (Figure 3.18). These programmatic strips clearly defined the area for the citizens, testifying to the powerful status of Tel Aviv civil society during the British Mandate. However, since the 1950s, the beach has become the locale of marginal groups, sewage has been dumped in the sea, and the city turned its back on the water until the initiation of new plans in the 1960s.

Atarim Square: Facing the Tourists

To improve the behavior of the citizen who comes to the beach. To help to maintain cleanliness and proper behavior there. It has been shown that proper bathing conditions create high behavioral standards that allow enjoying the beach while keeping it clean.[114]

FIGURE 3.18   *View of the Tel Aviv Strand Promenade, 01/07/1942. (Photo: Kluger Zoltan, Government Press Office)*

The establishment of the state in 1948 changed the balance of power among bodies operating along the beach. The boundaries of the city changed following the annexation of Jaffa and the demolition of the Menshiyeh neighborhood.[115] The City Council and the government, adopting a spatial-political perspective, took the beach as the western frontier of both city and state and planned to turn it into a tourist attraction intended to promote Tel Aviv as a secular center, in contrast to traditional religious tourist attractions such as Jerusalem, Nazareth, and Tiberius. This plan, in sharp contrast to the promenade layout of the 1930s that gave the beach to Tel Aviv's citizens, exemplifies the use of architecture as a sphere of mediation between the state and the city. However, the plan's lack of integration of citizens' needs and aspirations doomed it to failure.

The rationale behind the Atarim project was based on Tel Aviv as a tourist center with proximity to the airport. It envisaged different developments along the beach, by national-municipal companies (often with the mayor as the chairman) aiming to invest private capital in projects developed by publicly initiated plans.[116] This beach development was intended to advance municipal interests along with national goals. The state's financial and territorial assistance helped the city to sustain its status as a cultural and business center, thus maintaining its dominance over other urban centers and obtaining public resources for future development.[117]

FIGURE 3.19   *The beach in 1964: Jaffa (bottom right), Menshiyeh (middle center).*
(Photo: Willi Folender, Tel Aviv Municipal Archives)

The recognition of Jaffa and Tel Aviv as a central national asset requiring development resulted in a number of large-scale plans for three areas of the shore: Old Jaffa, Menshiyeh, and Machlul (see Figure 3.19). The Jaffa Development Company, established in 1962 in order to "develop old Jaffa as center for art, entertainment and tourism while preserving its unique character,"[118] operated in the south. Achuzot Hof Company, established in 1960 to develop a business center "to regenerate the poor neighborhood in the city center,"[119] was in charge of the Menshiyeh area, an Arab village destroyed during the 1948 War and later demolished by state order. The northern part of the beach—the Machlul neighborhood, a poor Mizrachi Jewish immigrants' community—was undertaken by the Atarim Company, established in 1969.[120] The City Council also ordered two additional plans, one of which was a general layout of the shoreline development (1963) made by the Italian town planner Luigi Piccinato, and the second was a master plan for Tel Aviv (1964) prepared by the Israeli town planner Zion Hashimshoni.

The rationale behind this double planning was to reinforce the city's image and obtain state support. The city image was to be achieved by transforming Jaffa from a hostile urban center into an "Old City," integral to Tel Aviv and its heritage. The promised public funding provided collateral for private investment while promising access to land entrusted to the state after the occupation of Jaffa. The master plan involved regenerating Jaffa to the south, a tourist center in the north, and a business center in between on the ruins of the Menshiyeh village. To understand the role of architecture in negotiating between the state, the city, and the citizens, we focus on the tourist center to the north, Atarim Square, built in the 1960s.

In an agreement between the City Council and the Treasury, the city was to evacuate the Machlul neighborhood and replace it with hotels, public gardens, and a promenade.[121] A national-municipal company was established,[122] but to accelerate the process, the City Council delegated the evacuation of Machlul to Ezra and Bizaron, an established state-municipal company (Figures 3.20, 3.21). At the same time, the Company for Developing Tourism commissioned a design for a commercial center, 25,000 square meters, by the architect Yakov Rechter. The main idea was to elevate the project above the six-lane motorway along the shoreline (Hayarkon Street), by creating a

(*Opposite*)

FIGURE 3.20 *Machlul neighborhood, 1959. (Photo: Willi Folender, Tel Aviv Municipal Archives)*

FIGURE 3.21 *Machlul neighborhood, 1961. (Photo: Willi Folender, Tel Aviv Municipal Archives)*

3.20

3.21

square and commercial buildings over a parking lot (see Figure 3.22). To generate additional development,[123] the center was to supply tourist services and display a permanent exhibition of export products.[124]

In 1963, the City Council also invited Professor Luigi Piccinato to prepare a master plan for the shoreline, to take into consideration all existing projects.[125] Piccinato visited the city and met with the architects and then presented a report opposing many of the projects. His plan, modest and sustainable compared to those of the Israeli planners, was to preserve Jaffa Hill and Menshiyeh Bay, thus creating three new focal points along the beach.[126] He argued that the layout for the proposed tourist center was too dense and inappropriate for the site.[127] He publicly criticized the suggested parking lot and the elevated construction above it as no more than economic speculation. He believed that Tel Aviv should avoid the establishment of big concrete blocks and that the residents must participate in the planning processes.[128]

The mayor and the City Council, asked to intervene in the dispute, submitted Atarim Square for redesign, asking architects to submit "plans that relate to Piccinato's suggestions but are substantially different from it."[129] This conflict about the size and economic feasibility of the project resulted in a compromise, reducing the construction area to 18,000 square meters (though the final plan, approved in 1965, consisted of 19,400 square meters).[130] It was implemented by the Atarim Company and intended to attract investment for future projects with 70 percent of premiere investments covered by foreign investors,[131] because—"This is how to combine public and private interests for the benefit of all"[132] (see Figure 3.23).

Disassociated from the urban context and from city life, Atarim Square clearly demonstrates the cooperation between capital, state, and city. The square is a purely commercial venture whereby architecture reconstructs the city with a national image, creating a dialectic relationship with Jaffa. Yet, despite considerable success in property sales, services and rents could not support business, and the local crowd avoided the place. It is customary to blame the project's failure on its design. This criticism, especially in postmodern architectural discourse, attacks the hierarchical separation between traffic and pedestrians and the objectification of the space. The difficulty of reaching the square and the passive resistance to using the space are usually pointed out. The size of the project and how it cuts the continuity between the city and the shore, the blocked views to the sea, the sealed façades, and the restaurants facing the city rather than the sea are all criticized (see Figure 3.24 a, b). However, the architecture is not solely responsible for its failure. If the planning process is a mediation sphere, in this case the relationship between all the participants has failed. The linear strips of the 1930s that changed into

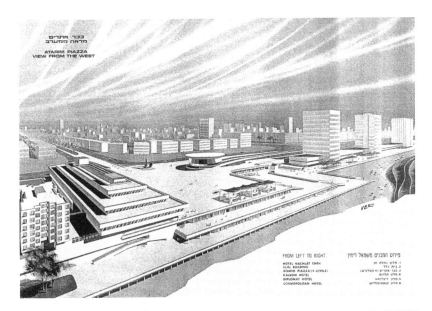

כבר אתרים
מראה ממערב
ATARIM PIAZZA
VIEW FROM THE WEST

VERD

FROM LEFT TO RIGHT:
HOTEL NACHLAT CHEN
CLAL BUILDING
ATARIM PIAZZA (4 LEVELS)
KALADIN HOTEL
DIPLOMAT HOTEL
COSMOPOLITAN HOTEL

פירוט המבנים משמאל לימין
1. מלון נחלת חן
2. בית כלל
3. כבר אתרים 4 מפלסים
4. מלון קלדיון
5. מלון דיפלומט
6. מלון קוסמופוליטן

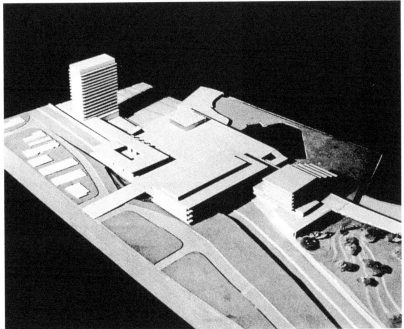

FIGURE 3.22   *Model and Perspective of Atarim Square, as designed by Yakov Rechter to reconstruct a national image in a dialectic relationship to Jaffa. (Photo: Tel Aviv Municipal Archives)*

FIGURE 3.23 *Atarim Square under construction. (Photo: Willi Folender, Tel Aviv Municipal Archives)*

focal centers along the beach in the 1960s have become a site that affects the city's everyday life. Beach development based on inward-facing centers with controlled circulation and regulated views clearly encourages consumerism and is not unique to Israel. One can only wonder where the State was and whose benefit it was serving in this development.

Tel Aviv's Beach in the 1990s

National consensus in Israel has been changing since the 1990s, with public debates questioning Zionist ideology[133] and privatization and globalization increasing amid the ongoing Israeli-Palestinian dispute[134] and its effects on the urban space. Tel Aviv's southern beach in the 1990s presents a picture of

FIGURE 3.24 (A) *Atarim Square, 2000. (Photo: Author)*

FIGURE 3.24 (B)   *Atarim Square, 2000. (Photo: Author)*

stiff monochromatic spaces on the one hand, and a sensual experience on the other. The office towers planned for Menshiyeh village in the 1960s are confronted with temporary areas of the beach organized for leisure activities, creating a complex social mosaic. Arabs and Jews share the grassy area stretching toward the beach, filling it with smells of food and voices of children. But all this was halted on Friday evening, June 1, 2001, when a Palestinian suicide bomber killed himself and youngsters crowding the entrance of a nearby disco (Figure 3.25). The funerals of the dead a few days later exposed the complex identities of the local population. Moreover, the attack on a Jewish leisure center in front of an Arab mosque exacerbated the situation. The next day, a Jewish crowd threw stones at the mosque and called for revenge.

This intersection of time and space characterizes the architectural processes of the 1990s and their connection to the ongoing Israeli-Palestinian dispute, the increasing immigration, and post-Zionism. Seizing this opportunity, the Tel Aviv Municipality tried to re-frame its vision of the city,[135] attempting to restructure itself "horizontally," free from the hierarchical order of the 1960s. Through professional discourse, Tel Aviv now emphasizes its significance as a "world city," an urban center capable of providing quality of life and services

FIGURE 3.25   *Dolphinarium, memorial monument, 2003. (Photo: Author)*

to suit the international businessman and the hi-tech community alike, with proximity to the airport, ample leisure areas, and expensive apartments modernized to international standards.[136]

Nine months after the violent act at the Dolphinarium, the City Council called a public forum to discuss demolishing the building. The Dolphinarium, designed in the 1960s as an ocean museum, had been partly abandoned since the 1980s and used by light commerce. Perceiving it as an obstacle to the continuity of the promenade and the green belt along the beach connecting Tel Aviv and Jaffa,[137] the municipality has offered to exchange its lease rights for a public open space located across the street, close to the Hassan Beq mosque. This exchange agreement provides the Dolphinarium's leaseholders with the right to construct tower buildings of twenty-six to thirty-six stories "continuous with the urban fabric" and enables the council to develop the promenade (see Figure 3.26). In a sophisticated marketing move, the project has shifted from commercial venture to promenade development and, in the name of "order," "continuity," and "regularity" for the "benefit of the public," has called for the evacuation of the Dolphinarium and the construction of new tower buildings near the mosque.

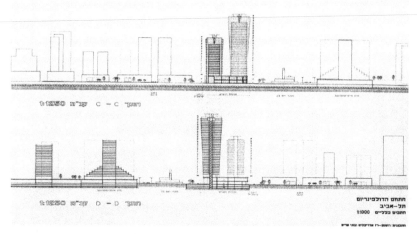

FIGURE 3.26   *Section of the Dolphinarium project. (Tel Aviv Municipal Archives)*

The plan for the Dolphinarium exemplifies the role of mediator played by architecture in the dynamic of state, city, and citizens. To better understand this, we can look at the public debate around this project and note the power relationships and strategies used by all the participants. As opposed to the 1960s, the municipality today avoids any large-scale plans, initiating only incremental projects whose programmatic and design features are decided without reference to a master plan. For statutory reasons, and for the sake of feasibility, the municipality prefers to operate only in designated areas and does not propose long-term or wide-scale plans. Limited municipal resources require private investments that often do not match the needs and aspirations of the city inhabitants. The absence of the state in this process strengthens the tension between the moneyed community and the public, and in the absence of an official public voice, the emergence of civil groups which criticize municipal initiatives is most interesting. In addition, as in the 1930s, criticism is also heard from the City Council itself. Does all this signify the emergence of a civil society?

The absence of a civic sphere in the 1960s changed in the 1990s to allow official public participation. Accordingly, the new Dolphinarium project debate has been taking place with the invited participation of professional civic bodies such as the Architectural Association and the Nature Reserve Society, not of the municipality but cooperating with it. These groups use trendy professional jargon but, like the municipality officials, they do not live in the area. Thus, they ask for "architectural alternatives" or argue that "the project is a mistake," referring to the 1960s Atarim Square failure.[138] However, none of them negates the project or demands that it be replaced; they only ask that it be updated to fit their perspectives. As Ophir argues,[139] these public hearings "up front" are based on rules that promise generality, though behind the curtains the debates are based on the production itself. Thus, as Ophir maintains, the questions are: Whose capital is invested? How can it be used or changed? Is it political, social, economic, or symbolic?[140]

The Dolphinarium debate embodies the hierarchies of the social order of the city and its citizens, but it also presents the contradictions inherent in the plan and the complex interests involved in its fulfillment. Despite formal public debates, any criticism and suggestions for alternatives are limited by the capitalist reality of the plan. The municipality, aware of these contradictions, admits that "public participation applies to everyone."[141] Nonetheless, as it proclaims, "citizens and City Council members are included, but the citizens are right to mistrust the participation process." This lack of citizen confidence in institutional mechanism (city and state alike) has been quite evident throughout the Dolphinarium debate. Thus, the public has no real influence but is used by the municipality, through public participation, to achieve ostensible cooperation.

From the architectural perspective, replacing the Dolphinarium with a public park and high-rise developments along the beach negates the 1960s planning concept. The current approach reverts to the linear beach/promenade/street/buildings strips of the 1930s. This, of course, is due to statutory constraints and land availability, but it also echoes the current neo-capitalist order—the segregation between private (rich) and public (poor). Thus, although the spatial organization of the current approach is similar to the 1930s plan, the buildings' height and scale resemble the constructions of the 1960s, so that even though the architectural language and materials have changed since the 1960s, the buildings are designed in the modernistic tradition, as isolated entities in space.

It is easy to see how the professional practice of the 1990s merges the urban perceptions of the 1930s with the national-capitalist character of the 1960s architectural projects. Obviously the present is a transitional phase of crossbred order between national and private market forces operating within complex global processes. This "glocalization"[142] and its spatial expression do not necessarily signify the power of society or of particular groups. It expresses the complicated relationship between nation and state that influences the architectural order and the everyday life of the citizens.

Mediation by Architecture

The ongoing acts of violence barely affect the capitalists' shoreline development (Figure 3.27). Consideration of Tel Aviv seashore development reveals how architectural practice, through mediation, is strengthened by spatial controversies. However, although this spatial arbitration takes place in the public domain, groups apart from state and city hegemonies often lack power, indicating that spatial production tends to reinforce the powerful and maintain inequality. It is evident that architecture often caters to the demands of authority and capital and disregards the citizens.

In the 1930s, the Gruenblatt Project attempted to reshape the beach. In the 1960s mega-architecture was recruited by state ideology to construct its image. These processes were further accelerated by the violent events of the 1990s, when destruction promoted reconstruction. However, these events were inadequate for fostering social change. Nationwide terrorist attacks, disconnected from local socio-spatial implications, merely increased capital production, so that the violence in Tel Aviv actually furthered and legitimized urban development.

Over the years, the Tel Aviv shoreline has revealed the marginality of the inhabitants' voices in development schemes. Unlike the 1930s, when citizens did participate in public debate, they have not been privy to the 1990s discussions. The municipality did initiate some public participation, proclaiming the need "to balance power in a democratic society and allow citizens' groups to affect decisions, including those with no political power or resources."[143] Nonetheless, exchanges of ideas took place mainly at the official level.

In the context of late capitalism, urban space no longer pretends to be an equal territory. Postmodern conditions increase the influence of capital on urban production. As Jameson explains, architecture is closely allied to economy, with which it develops unmediated relationships,[144] so that the architects' prosperity is attributable to the international business world. Aware of this, the Tel Aviv Municipality is attempting to regenerate its urban vision by "horizontal" restructuring free from the hierarchical order of the 1960s. Through professional discourse, it continuously searches for economic leverage. The White City's current recognition as a world heritage site by UNESCO[145] is another asset that will promote urban real estate development.

So the violent act, severe as it was, created a temporary meeting point for the two rival groups on the site. This moment of sober recognition could have created a conscious transformation, thereby influencing the production of space. However, analysis of urban production after the event does not indicate this. Rather than offering revision or change, it exposes the accelerated and

FIGURE 3.27 (A–B)   *West Façades (facing the beach) along the seashore, with Hassan Beq mosque. (Photos: Author)*

FIGURE 3.27 (C–D) *West Façades (facing the beach) along the seashore, with Hassan Beq mosque. (Photos: Author)*

FIGURE 3.27 (E–F)   *West Façades (facing the beach) along the seashore, with Hassan Beq mosque. (Photos: Author)*

automatic production of urban space. Furthermore, it only served as a catalyst to economic processes, giving them extra legitimacy.

Economic aims are further promoted in the context of the violent events. Destruction motivates reconstruction. The contradiction, however, is that although these events expose the complex social relationships among local groups, they are unable to mobilize processes that foster social change. As stated earlier, perceiving the attacks of violence at a national level, disconnected from their local socio-spatial implications, only increases the regular routines of capital production. Ironically, the violent act has given the developers further support and legitimization.

The Tel Aviv shoreline development proves, once again, the importance of spatial order in urban production. As argued by David Harvey, flexible accumulation is a leading force in the production of urban space, especially with regard to late capitalism and the radical forces of globalization. Demonstrating how the global system increases geographical processes of capitalism, Harvey shows that, ironically, the elimination of spatial barriers can work only by the formation of fixed spaces.[146] Capitalism thus produces landscapes appropriate to its own dynamic, only to have them destroyed and rebuilt to accommodate further accumulation. In Tel Aviv, these processes are accelerated by violent events, whereby urban construction is legitimized by destruction. Nonetheless, architecture and planning, by their very nature, aid this construction and assist urban production by transforming resources into a concrete reality. However, architecture and planning could also be used to mediate between interests and powers to negotiate between participants as well as between hegemonies and the fragile temporary order of everyday life. Taking the development process from its speculative stage into concrete reality, architecture makes the invisible visible.

In contrast to the seashore, which serves as an intersection point for different groups' lives, the third site—the Neve Shaanan neighborhood—may be considered the backyard of the city. In a trajectory that follows the rhythm of the daily lives of the inhabitants (Israelis, immigrants, and Palestinians who reside in this part of the city), we track the forces operating on the city's periphery, noting how political violence and the suicide bombings in 2003 expose the socio-spatial texture of the place.

Chapter 4

Urbanity, Immigration, and Everyday Life in Neve Shaanan

THE SUICIDE BOMBINGS AT THE CENTRAL BUS STATION, JANUARY 5, 2003

One Sunday afternoon, at 6:30 p.m., two suicide bombers blew themselves up, one after the other, on two parallel streets by the Central Bus Station. The first exploded in the pedestrian precinct of Neve Shaanan at the corner of Rosh Pina Street. The second exploded on Gedud Ha'ivri Street, parallel to the pedestrian street. Both bombers carried powerful explosive devices packed with metal screws and other items, killing twenty-three people and injuring another hundred in this double attack.[1] Significant damage was also done to property in the area. The violent acts and their spatial location in the southern part of the city exposed the complicity between the immigrant laborers and the Palestinians. Both groups, perceived as "outsiders" residing mainly in the southern area of Tel Aviv in Neve Shaanan, were trapped together in that moment.

Immediately after the violent act, the issue of the immigrant workers began to dominate the media reports. Most of them emphasized geographical concentration, describing the neighborhood as one with conflicted relationships between the "locals" (Israelis) and the "foreigners" (immigrant workers), with the locals seeing the immigrants as a criminal threat to their traditional way of life.

A few months later, on a Thursday afternoon, in the summer of 2003, a singer in a hip hop band,[2] Chemi, who lives in the neighborhood, unloads amplifiers in the empty lot outside a building in Matalon Street. Nearby, some immigrant workers are packing boxes wrapped in blue plastic into a brown shipping container (Figure 4.1). They are leaving by order of immigration authorities. From our balcony, we watch the shipping containers, looking like Lego houses, being steadily filled (Figure 4.2). In the meantime, loud music issues from Chemi's black amplifiers, causing people to stare, stand, hang around the site. Gradually, Chemi's friends arrive with some bottles of alcohol and everyone begins dancing to the beat. Other neighbors shout from their balconies, enraged at the noise. One neighbor calls the police. A patrol vehicle arrives and the police politely suggest ending the "happening" at 9 p.m. The other immigrants continue packing, smiling, amused by the event but not joining in. Another vehicle arrives with more boxes for packing and loading. It is nearly 9 p.m. and the patrol car returns. The crowd disperses. The place is again an empty asphalt lot.

Some years later, during the summer of 2007, out of nowhere, hundreds of refugees fleeing persecution in Eritrea, situated in south northern Africa, were dropped off in our neighborhood. They marched for months across the Sudan and deserts of Egypt, arriving in our working class low-income area of the city, where most labor immigrants reside. They were accommodated in crowded shelters with one restroom and a shower. I watch them on my way to work each morning and each evening, sitting on a low fence, gazing quietly. Having nothing to do and no ability to communicate in our language, they remain bored and displaced. In the evening, they drag their mattresses out of their stuffy shelters to the street to make sleeping bearable. Two volunteers pass, leaving boxes of food, pausing just long enough to offer useful advice. In the daily newspapers are many articles on the Israeli government's negotiation with Egypt regarding the increasing flow of refugees from the common southern border—a controversial negotiation that raises much debate about the neglect of the government and society in accommodating the refugees, who have suffered the horror of genocide. I wonder if they ask themselves why, out of all places in Israel, they found a shelter in this neighborhood.

FIGURE 4.1   *Matalon Street, Neve Shaanan, 2003. Immigrant workers packing boxes and neighborhood residents gathering for an open-air party. (Photo: Author)*

Using the suicide bombings at the Central Bus Station as a reference point, this section examines the complex economic disparity between local and immigrant laborers in the Neve Shaanan neighborhood, with the Central Bus Station as a key space in the city and in Israel. One should note that bus travel throughout Israel plays a dominant role in the movement of both inhabitants and visitors. The section below titled "Center and Periphery" addresses the role of capital in the reality of a conflicted city and its inhabitants. It focuses on Neve Shaanan, a southern neighborhood of Tel Aviv that was developed in the 1920s but has since been perceived as a social, economic, and demographic margin of the city. This has been reinforced by the presence of immigrant workers who replaced Palestinian workers after the Second Intifada. The section presents three architectural projects dating from the 1920s, the 1940s–60s, and the beginning of the twenty-first century (after the arrival of the immigrant workers), discussing the inherent tensions between the forces of economic production, marginal groups, conflicts, and architectural representations of the neighborhood. The second part, "Everyday," addresses how conflicts accelerate visibility both of the injured and of the attackers. It refers to daily implications of the revisioning strategies initiated by the state and the municipal institutions and the tactics initiated by

FIGURE 4.2 (A, B, C) *Urban containers. Spread all over neighborhoods, these shipping containers are used by immigrant workers. (Photos: Yoav Meiri)*

the inhabitants that expose the vulnerability of marginal groups and citizens in a conflicted social reality.

CENTER AND PERIPHERY
Economic Production and Urban Representation

The structuring and restructuring of the city through the spread of industrial capitalism was already apparent in the writings of Max Weber, Emile Durkheim, and Karl Marx.[3] They saw the city as the locus of class struggles engendered by capitalism and contestation over the control of space, a view further developed by the contemporary writers Manuel Castells and David Harvey, who argue that the geography of cities is not a result of "natural forces" but of capitalist power in creating markets and controlling the workforce.[4] All this has fostered questions about city locations and their advantages,[5] such as land values and proximity to services and sources, thereby arousing contestations over territory and power. These questions of political economy are highly related to the social reality of cities and to the social migrations affecting, and being affected by, the global economy. As a result, labor, infrastructures, and national identities are all being modified, thus redefining the culture of cities.[6]

This incremental effect of global capitalism is also evident in cityscapes in its symbolic and representational aspects,[7] such as the exclusion and inclusion of social groups in the production of cities.[8] In planning/architectural discourse, the role of the political economy and its symbolic representations has been addressed by scholars who integrated an analysis of migrations with spatial definitions in order to highlight the reciprocal relationships between economic production and the physical environment. But what exactly are these relationships? How are they are manifested in space? Do they have different expressions (morphological, visual, discursive) in different eras?

Economic Production and Architectural/Planning Practice

David Harvey argues[9] that planning practice responds to hegemonic order. It does not call for change or challenge that order, but translates the division of resources into physical forms, and thus expresses and reproduces the state's socio-economic agenda. Who is the main beneficiary of these spatial processes? Neo-Marxist scholars argue that the socio-economic agenda behind these spatial processes serves the hegemonic institutions of capitalist society.[10] These institutions are the powers of the "center," expressing order and repetition and tending to ignore the margins. These central powers, Lefebvre argues, aspire to homogeneity and stability and discourage competition by absorbing the marginal powers into the center.[11] These differences between central and peripheral forces are not simply numerical or geographical.[12] Marginal forces constantly change and move, making it difficult to categorize them. Conversely, central forces are repetitive, organized, and perceived as unable to integrate the multiplicity and flexibility of marginal minorities.[13]

Architecture and planning as practices within the nation-state use abstract tools (mapping, statistics) that follow the definitions of the center and often contribute to the exclusion of the "other" or to stereotyped representations that shove aside those that do not accord with the "normal" order. The construction of the stereotype normalizes and stabilizes hierarchies within society.[14] It also frames planning and architectural action so as to serve the central powers.[15] The awareness that mapping and knowledge define professional practice, means and aims of operation, and division of spatial resources raises critical questions, such as: If architecture and planning practices are merely tools in the hands of the central powers, serving government and entrepreneurs, then what latitude of action do they have in marginal spaces? Can they challenge the power relationships or operate in favor of the marginal groups? Can they foster social change?

These questions are explored here by considering planning projects in three discrete time periods in Neve Shaanan. Each project has been affected by socio-political conflicts, anchored in different economic contexts, and is a product of the architectural/planning discourse of its time. The first, completed in the 1920s, was originally developed as a private agricultural cooperative and was later acquired by the Municipality of Tel Aviv.[16] The *plan* of the district was designed in the form of a seven-branched candelabrum (a Jewish symbol) and was financed by private capital that was amassed on Zionist ideological and economic principles. In the 1940s, the neighborhood mutated from a space on the periphery of the city to a transport *center*, built with public and private capital on private land, which ultimately became a municipal and national hub. During the 1980s and 1990s, a new bus station was planned nearby as a public shopping mall to be constructed on a private land with a private capital. These spatial changes caused major social shifts in the character of the neighborhood in the early 1990s, when it became the locus of immigrants from the former USSR, to be replaced later in that decade by immigrant workers. The period was marked by expansion and recognition of the City Council's initiative in re-thinking the *image* of the place by creating a strategic plan to be implemented with private and public capital.

MAP 4.1   *The neighborhood area, Jaffa–Tel Aviv, 1936, British Survey of Palestine (Extract). The street layout, the seven-branched candelabrum, was planned by the architect and engineer Yosef Tishler and implemented in 1921. (Source: Department of Geography, Tel Aviv University)*

The Neighborhood as an Agricultural Center

The street layout, the seven-branched candelabrum, was planned by the architect and engineer Yosef Tishler and implemented in 1921 (see Map 4.1).[17] Despite this symbolic representation, apparent in maps of the district, the area consisted mainly of sheds.[18] The layout embodied the founders' dreams of a satellite agricultural area that would service Tel Aviv, all of which accentuated, and was embedded in, conflicts both with the municipal authorities and with the Arab community.

This ethno/capital conflict began after the Jaffa riots in 1921,[19] resulting in many displaced Jewish refugees. Most of the refugees lived in temporary dwellings along the seashore of Tel Aviv and were divided into two factions. One faction agreed to establish a neighborhood on land belonging to the Jewish National Fund.[20] The other group objected to the limitations and restrictions derived from building on "national" land and set up the Neve Shaanan cooperative together with private developers.[21] Their aim was to build private houses on private land. Neve Shaanan was thus created as a shareholders' company promoting social values such as the solidarity and heterogeneity of its members. As they describe it: "We published an announcement calling on the homeless to come to a general meeting to discuss acquisition of land for constructing houses on the basis of private enterprise. A large heterogeneous crowd attended the meeting, and it was decided to organize into an association to be known as *Neve Shaanan*."[22]

The dearth of apartments in Jaffa was also connected to the housing market and rent speculation.[23] But the main problem was the conflict with the Arab area community of Jaffa city: "We must deploy our institutional forces in order to create, in the near future, not palaces or large buildings but small two-roomed homes that most of the population requires. These new houses should be constructed on the outskirts of Tel Aviv, in order to be safe from attack and yet be accessible to Tel Aviv's educational institutions."[24] Following these statements, the leaders of the company selected the orchards in the south-east area of the city as the site for two-room houses, each with a balcony and a kitchen, to be owned privately by each member.[25]

After acquiring a 220-dunam (198,000 meters) plot of land, contractors were approached to build 200-300 units. To increase the economic viability of the project, an agriculture initiative was suggested to replace the produce—vegetables, eggs, milk—supplied by the Arab community. The protocol asks: "Why shouldn't we supply our neighbors in Tel Aviv and at the same time provide work for our unemployed?"[26] Based on this premise, the founders applied to the Jewish National Fund[27] for acquisition of 400 dunam for farming, plus a loan to each member who wished to establish a farm.

Despite its promises, the Zionist Federation never granted the loan.[28] The labor and the development of the small farms were inadequate, and the neighborhood remained isolated, on the verge of economic collapse. The location, outside the boundaries of the city, surrounded by Jewish and Arab orchards, exacerbated its spatial and geographical isolation.[29] From 1922 to 1931 the area was linked to Jaffa by a single road. In 1930, although the district was now within the city bounds, it was still disconnected from the city center. The request for a road[30] that would connect the district to the city was partially answered in 1931–1932, when a short service route[31] was constructed for Tel Aviv's first fair. As one resident wrote, "Each winter the neighborhood was flooded and it was sometimes impossible to move about. Later on, when they (the City Council) uprooted the orchard where the bus station is located, things improved. . . . This was because the Council organized Tel Aviv's first fair there. . . . We were lucky because the paved road passed near our house."[32] In their protocol the residents asked to connect the neighborhood to the city. The government and the Tel Aviv Council stated that they would love to pave the streets, but it could only be done with the agreement of the Arabs to sell their land.[33] Despite this promise, and although seven streets connected the neighborhood to the city, in reality the connection never took place.

However, even though the neighborhood committee acted legally, it was not part of the city governance. In 1924, the cooperative faced an argument among its members as to whether to remain independent or unite with Tel Aviv. At a meeting in November 1925, after forceful differences of opinion, it was decided that the cooperative would be dismantled and sold to the Geula Company, thus acquiring the city's services.[34] This was arranged two years later[35] after many disputes between the residents. The protocol states: "In the meantime, this neighborhood that, throughout its seven years of existence, has been a nest of dispute and humiliation . . . was stopped when the government dismantled the cooperative. Due to the intervention of the Council, the neighborhood returned to its miserable state. Arguments, conflicts and blows are daily events there. The Tel Aviv police have been given special authority by the government to patrol the neighborhood six times a day to prevent violence."[36]

Thus, the establishment of an autonomous, ideological settlement on the outskirts of the city failed. After the company was dismantled, the neighborhood was connected to the city's water supply. The City Council portrayed it as a blemish on the new modern city of Tel Aviv: "The area comprises long-established sheds and many modern buildings, interspersed with shanty towns. Building construction progresses and is changing the area, giving it a modern look; but here and there, like sores on a healthy, young body, there are areas whose neglected appearance, high density and depressing poverty remind us of the worst sections of Menshiyeh."[37] This and other descriptions reflect the increasing tension between the architectural representation of the center (international style) and that of the margins (any other buildings that are not in this category). The district changed during the 1940s with the development of an international-style transport terminus. The candelabrum plan has been forgotten, and the neighborhood has been subsumed into the city, evolving as an urban center.

A Center for Transport

In the early 1940s, the physical setting of the district's heterogeneous population was a hybrid of new and old buildings (wood and concrete) of one, two, or three stories.[38] The significant shift in the neighborhood's character occurred after the council's decision to create a transport center in the area—a decision linked to the significant growth of the city and its population, the deployment of the Jewish community for the forthcoming state, and the need to support the economic infrastructure of the city.

The process began with an attempt by the City Council to divert the railroad track from Lydda to Tel Aviv. Council members argued that the city's centrality and development necessitated diverting the route to include Jaffa and Tel Aviv.[39] This was more than a simple geographical issue. It was part of a struggle for the city's economy as opposed to the strategic needs of the British, who constructed the port in Haifa and the railway terminus at Lydda,[40] the north-south route that bypassed Tel Aviv.[41] The port served the economic needs of countrywide transportation[42] that employed the services of the Jewish Egged bus company.[43] The first British Commissioner, Sir Herbert Samuel, promised to shift the railway station from Lydda to Jaffa, with a station in Tel Aviv. At the same time, the City Council proposed a bus terminal for regional public transport. The designated area, an orchard in Neve Shaanan, was close to Tel Aviv's train station and was handed over without payment by its Jewish owners (Shafir Klein) in 1937. In return, the council gave the owners permission to build a small commercial center in proximity to the station. The exchange is confirmed in a letter to the mayor by the owners, elucidating the mutual interests of the City Council and themselves as private entrepreneurs in the development of the city, a collaboration that would be of financial benefit to both parties.[44]

This step was followed by an architectural competition, announced in October 1938 and managed by the municipal engineering department. Sixty-one plans were submitted, and the winning proposal was that of architects Zelkind, Vitkover, and Luria. The plan comprised both a bus yard and a railway station that included ticket and management offices, a cafeteria, newspaper stands, and a police station. The design distanced itself from the local architecture, both Arab and Jewish local residential, responding to the modernistic functional approach and aesthetic expressed in the horizontal composition of the façade, with its concrete pillars and roof.[45] Construction began, after some delay, in the 1940s.[46]

The transport center and adjacent railway station altered the commercial array of the neighborhood, and many stores and businesses moved to Ben

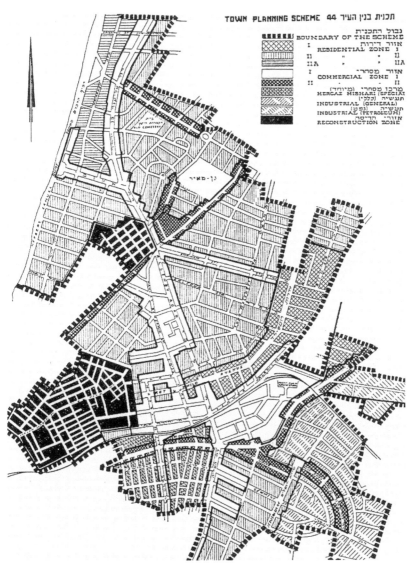

FIGURE 4.3   *Town planning scheme, 1938. (Yediot Iryat Tel-Aviv, Tel Aviv Historical Archive)*

Yehuda and Allenby streets.[47] Plan F (1941–1946) for Tel Aviv[48] also encouraged mixed use of residential, commercial, and industrial developments, significantly altering the character of the neighborhood and accelerating conflicts among developers, businessmen, inhabitants, and the council (Figures 4.3, 4.4, 4.5).

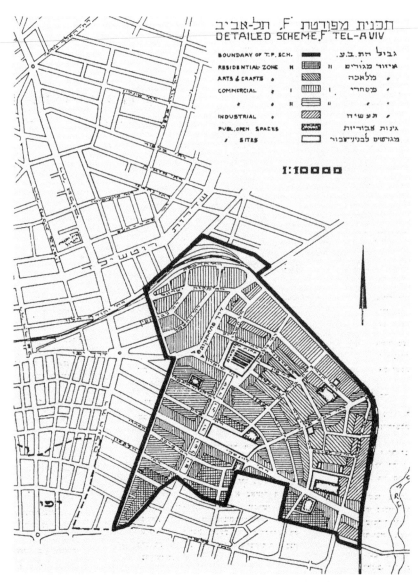

תכנית מפורטת .F תל-אביב
DETAILED SCHEME F TEL-AVIV

BOUNDARY OF T.P. SCH.	▬▬	גבול חת. ב.ע.
RESIDENTIAL ZONE א	⊞	איזור מגורים א
ARTS & CRAFTS ב	▨	מלאכה ב
COMMERCIAL ג	▥	מסחרי ג
ד	▤	ד
ה		ה
INDUSTRIAL ו	▨	תעשיה ו
PUBL. OPEN SPACES	▨	גינות צבוריות
SITES ז	☐	מגרשים לבניני-צבור

1:10000

FIGURE 4.4   *Plan F, Detailed plan for Tel Aviv. (Yediot Iryat Tel-Aviv, Tel Aviv Historical Archive)*

FIGURE 4.5 *The idle Central Bus Station during the curfew in Tel Aviv, 3/3/1947.*
(Kluger Zoltan, Government Press Office)

When the British Mandate ended in 1948,[49] this vulnerable, crowded center was damaged in an aerial attack by the Egyptian Air Force (Figures 4.6
a, b). The years following the 1948 War, with the occupation of Jaffa and its
surroundings by Israel, are marked with intense Council activities to re-think
the city's spaces, with the intention of dealing with the poverty.[50] Neve Shaanan was not, however, the highest priority.[51] The Council did attempt to deal
with its problems but focused, almost exclusively, on those arising from the
Central Bus Station, such as heavy traffic,[52] overcrowding, and possible aerial
attacks.[53] Additionally, the bus station became inadequate for the size of the
city, so a decision was made to build two stations—one to serve Tel Aviv's
southern district and another to serve the northern end.[54]

The problem was to find suitable space and funding to support this ini-

FIGURE 4.6 (A, B)   *Aerial attack by the Egyptian Air Force, 1948, Central Bus Station.*
(Photos: collection of David Elazar, Israel Defense Forces Archives)

tiative. As a first step, the council allocated space in the northern part of the city.[55] The planning process for the new station began in 1962[56] with the agreement to renovate the old station.[57] A plan was ordered from Vitockover, the station's designer. At the same time, it was understood that the station would have to be closed for some years, with buses either dispersed to other concentrations or allocated to an alternative temporary location. One site available for this purpose belonged to the developer Arie Piltz on Levinsky Street. Responding to the council's proposition, Piltz cleverly offered to establish a permanent station in the area with his own finances. The Council, disregarding all previous plans, responded to his suggestion in the affirmative so as to avoid renovating the existing bus station with public funds.[58]

A report from 1966 by the state comptroller affirms that there is no record of how the change of location was decided.[59] The Council explained to the Ministry of Transport that they had abandoned renovation of the bus station because they could not reach an agreement with the developers of Shafir and Kalien's property (the inheritors of the bus station plot). The state comptroller points out that there are no records of how, when, and under what circumstances these disagreements occurred. Furthermore, discussions between Piltz, the Council, and Mayor Yehoshua Rabinovitz did not include the Dan and Egged bus cooperatives.

In January 1965, the developer announced to the City Council that he was willing to establish a company to set up the project, asking for permission to develop the project on a commercial basis. Two months later, on March 11, 1965, the Ministry of Transport intervened, arguing that the project was a national rather than a municipal issue, to which the City Council responded on April 8, 1965, that they were not involved in the matter, which was managed by a group of capitalists and the Egged and Dan bus cooperatives. In May of the same year, all documentation of planning and location was transferred to the Ministry of Transport, which exacerbated tensions between the city and the government with regard to the use, scale, management, and realization of the project. The state comptroller argued that it would be difficult to estimate the advantages of the new project over renovating the existing station, and queried as to why the Council did not interest other developers in the project. Nor was the project included in the Council's master plan.[60] The city spokesman's response—that the process was confidential in order to avoid difficulties in evacuating inhabitants—illustrates the Council's economic interest in the production of the space, as opposed to a concern for its far-from-wealthy inhabitants.[61] The Council, claimed a city spokesman, did not wish to expropriate land or to spend significant sums of money on buying appropriate land. Thus, accepting this offer, in a relatively short time, would solve both the transport problem and the danger to the public of the existing station.[62]

Despite the critics, the project was commenced, managed by the Kikar Levinski Company, a joint venture that included the developer (50 percent), the Egged Bus Cooperative (35 percent), and the Solel Boneh construction company (15 percent). The design was, as the developer called it, "A City under One Roof" covering an area of 180,000 square meters (Figures 4.7, 4.8, 4.9). As described in the brochure distributed by the company:

> The Central Bus station is a city in its own right, a meeting place of bus routes, of movements of passengers, with a constant flow of crowds of people pouring into or departing from it daily and hourly. Here one can purchase items for the house and the office. Here one can eat or drink, get a haircut . . . shop in the evening . . . or get a bus home. For years we have been planning a modern bus terminus for Tel Aviv, and have been searching for the optimal response to the expanding needs of Israel's cities—a terminus that includes a lively center for trade, business and industry. Meticulous planning has given rise to a project whose completion will take about three years, culminating in the largest and most up-to-date construction— a township under a single roof with one of the biggest and most modern bus stations in the world.[63]

Three features characterized the new station as an architectural object. The six-story station with its high-density construction is a self-servicing giant shopping mall. This huge autonomous, metal and concrete complex[64] is in the tradition of Team 10,[65] which resisted Le Corbusier's functional city but was nevertheless committed to the concept of a multilevel city.[66] The second feature is its highly disputed mega scale. The Architect Ram Carmi justified the scale of the project by citing the necessity of encouraging the population to use convenient public transport.[67] His plan included concrete bridges, level with the first floor of residential buildings. This was implemented by evacuating residents living in proximity to the site. Construction of the bridges affected both the existing fabric of the neighborhood and the ecology of the area, accelerating the abandonment of the neighborhood. The third feature, the architectural language of the building with its blind ceramic-covered façades, and the planning of the project as a totally enclosed space, stands in stark contrast to the old bus station, with its noisy popular bazaars.

After the war in 1973, the project encountered financial problems and disagreements among the company's partners and was halted.[68] After extended postponement, the court declared in 1979 that the company should be dis-

FIGURE 4.7   *Aerial view of proposed project. (1967, Tel Aviv Historical Archive)*

FIGURE 4.8 *A. Under construction, the new Central Bus Station. (Photo: Willi Folender, Tel Aviv Municipal Archives) B. The project's logo: A city under one roof. (Tel Aviv Historical Archive).*

mantled, resulting in the Council freezing development of the area between the two stations.[69] Criticism of the project's failure and fear of possible ecological and sanitary damage[70] resulted in the 1982 establishment of a national committee to decide whether to renovate the old station or to continue with construction of the new one. Paradoxically, the committee favored the old

FIGURE 4.9 *The market in the old Central Bus Station. (Photo: Willi Folender, Tel Aviv Municipal Archives)*

station as better suited to its purpose in terms of location, size, and future transport goals.⁷¹ Their report concluded that renovating the old station would reduce expenses and provide more efficient operation, maintenance, and services both to the passengers and to the operators. However, funding for this venture would be provided by the state, whereas the funding for the new station would come from a private developer, the Levinsky Project, and was thus given priority, since it would be possible to use what had already been invested.⁷²

The new Central Bus Station was opened in 1993. As an urban project designed as a mega-structure complex reflecting the multiplicity of city life, it is not unique to the Israel of the 1960s, nor is the collaboration between the

FIGURE 4.10   *Bombs at the Central Bus Station, 1968. (Photo: Collection of Bamahane;*
Photographer: Miki Asted, Israel Defense Forces Archives)

FIGURE 4.11   *Central Bus Station, 1980. (Photo: Collection of Bamahane; Photographer:*
Eva Streitner; Israel Defense Forces Archives)

state and private capital. In point of fact, the project emulates the capitalist structure of the city and the power relations between city, state, and capital, leaving the residents with limited latitude of action. Disregard for the social configuration of the neighborhood and the residents' needs has been changing since the 1990s, with the entry of immigrant workers into the area.

The Neighborhood as Immigration Center

In the 1990s, the neighborhood became a focus for immigrants from all over the world, including massive immigration from the former USSR. During these years, the deterioration in security and the separation policy regarding Israelis and Palestinians created intense pressure by interested parties (contractors, developers, etc.) on the government.[73] Particularly with the Second Intifada and deteriorating security, Israel promoted a policy of separation between the two nations. Not only did this prevent the entrance of approximately 100,000 Palestinian workers, it also interfered with construction projects to accommodate the massive immigration from the former Soviet Union. Interested groups pressured the government to open the gates of the country to foreign workers, perceived as a viable solution for the problem, and in the 1990s, for the first time, the government invited foreign, non-Jewish immigrants to become residents of Israel. In other words, the Palestinians living in the neighborhood prior to the Intifada were replaced by the immigrant workers. Thus, the Intifada changed the immigrant balance in the city, increasing its population by 20 percent in 1993, of which 9 percent were labor immigrants. The neighborhood, perceived as a "vacant" space with its neglected infrastructure and environmental hazards, suited many of these (legal and illegal) immigrants. In 1996–1997, the Council acknowledged the presence of the newcomers and their importance for the city and prepared a strategic plan for a comprehensive development policy for the area. In other words, the Israeli-Palestinian conflict, together with the condition of the old Central Bus Station, was the catalyst for this development.

Eighty years after the establishment of this neighborhood, the City Council invited submission of plans for the area, to include the two bus stations. This decision derived from tourism, image, and economy.[74] Since the early 1990s, tourism has been endemic to the vision of Tel Aviv as a "world city" in which both the periphery and the daily vernacular contribute to its cosmopolitan image. Marginality is no longer perceived as blight, but new enclaves of immigrants contribute significantly to the ethnic, multi-cultural cityscape.[75] To quote the city's profile book:

This area has suffered from ongoing neglect by the Tel Aviv–Jaffa Council. Today it is seen as having much significance due to its renovation, and now functions as a vital residential area of the city.[76] . . . It is our intention to change the current problematic reality by nurturing its heterogeneity, and strengthening the area as an ethnic center with tourist attractions. Examples of such urban renovation based on nurturing ethnicity can be found in cities worldwide, including Amsterdam, Rome and Paris.[77]

Thus, and although the city's profile book appears to resent the presence of the illegal immigrants, emphasizing that most of the power is held by the government,[78] in practice the city recruits professionals in order to produce urban space that adapts to the global order and its transnational conditions. The task as seen by the council is to redesign the image of the neighborhood (i.e., to modify the image of the neighborhood in the collective consciousness).[79] In its neglected state, it is seen as a burden on the city, a negative image in spite of its role as an urban "shop window" for many visitors to Tel Aviv. This modification would also contribute to the urban economy. Namely, property prices in the area are relatively high, higher than the income from the neighborhood, so that, as suggested in the strategic plan, investment in developing the site would be compensated by the income (taking into account the interval between beginning the work and the levying of taxes).[80] This is also before taking into account additional benefits such as property tax and the positive chain of reactions to the district as a whole.

The plan does not propose radical changes. Rather, it suggests renovations of streets and infrastructures, urban reinforcement, and planning controls to be imposed by the building authorities. Daily maintenance such as cleaning and improving street furniture and lighting does not require much in the way of resources, but would be a positive asset for market forces and public and private initiatives—all of which would have significant impact on the image, economy, and physical environment, both of the district and of Tel Aviv–Jaffa as a whole.[81]

The title of the plan is "The Meeting Place" because, according to the planners, it will increase encounters between different populations and their activities (Figure 4.12). They explain that "meeting" encourages power and vitality in developed and new cities alike. Such a policy could assist in dealing with many of the conflicts that characterize the district today, turning the problems of the past into opportunities for the future.[82] The plan, significantly different from those of the 1960s and 1940s, is residential-based. It divides the district into three sections, each with its own distinctive, clearly defined population. For instance, in the temporary-residential and commercial areas,

תמונת העתיד

FIGURE 4.12   *The Planned Vision — meeting in Tel Aviv. (Tel Aviv Municipal Archives)*

the population would be mainly immigrant workers, students, young couples, and people working in the central business area. The permanent residential areas are intended to attract a young, educated, middle-class population. The third section is inhabited by those who work or have businesses in the area or who leave the city and the area in the evening. Meeting points and encounters will focus on the Central Bus Station and in public spaces that would resemble other such locales worldwide. This planning approach, emphasizing the boundaries among the groups operating in space, is quite surprising when one considers the time spent in social research for the plan.[83]

So why do the planners have difficulty in addressing social space? Is there a correlation between the information acquired and the prospective product? Would a better acquaintance with the neighborhood produce more rigid boundaries between the different areas of the neighborhood?

First, and more generally, this type of plan should be seen in the context of contemporary Neoliberalist strategies in urban planning, which dismantled the planning authority of the state, giving more power to local government and private developers.[84] Advocates predicted that decentralization of state planning would contribute to growth by giving power to the capital market and diminishing the control of national planning initiatives. Thus, there was a major shift in urban planning during the Neoliberalism period, in vogue since the early 1980s, from a welfare framework to a competitive market-driven framework. The critical instrument of this period was, and still is, strategic planning.[85] This type of approach is intended to generate participatory, integrated, and consensual development, implemented and managed by four fundamental actors: local government, producers (entrepreneurs), the knowledge sector (universities and laboratories), and the community. By defining objectives, conditions, and common benefits to the municipality or region, these actors set the priorities, plans, and programs and evaluate the projects, although the result of this process has not always been social equity, economic efficiency, and environmental sustainability. Nevertheless, the Neoliberalist strategy has paved the way for a shift from planners designing urban projects to managing them.

Second, there is no doubt that, for the first time, a comprehensive study of all the parameters of the neighborhood—social, physical, and economic—has been conducted, but it seems that each of these topics remains endemic to the space in which it operates. Would seeing the city as parallel systems of economy, society, and architecture produce the same representation? How do planning and architecture relate to marginality? It seems that, for the purpose of integrating national capitalism into the global order, marginality is an asset. This does not indicate that society is recruited to the "other" (Palestinians, labor workers) but that this socio-spatial sphere is a resource. In other words, if in the past the realization of an urban project called for the evacuation of groups, today such groups contribute to the authentic image of the place and its consumption by the other. This is not unique to this neighborhood, but it illustrates the way conflicts assist and function as catalysts in the contemporary socio-economic organization of the city and the state.

TABLE 4.1   CONFLICTS AS CATALYSTS FOR CHANGE IN
NEVE SHAANAN

	1920s	1960s	1990s
Geographical location	Outer	Central	Central
Conflicts as catalysts for change	1921 riots	1948 war	Intifada
Status of citizens	Active (Neve Shaanan cooperation)	Trivial	Initiated participation by the council
Status of the capitalists	Dominant: cooperation between capitalists and inhabitants	Dominant: cooperation between capitalists and council	Dominant: cooperation between capitalists and council
Perception of place	As marginal space	As central space and as economic center (1940s on)	As a center for marginal communities
Planning/ architectural representation	Symbolic: seven-branched candelabrum	Monumental: "Roofed City"	Traditional: "A Meeting Place"

Ideology, Capital, and Professional Action

What are the interests of the planner/architect in the production of space? What is the ideology that motivates the planner? The projects in Neve Shaanan have shown us that professional practice responds to economic order, a socio-economic order that responds to national conflicts in a manner serving the capitalists and the powerful. The profession is thus always controlled by capital or power, playing the role of mediator between both. This is particularly apparent in what are perceived as margins, where the power of the individual is minimal.

Thus, looking at three points in time reveals the different plan representations and their connection to the market and the nation-state (See Table 4.1). In the 1930s, the neighborhood was planned along abstract lines, correlated with a Jewish symbol, but with no actual physical layout. The Tel Aviv Council, operating autonomously within a capitalist framework,[86] put many obstacles in the way of the private company operating outside the Council's jurisdiction, leaving the site neglected and detached from the city's centers of action and public discourse. In the 1940s, the city planned the Central Bus Station as a cooperative enterprise by the municipality and private capital. In this instance, the municipality operated as the agent for an economic project serving capitalists, in which the citizen did not top the list of priorities. The neighborhood was still perceived as marginal, a status that was reinforced in the 1960s with the evacuation and compensation of residents, on the one hand, and capitalist power, on the other, during construction of the new bus station. The situation changed in the 1990s with the recognition of the "marginal," not as merely a phenomenon that must be overcome but as one that must be nurtured, an aspect of the city's cosmopolitan character. This approach should be understood not as an intervention in a particular place but as a policy integrating multiple plans and interests to realize the economic value of the neighborhood.

These dynamic processes illustrate the way the free market connects to the power centers of the city and the government, even when they seem to be in conflict. Obviously, the city is where these processes occur, but, like the free market, it is not an autonomous entity. The free market depends on the expansion and productivity of the state, and vice versa, for, contrary to general opinion, market processes do not weaken the government but rather strengthen its grip on the social processes, even when these processes do not accord with the popular culture. Moreover, for a government to gain legitimized national and/or imperial power, both the market and the city are vital aspects of its political platform.

To such socio-politics, the architecture and planning discourse responds reflexively, adapting itself to processes. In the 1960s, a mega-structure was imposed on the symbolic plan of a neighborhood, brutally disrupting its local fabric. This was modified in the 1990s, with a shift to the human scale, and to the preservation of the city center.

Recognizing that representations of space and knowledge encourage inequality in the division of resources, in recent decades planners and architects have been attempting to focus on social justice, an approach that challenges capitalist logic by offering alternative interpretations and actions in space, which should assist the interpretation and planning of space using "local" knowledge, as in the 1990s plan. The real problem is that, under the guise of "local knowledge," architects and planners are acting in marginal spaces without engaging with their daily life or comprehending their multiplicity, trying to order and align the spaces as aspects of the center. The basic question that arises from the analysis is: What is the meaning of "local knowledge" in the planning process? With what and how is the planner forced to familiarize himself with the space in which he operates? Does the professional knowledge of the planner, who often lives far from marginal environments (physically and mentally), suffice? From the events studied in this chapter, it seems that professional practice recruited to strengthen economic processes is not a significance factor in social change. Similarly, acquired local knowledge is not integral to the project, nor does it generate power; it is merely an additional source of knowledge. If the profession wishes to respond actively to conflicted situations, it must clearly embrace a social commitment to change.

EVERYDAY
Visibility and Temporary Urban Coalitions

Let's look again at the event that took place that Sunday afternoon in May of 2003 that underlies the relationships between the locals, labor immigrants, and the Palestinians and their spatial location in the southern part of the city. As stated, two suicide bombers blew themselves up at 6:30 p.m. in the Central Bus Station area. The horrendous event united the two groups for a moment, the Palestinians inhabiting the area prior to the Intifada and the labor immigrants encouraged by the government to replace Palestinian labor.[87]

Immediately after the suicide bombings, an intense debate erupted concerning the labor immigrants' role in Israeli society. Although there are labor immigrants countrywide, their concentration in the southern part of the city placed Neve Shaanan at the core of the discussion. Again the violent act affected the imagined and the concrete space, creating a reflexive relationship between the place, the violent act, the victims, and the revisions yet to come. In this particular case, these relationships gave rise to discussions about the "other," "urban marginalization," "legal and illegal inhabitants," and citizenship.[88] Furthermore, the heterogeneous and liberal frame of the city, exposed by these events, collapsed. To many Israelis, the boundaries were violated twice, once by the bombers (Palestinians) and then by the victims (illegal immigrants), both perceived as "outsiders." In July 2003, the "self evacuation" project was announced by the immigration administration,[89] a project that placed the city's liberal policy at risk. On the one hand, the government readdressed the question of formal or authorized residence; on the other, the city initiated a rehabilitation plan for the neighborhood based on the immigrants' presence. Amid these contradictory forces of violence, cosmopolitanism, image, and economy, the inhabitants and the government institutions became embroiled in an ongoing dispute. Reading the relationship between city, state, and citizens in the context of violence bypasses the banal "marginalized" representation of the place and illuminates the social complexity of the area, not merely as a passive representation but as an active force that responds to changes accelerated by violence. The reciprocal relationships between everyday tactics (by individuals or groups) and strategies that construct the everyday (of institutions), all embedded in the cycle of political violence, depict the daily national conflict.

Neve Shaanan: A "Marginal" Neighborhood

According to a statistical analysis by the Tel Aviv City Council, Neve Shaanan includes the adjacent neighborhoods of Shapira, Kiryat Shalom, and Florentine. The municipal pamphlet "Who's Who in the Southern Area of the City" identifies three different groups as inhabiting these neighborhoods: The first group is comprised of old residents, those who remain in their homes because lack of resources prevents them from moving to a better residential environment. The second group is a transient population of young Israelis, some with bohemian lifestyles, and new Jewish immigrants (from the former Soviet Union) who live mainly in Shapira and Kiryat Shalom. The third group consists of immigrant workers who, in some areas, comprise 50–70 percent of the population, and includes different nationalities, families and singles, and legal and illegal workers.[90]

These statistical data were collected between 1960 and 2000, when the population of the south declined in general. In 1960, the inhabitants numbered 46,000, 12 percent of the city's population. In 2000, the population was at its lowest, at only 7 percent. Despite the increase in the early 1990s, due to an influx of immigrants from the former Soviet Union, the neighborhood balance remained negative.[91] There are differences among these neighborhoods. Florentine is "young" (47 percent between 25 and 44 years old), Neve Shaanan is "old" (20 percent aged 65+), and Shapira and Kiryat Shalom neighborhoods are characterized by families with young children (22–24 percent).[92] Overall, these neighborhoods have a low socio-economic base, with high density (3.9 per dunam, as compared to the 3.2 average in other parts of the city).

Despite its social complexity, Neve Shaanan is essentially defined according to a quantitative analysis of the area in which socio-economic gaps are typical.[93] Accordingly, urban researchers demarcated this area as a poor neighborhood that should be rehabilitated. As Naomi Carmon writes: "After the State of Israel had safely passed the first turbulent decade of its history, it faced the fact that it had to take care, not merely of the safety of new immigrants and the heroic settling of the periphery but also of the poor, expanding neighborhoods and their locations, including the city center."[94] In the same spirit, Gila Menahem points out that the south is "a deteriorating area with mixed commercial and industrial uses within residential environments. In many cases, the buildings are in poor condition and there is a high percentage of unoccupied apartments and buildings" (relating to statistical data from 1991).[95]

Although different development approaches have been attempted in some of the southern neighborhoods (Shalom Village, Florentine, Neve Eliezer), Neve Shaanan was never included in these rehabilitation projects. The conditions of the new immigrants from the former Soviet Union supported the claim that this rehabilitation resulted in positive feedback from the newcomers.[96] In her research, Menahem claims that Neve Shaanan's deterioration was one of the main reasons residents left after a few years. As she says, "Although there was a strong attraction to the communities from their countries of origin, the attraction of low rents, and the hope of a new (though modest) start, the social price of living in a run-down neighborhood with hardly any public services was too high, from the families' point of view."[97]

When the Jewish immigrants left the neighborhood, another discussion arose concerning the arrival of foreign workers.[98] As noted earlier, these immigrant groups should be viewed in the context of the Palestinian-Israeli conflict and the government decision to invite foreign, non-Jewish immigrants to become residents of Israel.

Tel Aviv has been radically influenced by this process. Since 1993, the city has been transformed from a place without new residents to a city that has increased its population by 20 percent, of which 9 percent are labor immigrants. Neve Shaanan, Hatikva, and Shapira became focal residential areas for these varied communities, many of whom are illegal residents. This immigration and its consequences have generated new municipal strategies that, in part, contradict government policies, defining Tel Aviv as a trans-national space in the context of global capitalism and immigrants in the labor market.[99]

The Municipal Council was preoccupied with the competition between labor immigrants and low-income families in the area. Nonetheless, in 1996–1997, the Council recognized the presence of the labor immigrants, realizing the need for a policy that would take into account their contribution to the city. In 1999, Tel Aviv established the Mesilla Center for the foreign community, offering social services for the labor immigrants and collating information about this new population. In addition, the organization asked the immigrants to nominate representatives to mediate between the different communities and the authorities. According to Adriana Kamp and Rivka Reciman, this suggests that Tel Aviv's policies with regard to the labor immigrants (legal and illegal) and those of the state were conflicting.

However, the discourse concerning Neve Shaanan has remained limited, dealing primarily with the arrival of new groups and ignoring the residents of the neighborhood. In other words, Neve Shaanan is perceived as a void, an empty space to be filled. The diversity of the population is minimized by a quantitative approach and oversimplified by ignoring the relationships between the different groups. Most of the representations are detached from the actual physical space, defining this neighborhood merely as a neglected space filled with marginal groups, rather than as a vital dynamic space with its own social complexities.

Schematic discourse about the neighborhood also characterizes the planning discourse that sees the solution to the problems of southern Tel Aviv as physical rehabilitation. As elaborated in the 1960s Master Plan, "Tel Aviv is a young city as compared to other cities in the world. How is it that, in such a short period, one third of its population lives in areas requiring regeneration? The main reason is that the development of the city and its construction were conducted under strong demographic pressure. Israel is a state of immigrants. Tel Aviv's economic and social activities have attracted large numbers of immigrants."[100]

Lately, a forceful debate in architectural discourse has begun over the double image of Tel Aviv as *White City* and *Black City*. The engagement with the White City is connected to the 1980s concept of "Bauhaus Tel Aviv," the 1930s architectural image of the city.[101] Contrary to this "white city" impression of central Tel Aviv, Sharon Rotbard[102] suggests *Black City* as a neat epithet for all the other areas not represented in the architectural-historical discourse of the city. As he writes, the *Black City* is clearly evident at the bottom of each map and each table in the annual statistics of Tel Aviv, namely Areas 7, 8, and 9—i.e., the invisible city, everything that is not included or acknowledged in the story of the *White City*. This is the city that no one talks about, writes books about, or creates exhibitions about. The *Black City*, and Rotbard's discourse about the Central Bus Station, adapts the terminology of the center of Tel Aviv to the disadvantaged south. Yet, Rotbard's binary perception offers no alternative reading of the neighborhood, but adopts a hegemonic discourse and clearly labels it.

Most of the extant representations ignore the concrete spaces and tend to ignore their reciprocal social relationships. These representational limitations

are being addressed in works that deal with the daily life of the inhabitants
of the area and how they occupy space,[103] as well as in works discussing the
influence of identity on perception of space and its impact on the production
of space.[104] The following text explores how these diverse groups act in space
and how their actions are affected by cycles of violence and the authorities'
violence-related strategies.

Responding to Violence: Tactics and Strategies

What are the "Everyday" theories, and can they challenge the social and
planning representations described above? Can they help us to understand
the neighborhood conflicts and the deportation of thousands of immigrant
workers? The basic assumption is that people live in a space and thereby construct it. They are not merely present in space, or looking at it as in a mirror,
but acting in interrelated juxtaposed circles. This perception, which sees the
historical evolution of a place as secondary, may assist in understanding the
complexity of space.[105]

   The concept of the "everyday" was first developed in anthropology and eth-
nology,[106] arising from interest in the ordinary "lived experience," an attempt
to understand culture as derived from common shared values, with the latter
translated into the norms and rules that regulate society.[107] Henri Lefebvre's
writings concerning the relationship between the everyday and modernity
discuss the ability of the everyday "spontaneous conscience" to resist the oppressions of daily existence. De Certeau,[108] disregarding the monotonies and
tyrannies of daily life, stressed the individual's capacity to manipulate situations and create realms of autonomous action as "networks of anti-discipline."
Anthony Giddens[109] perceived everyday practice as a potential challenge of
the modern nation-state whereby daily routines of skilled participants construct a liberating social order through originality and creativity. Thus, personal actions create cultural and social redefinitions that can affect change.

   Theories of the everyday include analysis of local versus global lifestyles,
focusing on typologies of urban daily life.[110] Tracing day-to-day routines and
social interactions in urban environments offers correlations between human
activity and technological, physical, and social processes. However, this approach also disregards the complexity and multiplicity of the everyday. The
non-discriminatory and rather romantic theories of day-to-day practices
blur the boundaries between power relations, arbitrarily classifying the actions of individuals and/or groups as related to social class, ethnicity, age, and
gender.[111]

   Consideration of the everyday as a critical construct has attracted the attention of architects, essentially in reaction to the universality of globalization, and as an attempt to resist commodification and consumption.[112] They see the everyday as a lived experience, a political struggle against capitalist economy and professional complicity with governments. This resistance, as Harris insists, "lies at the focus of the quotidian, the repetitive, and the relentlessly ordinary." Accordingly, the everyday is defined as "that which remains after elimination of all specialized activities."[113] This is clearly an attempt to extend the premises of architecture beyond the traditional notions of convenience, strength, and beauty[114] to include spaces that are outside the scope of architecture[115] and present new professional agendas. This extension calls for engagement with the temporal, "the spontaneous event, the enjoyment of diversity and the discovery of the unexpected," defined by Karen Frank and Quentin Stevens as "looseness."[116] Obviously, such inclusiveness enriches architecture with spaces not traditionally included in the architectural canon.

However, even this professional interest in the everyday seems to have degenerated into a mere aesthetic celebration of the picturesque. Attempts by architects to celebrate "ordinary," "banal," and "less photogenic" spaces have, in effect, fostered a post-modern search for authenticity, frequently promoting the everyday as a commodity. Avant-garde responses to the everyday have created a useful framework for the exotic "other." Even the claim that everyday reality "on the ground" can confront modernist utopias[117] seems to support professional presentations of architecture as the beautification of elements in space.

Yet, this architectural understanding of the concept of everyday does not construe it as one element of a complex economic, social, and cultural reality. It is often divorced from political circumstances. In the context of the developing world, the everyday is not considered against the old or new forms of Western dominance so often embedded in local patterns of control. Thus, it disregards the political implications and the intricate ways in which a nation-state engages in constructing the everyday.[118] As Ananya Roy argues, informality is not a territory separated from the state, but a practice supported by the state and its apparatuses. Understanding informality thus requires figuring out how the state operates, both through planning and through the unplanned and the "unplannable."[119] This mode of thinking about the everyday necessitates seeing it as a state-constructed mechanism that manifests order, land distribution, and wealth—all having political implications. In light of the current preoccupation with planning from below (which has often resulted in lack of attention to the "top down" mechanisms of the public sector),[120] the everyday deserves reconsideration in order to challenge the prevailing assumptions regarding the means by which the urban environment is manufactured and controlled.

Planning discourse, especially over the last two decades, has acknowledged that its institutions are not the only participants in the production of space. This has resulted in an ongoing search for innovative approaches to re-reading the space that can include additional voices and representations of those who are absent from the planning discourse, historiography, and acts.[121] From this awareness, approaches such as advocacy planning[122] and communicative planning[123] have emerged. They encourage the idea of planning-from-below, which has also shifted professional focus from the city itself to action-oriented participation. These strategies, which expose the requirements of different groups, deal primarily with distribution of resources, and operate within an existing order. As a result, the planning process has become a matter of inclusive negotiation and no longer fosters macro-visions of social justice. Furthermore, although engaged with distribution of process, planning discourse is still lacking in ways that discuss the role of dynamic, temporary, and conflicted daily practices. These issues are particularly significant in the context of Israel, where the "other" is allegedly located outside the Jewish collective, and has become an exotic entity, without context, that allows beautification of socio-spatial readings.[124]

One way of addressing the everyday from a critical perspective is to assess the reciprocal relationships between tactics (by individuals or groups) and strategies (of institutions). For Michel De Certeau,[125] strategies and tactics alike operate in space and time. Strategy is recognized as enacted by authority—an institution, a commercial enterprise, or an individual whose status is that of the dominant order. Strategy manifests itself physically in its site/s of operations (offices/headquarters) and in products (laws, language, rituals, commercial goods, literature, art, invention, discourse). Unlike strategy, which inherently creates its own autonomous space, a tactic is "a calculated action determined by the absence of a proper locus. . . . The space of a tactic is the space of the other."[126] A tactic is deployed "on and with a terrain imposed on it and organized by the law of a foreign power." One who deploys a tactic "must vigilantly make use of the cracks that particular conjunctions open in the surveillance of the proprietary powers. It poaches in them. It creates surprises in them."[127] Tactics are thus isolated actions or events that take advantage of opportunities offered by the gaps within a given strategic system. Tactics cut across strategic fields, exploiting gaps, to generate novel and inventive outcomes.

Looking at the political construct of the everyday[128] in the neighborhood helps us to further understand the way strategies and tactics are embedded in cycles of violence and reciprocities. This ongoing process constantly shapes and reshapes the dynamic between state, city, and citizens. As James Holston says, "Membership in the State has never been a static identity, given the dynamics of global migrations and national ambitions. Citizenship changes as new members emerge to advance their claims, expanding its reality and, as new forms of segregation and violence counter these advances, eroding it."[129] Thus, violence becomes a tool of negotiation through which "outsider" groups, but also those within a regime, battle over meaning. The outcome of a negotiation expresses the power relationship between the groups, which cannot be reduced to economics or legislation. In this sense, revisioning acts (tactics or strategies) are not predetermined but are rather social constructions of power in which new possibilities and events can occur. How does this process affect the social arena of a place? To answer this question, we present the case of Matalon Street in Neve Shaanan as a microcosm of the strategies and tactics used by the city, the state, and the citizens in constructing a spatial order and meaning.[130]

Strategies and Tactics on Matalon Street

There is nothing special about Matalon Street, a residential street with four- or six-story buildings. Originally the ground floor was designated for small commercial enterprises, but today there are only a few shops and workshops on the street. At the corner of Matalon and Chlenov streets, there is a 24-hour kiosk/grocery store. The other end of the street backs onto the rear of the Central Bus Station. In the middle of the street, there are two empty asphalt plots enclosed by metal barriers 50 centimeters high, blocking access to vehicles. Here, people sit, play, and walk their dogs.

Who lives on the street? Some old residents who have been there since the neighborhood was established; young people (artists, bohemians) who enjoy the character of the neighborhood; other young people who see it as a good property investment; and immigrant workers who live on Matalon Street (as in other parts of the city) because of low rents, availability of apartments, and proximity to public transportation. These immigrant workers are a strong presence on the street, partly because some have built communal meeting places such as the improvised churches in the basement of Matalon 75, the pub, also at Matalon 75, and cafés. Since many people share crowded apartments, these public spaces are important as gathering places. In general, these immigrants tend to spend time outdoors, queuing for public telephones, watching television in the kiosk, drinking beer, and so forth. During the day, one sees children playing in the vacant plots, and in the evenings people gather at the pub and the café. The "happenings" in these spaces reinforce the visibility of this urban space, with regard to authorities and the street's other inhabitants.

The visibility of this space is seen by the City Council as contributing to the city's cosmopolitan image and as a social boost to the downtown area. This has given the labor immigrants recognition, which later became a strategy of rehabilitation for the neighborhood.[131] Conflicts between Israelis and immigrants occur, but on a verbal level rather than on a physical level. The newcomers changed the exchanged value of the area with rents rising, vacant apartments are occupied, commerce flourishes, and the presence of people in the streets has heightened the sense of safety and vitality.

This was one result of the macro-scale strategies of Israel to decrease violence by increasing separation between Israel and the Palestinian Authority, placing a curfew on Gaza and then on the West Bank, thereby preventing the entrance of 100,000 Palestinians. In other words, the state's strategy affected the lived space of the city and accelerated urban strategies, which partly contradicted the state's own policy. After the suicide bombings the visibility of the labor immigrants and the conflicting policies of the state and the city towards them received national exposure. If previously the focus after the suicide bombings was on the victims as "us" (Israeli society), in this case the focus was on "them" (Palestinians and immigrants). Thus, although violent events in the city usually increase national cohesion, and locus becomes sacrosanct, in this instance both locus and society were perceived as the backyard of the illegal residents.

Although there seems to be little connection between then prime minister Ariel Sharon's declared aim of deporting these workers in 2002 and the suicide bombings, two months after the attacks (in July and August) leaflets were dropped from the air, reading as follows: "The Government of Israel calls on you to prevent an unpleasant situation. The State's new policy in regard to foreign citizens allows illegal aliens to leave the country without criminal charges or fines being leveled on them . . . and intends to enforce the law by any means necessary."[132]

A part of the Israeli-Palestinian cycle of violence, this strategy was clearly an invasion by the state into the lived space of the city. Meanwhile, the City Council continued to deal with, and care for, legal and illegal immigrants alike through the Mesila Organization. The immigrant administration and police operated throughout the streets of the city, looking for illegal workers who had not left. Visibility became dangerous, and most streets seemed nearly deserted. On Matalon Street, the café, bar, and churches were closed, creating a vacuum that benefited the drug dealers and drug addicts, who invaded all the vacant spaces, public and private. At first glance, these dealers and addicts appear to be beyond the state's jurisdiction, but in actual fact they are in contact with the police, who designate their precincts in order to keep them under surveillance. Thus, like the immigrant workers, the junkies overran the vacant spaces and the courtyards, choosing the end of the street as a good escape route, from the police, onto the highway (the adjacent streets are one-way).

Controlling the scene gave rise to another initiative. For the first time, a temporary coalition among residents of Matalon and the adjacent street was formed.[133] This committee did not have a unified agenda, but was a tactic for promoting their own visibility and accelerating distribution of resources and recognition by the authorities. As such, the group became extremely vocal about the Council's intention of refurbishing a former synagogue and transforming it into a rehabilitation center.[134] The committee's tactic was twofold, at the city and the state level,[135] demanding the sealing of abandoned buildings and general maintenance and infrastructure of the streets, by gardening, paving, lighting, etc. These projects were perceived by the committee as signs of habitation that would discourage the addicts from living in the street. At the government level, the committee contacted the police, who had "assumed that no-one lives here . . . ," an interpretation or reading of the place as a marginalized space[136] in which the inhabitants were invisible. The residents' tactic of increasing their own visibility influenced the national institutions to acknowledge their presence and assist them in modifying the social order. This visibility was further strengthened when one member of the committee decided to open a community center on the street (the Sisters' House), an organization offering information and advice to the residents in the neighborhood.[137]

As noted previously, to this socially complex picture the planning authorities responded by suggesting a strategic plan, known as "The Meeting Place." It proposed reinforcing the socio-physical character of the area. The plan underlined the intention of the planners to moderate conflict, defining its goals as "renovating and improving the area by integrating it with the social, economic and physical fabric of the city, moderating conflict, ordering and reducing environmental nuisance and economic, social and physical leverage."[138] As noted the plan divides the area into three sections—temporary residential and commercial area, permanent residential area, and central business district—and clearly defines the population characteristics of each area. It is obvious that the plan acknowledges the diverse character of the environment, but at the same time it fixes the existing social segregation patterns in order to enhance the city's image as a cosmopolitan city.

FIGURE 4.13   *Image of daily life in the neighborhood. (Photo: Author)*

FIGURE 4.14   *The park (at the back, the Central Bus Station). (Photo: Author)*

TABLE 4.2   STRATEGIES AND TACTICS

Strategy (state)	Strategy (city)	Tactic (inhabitants)
Permitting labour immigrants (1993)	Founding Mesilla, an information and advisory center for labour immigrants	Strengthening visibility in daily life. Improvising community centers, churches, bars, cafés. (Immigrant workers).
Self evacuation project (2003)	Supporting Mesilla	Immigrant workers leave, increased visibility of drug addicts and dealers. Crime and street violence
Police help to combat drug addicts and dealers (2005–2007)	Developing "The Meeting Place" Plan	Inhabitants' call to fight crime in the street. Establishing visibility through community center (NGO) and neighborhood committee.

The plan is being implemented gradually. One of the first steps is the renovation of a public park at the end of the street. Mainly occupied by drug dealers and addicts, the park was neglected for many years. The Council's strategy was to evacuate the junkies by force and to patrol the area day and night. In the first days after its re-opening, the place was deserted, but today it has become a meeting place for all, with labor immigrants (legal and illegal) dominating, sitting, eating, and playing. An interesting (illegal) phenomenon is the stands with home-cooked food sold by immigrants to visitors. This is in direct violation of the regulations and rules of the state (tax regulations and permits). However, this secure, colorful place is exactly what the city hopes for in order to support the city's cosmopolitan image, with its trans-national park further blurring social disparities and inequalities.

Table 4.2 summarizes the strategies and tactics described. What does all this imply? The description of the changes in social mobility in the street portrays the complex relationships between state, city, and citizens, mirroring the increasing violence in cities worldwide, which occurs because cities are strategic arenas for developing citizenship and contribute to social mobility.[139] As shown, the city provides a forum for different kinds of civic negotiations that are part of the struggle for order and are directly affected by violence, which is a viable strategy to help the city and the state modify and enforce change. In this state of affairs, visibility—through violence (as in the case of the Palestinians) or through setting up temporary communities (labor immigrants) or through organized committees (the street's residents)—is the citizen's main tool.

The dynamic of violence also creates tensions between state and city. Routinely, the lived space is cared for by the municipality (infrastructure, welfare services, construction), but most of the power remains in the hands of the government that sets policies. This state of affairs changes dramatically in cases of threats or violence, when the government tightens boundaries, both physically and symbolically, and can modify policies and strategies. The hierarchy of state and city becomes blurred, and direct force is applied to the inhabitant or the citizen. The citizen does not necessarily "resist" these policies, but a complex relationship of collaboration and objection occurs that essentially aims to alter and settle the existing situation as part of the negotiation over place. Since the lived space is where tactics and strategies acquire form, it is also the sphere where coalitions and fights over resources take place, including resistance to, or collaboration with, the state's mechanisms. Violence does not necessarily stabilize the role of individuals or groups, but it can influence society and social mobility in unforeseen ways.

Interpreting space as a dynamic aggregate of strategies and tactics suggests an alternative portrait of the city's social coalitions. It shows how social imagination plays a key role in manifestations of conflict or change through conflict. Thus, understanding processes of violence requires an understanding of the paradoxes of an imagined social and physical future. Analyzing the relationships between institutional strategies and residents' tactics in space shifts engagement with "marginality" to a better understanding of the place, from recording space as an abstract map of uses, identities, and actors to recording it as a series of conflicted actions over norms and resources.

‖ The Routine of Violence

I am walking down Eben Gvirol Street in Tel Aviv on a lovely sunny day. It is September 5, 2008, and I am on my way to the City Council to collect some additional archival documents for finalizing my book manuscript. At the entrance stands a weary security guard, who looks past me but nods for me to stop. Without thinking, I hand him my bag to search. He opens it and rummages through it indifferently, handing it back without making eye contact. Picking up an electronic device, he scans my torso and back in one mechanical movement, then turns away to scan the next person in line. I wish him a good day, but he is obviously too distracted or too tired to respond. I know that, just as I am invisible to this man, he is invisible to the many people who come into the building. I wait for the elevator to arrive. Minutes pass. I wait longer, thinking about all the checkpoints in the city and beyond, in Palestine, along "the separation wall," that have become part of our daily landscape, and about how the routines of violence—practiced by both Palestinians and Israelis alike—have crafted urban ghettos on both sides.

The countless violent acts in Tel Aviv have become almost routine, followed by revisioning moments enacted by the government, media, municipalities, police, and citizens that have themselves become habitual practices touching all levels of society.

In this book, we have looked at Tel Aviv through an analysis of violent acts in three key sites. By looking at Rabin Square, the city's distinctive socio-spatial historical constructions are illuminated; examining particular moments in the history of Rabin Square tells us about the political history of the Jewish community. Analysis suggests that the form of public assembly and the physical space in which it occurs are indivisible, thus ratifying architecture's contribution to the shaping of citizenship. This cohesive relationship of space and ritual was also present during the most dramatic event in the Square, fixed forever in the national (and international) consciousness: the assassination of Prime Minister Rabin on November 4, 1995. Rabin's murder exposed the deep fissures in Israeli society and triggered ongoing public debate about how to repair them. The Square became the locus of memory of the murder (in other words, changing the name of the Square was a memorial ritual, as was placing a monument on the exact spot of the assassination) and a constant reminder of the tensions that led up to it. These acts reinforced the political formalization of the space and its assemblies, adding further symbolic meaning and magnifying the importance of the Square's ritual and theatrical attributes. Analysis of the discourse concerning proposed new underground parking facilities has further exposed the discrepancies between the temporality and everyday life of the Square and its role as a memorial space. Looking at the seashore, we gain a sense of the role of architecture in constructing boundaries in the urban space and between communities. A historical examination of the production of the seashore exemplifies how the Jewish community used spatial tools to define its discrete cultural and social space. Unlike Rabin Square, the beach has been a conflicted site since the early twentieth century and the violent acts occurring in the area can be seen as part of its confused identity. The site presents spatial typologies—the door, the bridge, and the gateway—giving rise to discussions about architecture and planning as border-making practices. Until today, architecture and planning were part of "the separation discourse,"[1] contributing to conflict and to ethnic and physical barrier-making. With the suicide bombing at the Dolphinarium Discothèque on the beach, the temporary meeting point of two rival groups on the site became part of its historical controversy, exposing the social groups and making them visible to each other and to the municipality and the state. Unfortunately, this violence has only confirmed the discourse of rivalry and separation, both politically and physically. By examining the Central Bus Station in the Neve Shaanan neighborhood of the city, we see how architectural and planning practice responds to the dominant economic order, without calling for change but rather producing a spatial order that responds to national conflicts. The history of the neighborhood exposes its social and economic conflicts, while professional practices focus on the organization and beautification of the place. Here, the violent act again (as in the suicide bombing at the Dolphinarium Discothèque) exposes the social complexity of groups operating in the area; once again, national and economic forces influence architects' and planners' actions.

Another way to summarize what the book has been offering is to follow the chronological thread elucidated in the narrative about three significant periods of architectural and planning production in Tel Aviv during the 1930s, 1960s, and 1990s. As we saw, these three decades are intensely associated with conflicts in which architecture participated as an active agent. For each of these periods, it is clear that the architectural and planning discourse did not operate autonomously, but was rather synchronized with international professional discourse and was also recruited by the local national-political discourse. What we learned is that, during the 1920s and 1930s, the three sites became embedded in ethno-national struggles (Rabin Square and the Central Bus Station), and against capitalist ownership (the Dolphinarium). The neighborhood of Neve Shaanan, for example, was developed after the riots of 1921 in Jaffa; Menshiyeh quarter became a shelter area; and Summeil village, designated as a square by the Geddes plan, became an area for protests and gatherings opposing the British policy and the Arab community. In the 1960s, architecture and planning adjusted their discourse, mimicking national efforts to blur internal conflicts among social groups. During this period, spaces were redefined through large-scale projects funded by the state and private capital. All sites were redefined as key points of the city: a public center (Rabin Square); a tourist center (the seashore); and a public transport center (Neve Shaanan). This collaboration between the city and the state changed in the 1990s due to global-economic processes and local-political demands, necessitating another shift in the spatial definition of space: to a focus on updating architectural fashion and creating a rentable image. From this aspect, the violent acts of the 90s did not change or modify space, but they were significant catalysts for discursive modifications. These acts emphasized the cohesive triangular relationship between national conflicts, architecture, and daily life. Moreover, architecture and planning were active and central participants in a process in which construction and destruction were not binary but, rather, complementary forces.

Finally, a thematic reading presented the terminology that has shaped Tel Aviv's development since its early days. The terms appearing in the book— *ideology, memory, boundaries, center, periphery, order,* and *everyday life*—mark the changing ideological constructions as vital elements through which groups define themselves and negotiate, sometimes by means of violence, to establish their claims to the city. Thus, as we have seen, contestation through violence is not merely a competition over material resources but also over language and vocabulary, influencing how we perceive and later implement them into concrete development projects. Consequently, grounding these terms in the contested production of urban space enables us to assess their influence on the built environment of Tel Aviv. These terms are of particular significance to the architectural and planning practices that transform ideas into reality. However, architects and planners can also challenge these terms, and thus mediate between interests and powers, and negotiate between participants by offering other interpretations. Yet, in most cases the shortcomings of professional practice lie in accepting this role without any real attempt to challenge it.

The Dynamics of Violence

As previously stated, violence and revisioning moments are creative acts. Violence is born from imagined conflict. Revisioning moments are born from the memory of conflict and become reconciliatory acts. Both derive from friction between rival groups in which legitimacy of power is at stake. The Israeli/Palestinian conflict is based on this dynamic, which becomes a source for production that "constructs" a worldview, legitimizing one group's truth over the other. But has the dynamic of violent acts on both sides fostered change? Is it socially and spatially influential?

Because of the loud voice of these acts—and the way these acts have been embraced by the state and the media—the focus has been shifted from personal casualties to a larger political context. This has resulted in a reformative process that has exposed the Israeli-Palestinian social complexities and also has defused the process so that it reverts back to its more simplistic, binary form. This is evident in the case of the assassination of Prime Minster Rabin in the Square, which exposed the rivalry between groups in Israeli society. The suicide bombings in the Dolphinarium Discothèque exposed the different groups who occupied this space—the Palestinian community and the Jewish immigrants from Russia, both perceived as marginal and vulnerable. As the book suggested, the same dynamic applies to the case of the suicide bombing at the Central Bus Station, where labor workers, Palestinians, and Israelis reside. In both cases, the arbitrary bombings initiated a discourse about the spatial interactions and power hierarchy of these groups. One might say that, as opposed to criminal violence, the political violence actually accelerates public debates about society's composition, memory of events, political reactions, etc. Thus, the cases presented in this book showed how the national conflict in the urban center of Tel Aviv was made real to its citizens; however, this reality failed to foster a radical discursive shift.

To a certain extent, conflict did accelerate economic development. It is, in fact, difficult to separate the *destructive* dimension of violence from its various *productive* economic forces, examined here. Thus, for example, after the assassination of Rabin, elements were added to the Square—a memorial wall with some graffiti, a commemorative plaque, and the annual ceremonies, turning the Square into a tourist attraction. In contrast to the assassination itself, which added these elements to the existing fabric to "fill in" the deep fissures in Israeli society, the suicide bombings gave legitimacy to the revision of space. Unlike the well-maintained Square, the site of the Dolphinarium was not restored, but it did lead to the acceleration of new development. This also applies to the new development plan for the Central Bus Station that celebrates the place and its inhabitants (the labor immigrants), preferred as an image of consumption by authorities over the image of low-income Israelis and over the image of Palestinians who are perceived as the enemy. This implies that the memory of violent acts is selective, as seen in the way the city reacts to conflicts and uses them to erase and/or develop spaces. Thus, capital is not merely a means for ordering and regulating space to maintain stability; it is also a tool through which the state systematizes and synthesizes memory. In this sense, Tel Aviv and its geographic-capitalist order and its political conflicts are not unique. This order can be seen in other parts of the world as a conglomeration of contradictory forces that transform conflicts and violence into productive forces and generators of mobility.[2]

As clearly indicated in the book, these conflicts and violent acts strengthen the role of planning and architectural discourse and generate change in their public role (Table 5.1). This change, in which the discourse articulates differences among groups, happens because of the shifting of the core of violence into the city centers. As opposed to the wars of 1967, 1973, and 1982, the Israeli-Palestinian conflict of the 1990s is being fought in the urban arena, magnifying the involvement (by choice or accidentally) of different groups and their accessibility to resources. In other words, tensions after violent acts accelerate individuals' and groups' responses, leading to engagement with their surroundings. These tensions can be seen as a socio-cultural process in which physical space plays a key role. However, as evident in the different public forums on the three sites, inequalities remain. Public participation in this forum is somewhat normative, which keeps the power in the hands of authorities. Although architecture and planning discourse plays a role in this participatory process, it responds mainly to the power of authorities, barely responding to citizens. Operating within the context of conflict, architecture and planning are, unfortunately, detached from their societal role.

	Rabin Square	*Dolphinarium*	*Central Bus Station*
Conflicts in the 1930s	Cultural-ideological strife within the Jewish community and different groups, a unified ethno-national struggle	Ethno-national clashes between Jewish and Arab communities over place; and between Jewish communities against capitalist interests	Ethno-national conflict between Jewish and Arab communities, and between communities and Zionist and urban institutions
Architectural practice	—	—	The neighborhood plan as a symbol: the seven-branched candelabrum of the Temple
Conflicts in the 1960s	Repressing differences and clashes among Jewish groups, recruiting all to the national ethos	1948 war, occupation eviction, and destruction	Tensions between city and state
Architectural practice	Construction of a city/state representational space	Grand-scale projects based on cooperation between state and private capital; destruction of urban fabric, with citizens playing no role in decision making	Grand-scale project based on cooperation between state and private capital, with citizens playing no role in decision making
Conflicts in the 1990s	Ideological, internal, over the meaning of place; national appropriation of the square	Ethno-national clashes, including suicide bombings and events of October 2000	Ethno-national including suicide bombings; with the increase of labor immigrants, radical change in the social configuration of the neighborhood
Architectural practice	Reinforcing daily and capital value of the site; City Council uses participatory mechanisms in planning	Grand-scale project based on cooperation between the state and private capital; preservation and conservation of the urban fabric that was destroyed in 1950s-60s	Grand-scale project based on cooperation between state and private capital; regeneration of the site as a tourist area; strengthening its image as a global city

The Cyclical Power of Revisioning Moments

The discourse of violence is rooted in the State's actions, and on the assumption that its citizens are willing to fight (and die) for it. In other words, the State is constructed through violence that maintains its sovereignty. Even when a State seems peaceful (internally and externally), physical violence is still a tool that the State uses—made permissible by its citizens. Furthermore, the increase in violence in cities all over the world is not only due to a contestation over symbols, infrastructure, and resources, but also because this contestation focuses on the meaning and physicality of citizenship in urban centers.[3] This is why we cannot anymore perceive the city as just an arena for the residency of local citizens, foreigners, and labor immigrants, but rather as a forum for contesting different types of citizenship.[4] Still, this heterogeneous framework of citizenship within cities often collapses in cases of violent acts, when the division between the citizens of the territorial nation-state and other inhabitants (immigrants) is exacerbated by the State's desire for immediate normalization and closure. This kind of discrimination during acts of violence is determined by the degree of disparity between the city's dense and heterogeneous lived spaces and the nation as an idealized construction.

In addition to the debate over citizenship, violent acts destabilize the illusion that the State provides order and security. This destabilization reminds us that uncertainty and improbability are inherited in our social reality—thus fracturing what Slavoj Žižek calls a "social fantasy."[5] Holding onto this fantasy by both the regime and its citizens requires some sort of ideological symbolism to conceal the fragility of a State that could collapse at any moment. This fantasy is restored by the revisioning moments of citizens and political actors alike, urging us to go back to what we have lost, the illusion of unity and safety. As Dominique LaCapra says, in a secular context, the commonly desired objective is total unity, community, and consensus, usually because of the intrusion of others (regarded as outsiders or polluters) of the city or the body politic.[6] Thus, the revisioning moment is a response, not so much about who we are but rather who we were. This responsive process of forgetting and remembering creates a linear narrative of the event. This process is contentious. As such, the violent acts might lead to change, but it is doubtful they would do so. The reason is that there is increased insecurity and anxiety about social order and personal welfare. As such, this is a circular process, in which the violent acts are perceived as chaotic and accidental and are then reorganized, both spatially and discursively, until the next violent act occurs, and the cycle continues. In this cycle, rulers and citizens actively forget and remember as a means of creating social order, which has become the most significant tool of ruling parties for both imposing discipline and creating meaning.[7]

The discourse of architecture and planning in this post-traumatic situation accentuates power differences between groups. By planning for the future, it calls for transformation of daily life. In its essence, it is part of the process of spatial order for gaining normalization and security, based on tangible physical signs that can be read by citizens. This particular quality is what could potentially make the professional practice a mediator that integrates spatial production with political discourse, a role often ignored by professionals who do not fully embrace the opportunity to contribute to meaningful place-making. Thus, understanding the social characteristics of violent acts and revisioning moments contributes to our understanding of the different socio-spatial aspects of the conflict. Conversely, perceiving political conflicts at a national level only, with no socio-spatial implications, often merely maintains the status quo of capitalistic reality.

Epilogue: A Letter to Architects and Planners

Conventionally, Tel Aviv is described through its architectural and planning projects; however, as the study of violence and revisioning moments reveals, citizens play a meaningful role in the production of space. This narrative, presented as a complex picture of the multi voices and multi powers operating in Tel Aviv, leads to a more comprehensive understanding of cities. But we still have to answer the question of whether architects and planners can adopt a more active role to become mediators between regime and citizens. This can, however, only occur when professionals fully grasp the kind of basic principle of practice that addresses concrete, everyday needs of citizens, on the one hand, and a new vision of the city, on the other.

As noted earlier, this is particularly significant within the contemporary context of the Neoliberalist decentralization of urban planning, which dismantled the State's planning authority, giving more power to local governments and private developers. Of course, one significant flaw with having urban planning agendas set by developers is that their priorities often stand in contradiction to the social and environmental welfare of the city as a whole. However, only by addressing the welfare of the city as a whole will the profession shift from its marginal role to become a key player in the production of socio-spatial space. I mean here that we need to go beyond the various methods of integrating citizens in the planning process, often called "planning from below," which has shifted the professional focus from the object itself (i.e., the city) to action-oriented participatory practices.[8] Unfortunately, these practices that map the requirements of different groups deal primarily with distribution of resources and operate within an existing order without being able to challenge it. As a result, the planning process has become a matter of inclusive negotiation and no longer fosters macro-visions of social justice. Hence, mediation as defined here, both invents new forms of citizenship and also bridges the vision of groups by suggesting original solutions.

In the age of late capitalism, architecture and planning disassociate themselves from the practice of visioning and utopian thinking. But we have to ask, what does utopia mean to society today? Is it at all significant? If the answer is no, argues Frederick Jameson,[9] it is because of the polarity of the contemporary global order: the world of poverty, unemployment, violence, and death, in which the idea of utopia seems irrelevant and frivolous and the world of wealth and commercialization, in which these ideas seem outdated and boring. However, utopia is more than an idealized vision. It is a method of reflecting, of imaginatively challenging divisions and conventions, and a place where we can address many of our daily struggles for existence.[10] It is also an intellectual sphere that allows us to move from mapping and organizing cities to inventing new strategies of thought and action.

Aversion to Utopian discourse is partly a result of the twentieth century's simplistic assessment of Utopia as either a success or failure. This, in addition to critical discourse on knowledge, power, and truth,[11] has resulted in an acute separation between the lived experience and the imagined Utopian space, accentuating what Bernard Tschumi called "the architectural paradox."[12] Contemporary architecture cannot reconcile its need to both address everyday life and also reject the existing realities in order to find alternatives. This paradox is extremely evident in contemporary Israeli architectural discourse (but also in other places), which is currently polarized so that one group is committed to social change but ignores questions of form and material, while the other group is committed to technology, computation, and morphology but avoids social issues. This extreme polarization has created a state of detachment and aridity: theoretically, the first group of socially oriented professionals is also able to operate beyond the boundaries of the discipline. The second group operates within the domain of spatial form, presenting a limited reading of the city and its inhabitants, and thus marginalizing architectural practice. At the end of the day, both groups are detached from the production of space at large and do not significantly influence practice.

Reviving utopian thinking does not mean returning to the idea of spatial form as a tool for social change. It is a method of thinking and searching for alternatives to the free market. This is particularly vital in contested zones, where perceiving political conflicts at a national level, disconnected from local socio-spatial implications, all too often intensifies the capitalistic dynamic.

So, are architectural practices in Israel visionary? In other words, do these practices enrich the fundamental values of our society so they can initiate new reforms or present alternatives? *Not yet.* What we do have is a start, a forum for critical architectural debate influenced by discourses in sociology and geography, not yet translated into action. Why hasn't there been action? One reason is that Israel's architectural and planning discourse sees the Palestinian-Israeli situation as opposing one another. This binary opposition (occupier and occupied, guilty and just) has moved away from the core issue of human society inhabiting space, from the creation of mutual habitation patterns, and from enhancing similarities as well as differences. Thus, although revealing the limitations of the current discourse, the critical voices are unable to affect real change.

There is no doubt that the professional discourse in Israel has reinforced the social and political dimensions of the profession. Different from the modernist movement of the 1950s, which was used as a national tool to territorialize the Israeli environment, planning's contemporary discourse does not aptly consider questions of spatial form. And yet a lack of new spatial patterns is atrophying the logic of our profession. How can we then shift from a language of opposition to a language that addresses shared values? The only way is to suggest alternative methods that are discerning but, at the same time, constructive. Thus, along with acknowledging the destruction caused by violence and war, the mission of professionals and critics is to look through a multicultural lens and thereby initiate new socio-spatial patterns of humane and just environments. In the end, visioning may help us understand not merely where we came from but where we are going.

Finally and without doubt, the role of both architects and planners is complex and controversial. Over the last decade, professionals have, by and large, become disengaged,[13] detached from the socio-political arena. Thus, echoing Antonio Gramsci, we can acknowledge two types of professionals: the traditional and the organic.[14] The traditional ones, whether operating independently or within institutions, do not see themselves as ideologists. They conserve, stabilize, and recycle ideas without doubting them. Conversely, the organic professional participates in the socio-political struggle and recognizes knowledge as a key component of modern power, and as a condition critical to the creation and growth of society. With this organic approach, the architect and planner can shape society. At present, we have three options. The first is to deny, or refuse to believe in, our own influence on society, and thus to reject responsibility by adopting pragmatic arguments without offering solutions. A second option is to acknowledge we have the ability to influence society but refrain from doing so. Thirdly, we can accept the responsibility and deal with its complexities. This approach contradicts those who see architecture and planning merely as a profession that deals with space, either politically (with the aid of the nation-state) or economically (with the help of capitalists). It also contradicts those who separate theory from practice. Only by actively enriching the discourse of space with a political and social consciousness can the profession hope to make an enduring contribution.

Key Dates and Events

The following list is not comprehensive; it refers mainly to events and dates mentioned in the manuscript, with key historical dates.

1880	Menshiyeh quarter is established in the north, adjacent to Jaffa.
1887	Neve Tzedek, the first Jewish neighborhood outside Jaffa's walls, is established.
1906	Ahuzat Bayit, a corporation for building houses, is founded.
April 11, 1909	The first cornerstone of Ahuzat Bayit is established, and its members organize a parcel lottery.
May 21, 1910	Ahuzat Bayit is renamed as Tel Aviv.
November 2, 1917	Balfour Declaration, a policy statement mandated by the British government on the partition of the Ottoman Empire in the aftermath of World War I, of supporting Zionist plans for a Jewish homeland in Palestine.
November 17, 1917	The British Empire occupies Tel Aviv and Palestine, forcing out the Ottomans.
May 1, 1921	Riots and confrontation occur between Arabs and Jews in Tel Aviv and Jaffa during the May 1 parade led by Tel Aviv workers.
May 11, 1921	Tel Aviv is recognized as a separate township from Jaffa.
August 25, 1929	Riots and confrontation occur between Arabs and Jews in Tel Aviv, starting at the Hassan Beq Mosque.
January 12, 1934	Tel Aviv is declared a Municipal Cooperation, implying a total separation from Jaffa.
April 19, 1936	Riots and confrontation occur between Arabs and Jews in Tel Aviv and Jaffa.
September 9, 1940	Second World War, Italian Air Force attacks Tel Aviv.
November 29, 1947	UN General Assembly votes in favor of a resolution to adopt

	the plan for the partition of Palestine, recommended by the majority of the UN Special Committee on Palestine (UNSCOP). Jaffa is designated an Arab enclave in the Jewish state.
December 1947	A new Central Bus Station is opened.
May 14, 1948	The State of Israel is established, with Tel Aviv as its temporary capital.
May 14, 1948	War breaks out, during which Jaffa is occupied.
October 5, 1949	The government declares Tel Aviv–Jaffa a unified city.
1962	New plans are begun to replace the old Central Bus Station.
1963	Initiation of the "City Project" for "a new heart for Tel Aviv–Yafo [Jaffa]" in Menshiyeh.
1965	The City Council moves to its new building in Malchei Israel Square, later to be renamed Rabin Square.
January 17, 1991	Missiles hit Tel Aviv during the first Gulf War.
1993	A new Central Bus Station is opened.
August 20, 1993	The Oslo Accords, officially finalized as the Declaration of Principles on Interim Self-Government Arrangements, or the Declaration of Principles (DOP), is considered a milestone in addressing the Israeli-Palestinian conflict.
1993–1995	Suicide bombings throughout the country and in Tel Aviv.
November 4, 1995	Prime Minister Rabin is assassinated in Malchei Israel Square during a peace rally supporting the Oslo Accords.
September 2000	The Second Intifada, also known as the al-Aqsa Intifada, is the most recent wave of violence between Palestinians and Israelis, which began seven years after the end of the First Intifada.
June 1, 2001	Suicide bombing at the Dolphinarium Discothèque.
January 1, 2003	Suicide bombing at the Central Bus Station.
June 7, 2004	UNESCO announces Tel Aviv as "a world heritage" site.
2009	Tel Aviv celebrates its Centennial Events.

Tel Aviv in Numbers

TABLE 6.1 POPULATIONS' CHARACTERISTICS; THE POPULATION OF PALESTINE, TEL AVIV AND JAFFA, DURING THE PERIOD OF THE BRITISH MANDATE (SOURCE: YODFAT ARIE, *60 Years in Tel Aviv's Development*, TEL AVIV: TEL AVIV—YAFO MUNICIPALITY, 1969)

Year	*Tel Aviv/ Jaffa*	*Total*	*Jews*	*Non-Jews*
1922*	Tel Aviv	15,185	15,065	120
	Jaffa	32,524	5,087	27,437
1931**	Tel Aviv	46,101	45,564	537
	Jaffa	51,866	7,209	44,657
1937***	Tel Aviv	150,000	150,000	—
	Jaffa	69,400	14,200	55,200
1944***	Tel Aviv	166,660	166,000	660
	Jaffa	94,310	28,000	66,310

* Government Census
** Municipal Census
*** Estimate

Year	Total	Jews	Non-Jews
1950	335,000	330,000	5,000
1951	345,500	340,000	5,500
1955	359,700	354,000	5,700
1959	379,300	373,500	5,800
1961	386,070	380,288	5,782
1972	363,750	357,400	6,350
1973	365,100	358,400	6,700
1974	360,300	353,300	7,000
1975	353,800	346,600	7,200
1976	348,500	341,100	7,400
1977	343,200	335,500	7,700
1978	339,800	331,900	7,900
1979	336,300	328,100	8,200
1980	334,900	326,500	8,400
1981	329,500	320,900	8,600
1982	325,700	316,700	9,000
1983	327,265	317,810	9,455
1984	325,370	315,400	10,000
1985	322,770	312,600	10,200
1986	320,258	309,800	10,500
1988	317,806	306,700	11,100
1989	321,715	310,200	11,500
1990	339,354	326,965	12,389
1991	353,242	339,683	13,559
1992	356,911	341,906	15,005
1993	357,367	341,386	15,981
1994	355,197	339,642	15,555
1995	348,245	328,445	19,800
1996	349,217	330,917	18,300
1997	348,570	329,262	19,308
1998	348,117	328,136	19,981 [12,823 Palestinians]
1999	350,753	328,508	22,245 [13,213 Palestinians]
2000	354,428	329,979	24,449 [13,627 Palestinians]
2001	358,800	332,400	26,400 [14,100 Palestinians]
2002	360,400	333,000	27,400 [14,400 Palestinians]
2003	363,387	335,151	28,236 [14,898 Palestinians]
2004	371,400	341,847	29,800 [15,400 Palestinians]
2005	378,902	347,847	31,055 [15,924 Palestinians]
2006	384,400	351,800	32,600 [16,300 Palestinians]

Notes

FOREWORD

1. http://www.white-city.co.il/english/mayor.html
2. http://www.jewishvirtuallibrary.org/jsource/vie/Telaviv.html
3. *Urban Leviathan: Mexico City in the Twentieth Century* (Philadelphia, Penn.: Temple University Press, 1994).
4. With apologies to Andres Duany.

INTRODUCTION

1. Wenona Giles and Jennifer Hyndman (eds.), *Sites of Violence: Gender and Conflict Zones* (Berkeley: University of California Press, 2004), pp. 3–23; Elaine Scarry, *The Body in Pain: The Making and Unmaking of the World* (New York: Oxford University Press, 1985), pp. 3–23.

2. Michel Foucault, *"Society Must Be Defended": Lectures at the Collège de France, 1975–1976*, edited by Mauro Bertani and Alessandro Fontana (New York: Picador, 2003), pp. 23–24; Anthony Giddens, *The Nation-State and Violence* (Berkeley: University of California Press, 1985), pp. 7–34.

3. Vittorio Bufacchi, "Violence," in Iain McLean and Alistair McMillan (eds.), *The Concise Oxford Dictionary of Politics* (Oxford: Oxford University Press, 2003).

4. Johan Galtung, "Violence, Peace, and Peace Research," *Journal of Peace Research* 6, no. 3 (1969): 167–191; Johan Galtung, "A Structural Theory of Aggression," *Journal of Peace Research* 1, no. 2 (1964): 95–119. On the limitations of Galtung's theory see Kjell Eide, "Note on Galtung's Concept of 'Violence,'" *Journal of Peace Research* 8, no. 1 (1971): 71.

5. Charles Tilly, *The Politics of Collective Violence* (New York: Cambridge University Press, 2003), p. 26.

6. According to Grinberg, at times politics in Israel leads to what he calls "tribal

politics," which is based on an imagined national identity that emphasizes public hate and fear of new forces (outside and inside the nation-state). This type of politics silences and negates the legitimacy of the "others" and the need to talk with them. Lev Grinberg, *Imagined Peace, Discourse of War* (Tel Aviv: Resling, 2007; in Hebrew), pp. 30-31.

7. Tilly, *The Politics of Collective Violence*, pp. 130-50.

8. Ibid., pp. 194-220.

9. Ibid., pp. 81-101.

10. Hannah Arendt, *On Violence* (New York: Harcourt, Brace and World, 1970), p. 4.

11. Ibid., p. 7.

12. Harold Garfinkel, *Studies in Ethnomethodology* (Englewood, N.J.: Prentice Hall, 1967).

13. The urban rhythm is significantly different from the mechanical rhythm of a clock. Henri Lefebvre pointed out that the mechanical movement of the clock reproduces itself, as a repetitive process. The daily rhythm of life has a repetitive component too, but it preserves some qualities and changes others—thus, creating constant modifications. Henri Lefebvre, *The Production of Space* (Oxford, U.K.: Blackwell, 1991), pp. 205-207.

14. Max Weber, "The Profession and Vocation of Politics," in *Weber: Political Writings*, edited by Peter Lassman and Ronald Speirs (Cambridge: Cambridge University Press, 1994), pp. 309-369.

15. Stephen Graham, *Cities, War, and Terrorism: Towards an Urban Geopolitics* (Cambridge, Mass.: Blackwell, 2004), pp. 1-25.

16. Mary Kaldor, *New and Old Wars: Organized Violence in a Global Era* (Stanford, Calif.: Stanford University Press, 1999), pp. 1-14.

17. Paul Virilio, *Speed and Politics* (Cambridge: MIT Press, 2007), pp. 7-26.

18. Kim Booth and Tim Dunne, *Worlds in Collision: Terror and the Future of Global Order* (New York: Palgrave Macmillan, 2002), pp. 74-94; Craig Calhoun, Paul Price, and Ashley Timmer (eds.), *Understanding September 11* (New York: New Press, 2002); Slavoj Žižek, *Welcome to the Desert of the Real! Five Essays on September 11 and Related Dates* (London and New York: Verso, 2002), pp. 58-82.

19. Graham, *Cities, War, and Terrorism*, p. 6.

20. Sharon Zukin, *Landscape of Power: From Detroit to Disneyworld* (Berkeley: University of California Press, 1991), pp. 3-24; Sharon Zukin, *The Cultures of Cities* (Cambridge: Blackwell, 1996), pp. 1-48; Iris Marion Young, *Justice and the Politics of Difference* (Princeton: Princeton University Press, 1990).

21. Mike Davis, *Ecology of Fear: Los Angeles and the Imagination of Disaster* (New York: Metropolitan Books, 1998), pp. 3-56.

22. Emmanuelle Lequeux, "Reinventer les formes de la cité," *Beau Arts Magazine* 260 (February 2006): 76-83; Claude Parent, "Claude Parent: La citta ribelle / Claude Parent: The Rebel City," *Domus* 887 (November 2005): 68-71.

23. Azmi Bishara, "Reflections on October 2000: A Landmark in Jewish-Arab Relations in Israel," *Journal of Palestine Studies* 30, no. 3 (2001): 54-67; Or Theodore, "The Report by the State Commission of Inquiry into the Events of October 2000," *Israel Studies* 11, no. 2 (2006): 25-53.

24. Arjun Appadurai, *Modernity at Large: Cultural Dimensions of Globalization* (Minneapolis, Minn.: University of Minnesota Press, 1996), esp. p. 152.

25. Saskia Sassen, "Governance Hotspots: Challenges We Must Confront in the Post September 11th World," in Kim Booth and Tim Dunne (eds.), *Worlds in Collision: Terror and the Future of Global Order* (New York: Palgrave Macmillan, 2002), pp. 24-313.

26. Giorgio Agamben, *Homo Sacer: Sovereign Power and Bare Life*, trans. Daniel Heller-Roazen (Stanford, Calif.: Stanford University Press, 1998), pp. 15-29.

27. Mark Wigley, "Editorial," *Assemblage* 20 (Violence, Space) (1993): 6-7.

28. Roy Coleman, *Reclaiming the Streets: Surveillance, Social Control and the City* (Cullompton, Devon: Willan, 2004), pp. 1-12; David Lyon, *Theorizing Surveillance: The Panopticon and Beyond* (Cullompton, Devon: Willan, 2006), pp. 3-19.

29. John Friedmann, "City of Fear or Open City?" *Journal of the American Planning Association* 68 (2002): 237-243.

30. For example the studies by Alice Coleman, *Utopia on Trial: Vision and Reality in Planned Housing* (London: H. Shipman, 1990); Oscar Newman, *Defensible Space: Crime Prevention through Urban Design* (New York: Collier Books, 1973); Barry Poyner, *Design against Crime: Beyond Defensible Space* (London and Boston: Butterworths, 1983).

31. See numerous papers in the journal *Environment and Behavior*, e.g., Kuo E. Frances and William C. Sullivan, "Aggression and Violence in the Inner City: Effects of Environment via Mental Fatigue," *Environment and Behavior* 7, vol. 33 (2001): 543-571; Ben J. Refuerzo and Stephen Verderber, "Effects of Personal Status and Patterns of Use on Residential Satisfaction in Shelters for Victims of Domestic Violence," *Environment and Behavior* 7, vol. 21 (1989): 413-434.

32. For example see the studies by Scott A. Bollens, "City and Soul: Sarajevo, Johannesburg, Jerusalem, Nicosia," *City* 5, no. 2 (2001): 87-169; Usama Makdisi and Paul A. Silverstein, *Memory and Violence in the Middle East and North Africa* (Bloomington: Indiana University Press, 2006), pp. 1-25; Amartya Sen, *Identity and Violence: The Illusion of Destiny* (New York: W. W. Norton, 2006), pp. 1-17.

33. Rafi Segal and Eyal Weizman, *A Civilian Occupation: The Politics of Israeli Architecture* (London and New York: Verso; Tel Aviv: Babel, 2003); Haim Yacobi and Shelly Cohen (eds.), *Separation: The Politics of Space in Israel* (Tel Aviv: Xargol and Am Oved Publishers, 2006; in Hebrew).

34. For discussion on medieval cities see Iain Borden and David Dunster, *Architecture and the Sites of History: Interpretations of Buildings and Cities* (Oxford: Butterworth Architecture, 1995); George Broadbent, *Emerging Concepts in Urban Space Design* (London: Van Nostrand Reinhold, 1990), pp. 15-34.

35. Joachim Schlör, *Tel Aviv, from Dream to City* (London: Reatkin Books, 1999), pp. 34–49; Yacob Shavit and Gideon Bigger, *History of Tel Aviv (1909–1939)* (Ramot: Tel Aviv University Press, 2001; in Hebrew), pp. 52–89.

36. Stanley Buder, *Visionaries and Planners: The Garden City Movement and the Modern Community* (New York: Oxford University Press, 1990), pp. 133–156; Peter Hall, *Cities Tomorrow: A Peaceful Path to Real Reform*, later published as *Garden Cities of Tomorrow* (Oxford: Blackwell, 2002), pp. 87–141.

37. See for example the studies by Zeynep Çelik, *Urban Forms and Colonial Confrontations: Algiers under French Rule* (Berkeley: University of California Press, 1997), pp. 58–86; Robert Home, *Of Planting and Planning: The Making of British Colonial Cities* (London: E. and F. N. Spon, 1997), pp. 151–157; Jane M. Jacobs, *Edge of Empire: Post-Colonialism and the City* (London: Routledge, 1996), pp. 13–37; Anthony King, *Colonial Urban Development: Culture, Social Power and Environment* (London: Routledge, 1976).

38. High Commissioner for Palestine, Letter, 6.7.36, *Public Record Office*, 1936, file CO 733/313/6; High Commissioner for Palestine, Letter, 29.12.37, *Public Record Office*, 1936, file CO 733/341/14; Herbert Samuel (High Commissioner), "Report to the Colonial Secretary on the Situation in Palestine," Oxford: *Middle East Archive Centre*, St. Anthony's College, 1924, HAYCRAFT file GB 165-0139 [25.1.24]; Wauchope, "Extract from a Letter, 18.7.36," *Public Records Office* 1936, file CO 733/313/6.

39. Tom Segev, *One Palestine Complete: Jews and Arabs under the British Mandate* (U.K.: Little, Brown and Company, 1999), pp. 173–190.

40. Patrick Geddes, *Town-Planning Report, Jaffa and Tel Aviv*, Tel Aviv Municipal Archives, 1925.

41. On the formal decision of 8.4.21, see *Yediot Iryat Tel Aviv*, Tel Aviv Municipal Archives, 1921.

42. Though it did not get a formal approval, the Kauffmann plan from 1921 was a significant cornerstone in the conceptualization of the city's development and image. Kauffmann's Palestine Land Development Architect vision of Tel Aviv was based on the Anglo-German garden city. His plan showed a town oriented toward the sea, coherently planned and set amid gardens. The shoreline was to be the focus of urban life. A broad promenade with squares, markets, parks, and cultural and recreational centers was planned. The regularly spaced east-west routes were particularly emphasized as tree-lined avenues. Squares with public institutions were placed where these avenues intersected with the promenade. In order to maintain the original garden city character, Kauffmann suggested that the minimum plot size should be increased from 300–400 to 569–1,000 square meters and that the permitted building volume should be limited (Goldman, 1994). Pe'era Goldman (1994), "Tel Aviv: Transformation of a Suburb into a City, 1906-1935," in I. Kamp-Bandau and N. Winfried (eds.), *Tel Aviv Modern Architecture, 1930–1939* (Berlin: Wasmuth, 1994).

43. Geddes's initial report appeared in 1925. A plan based on this report was drafted in 1926.

44. Baruch Yoscovitz, "Urban Planning in Tel Aviv-Yafo: Past, Present, and

Future," in *Social Processes and Public Policy in Tel Aviv-Jaffa*, ed. David Nachmias and Gila Menahem (Tel Aviv: Ramot Publishing, 1997), pp. 347–365.

45. For further information please see the municipality website (Hebrew version): http://www.telaviv.gov.il/Hebrew/Strategic/Index.asp

46. In keeping with the argument made by Gurevitch and Aran, Israelis' sense of place consists of belonging to two places—the big place and the small place. The sense of locality—belonging to the small place—can be characterized in terms that bring to mind ideas of nativity, such as belonging to a specific locale, to a home, a street, or a childhood landscape. On the other hand, the sense of belonging to the State—the big place—is beyond specific places, being a collective idea. The big place is not a direct continuation and expansion of the small place—there is no continuum of home, neighborhood, city, and country—but rather a leap from the current local reality to an idea. Zali Gurevitch and Gideon Aran, "On the Place (Israeli Anthropology)," *Alpiem* 4 (1991): 9–44; in Hebrew.

47. Meron Benvenisti, *City of Stone* (Berkeley: University of California Press, 1996), pp. 1–49.

48. Gurevitch and Aran, "On the Place (Israeli Anthropology)," p. 43.

49. The Second Intifada, also known as the al-Aqsa Intifada, refers to the second Palestinian uprising, which began in September 2000. Palestinian tactics ranged from carrying out mass protests and general strikes, as in the First Intifada (1987–1993), to mounting suicide bombing attacks and firing Qassam rockets into Israeli residential areas; Israeli tactics ranged from creating checkpoints and constructing the West Bank barrier to conducting arrests and targeted attacks upon terrorist leaders.

50. Tali Hatuka and Leslie Forsyth, "Urban Design in the Context of Glocalization and Nationalism: Rothschild Boulevard, Tel Aviv," *Urban Design International* 10, vol. 2 (June 2005): 69–86.

51. Maoz Azaryahu, *Tel Aviv: Mythography of a City* (Syracuse, N.Y.: Syracuse University Press, 2007); Tamar Berger, *Dionysus at Dizengoff Center* (Tel Aviv: Hakibbutz HaMeuhad, 1998; in Hebrew); Mark LeVine, *Overthrowing Geography: Jaffa, Tel Aviv, and the Struggle for Palestine, 1880–1948* (Berkeley: University of California Press, 2005); Barbara E. Mann, *A Place in History: Modernism, Tel Aviv, and the Creation of Jewish Urban Space* (Stanford, Calif.: Stanford University Press, 2006); Sharon Rotbard, *White City, Black City* (Tel Aviv: Babel, 2005; in Hebrew).

52. For further reading on the relationship between time, space, and the idea of "spatial trajectories" as a tool to understand the ongoing development of space, see Doreen Massey, *For Space* (London: Sage, 2005), p. 25, p. 59.

53. Methodologically, the study is based on a variety of documentary and analytical techniques. The investigation is based on Hebrew and English documents collected in Israeli and British archives: Tel Aviv Municipal Archives, Zionist Archive Jerusalem, Israel Defense Forces Archives, Public Office Record (UK National Archives), Palestine Exploration Fund, London, St. Anthony's, Middle East Center, Oxford; on observations at different sites, on interviews with key figures and architects, and on interviews with members of the resident communities.

CHAPTER I

1. David Riches (ed.), *The Anthropology of Violence* (Oxford, UK; New York: Blackwell, 1986).

2. Bettina E. Schmidt and Ingo W. Schröder (eds.), *Anthropology of Violence and Conflict* (London and New York: Routledge, 2001), p. 3.

3. Nigel Thrift, "Immaculate Warfare? The Spatial Politics of Extreme Violence," in Derek Gregory and Allan Pred (eds.), *Violent Geographies: Fear, Terror, and Political Violence* (New York: Routledge, 2007), pp. 273-294.

4. Ibid., p. 28.

5. Much has been written on the relationships between the media, politics, and war (in particular in the context of the Iraq and Afghanistan wars). See, for example, Ariella Azoulay, *Death's Showcase* (Cambridge: MIT Press, 2001), pp. 4-8; Matthew Baum, *Soft News Goes to War* (Princeton, N.J.: Princeton University Press, 2003), pp. 1-14; Pippa Norris, Montague Kern, and Marion Just (eds.), *Framing Terrorism: The News Media, the Government, and the Public* (New York: Routledge, 2003), pp. 3-25; Shanto Iyengar, *Is Anyone Responsible? How Television Frames Political Issues* (Chicago: University of Chicago Press, 1991), pp. 11-16.

6. Schmidt and Schröder, *Anthropology of Violence and Conflict*, p. 6.

7. Thrift, "Immaculate Warfare?" p. 274.

8. "Regime." *Dictionary of the Social Sciences.* Craig Calhoun, ed. Oxford University Press, 2002. Oxford Reference Online. Oxford University Press. Massachusetts Institute of Technology (MIT). June 21, 2007. http://www.oxfordreference.com/views/ENTRY.html?subview=Main&entry=t104.e1420

9. For discussion about types of regimes and their classification see, Charles Tilly, *Regimes and Repertoires* (Chicago: University of Chicago Press, 2006), pp. 1-2.

10. Frantz Fanon, *The Wretched of the Earth* (commentary by Jean-Paul Sartre and Homi K. Bhabha) (New York: Grove Press, 2004); Arendt, *On Violence*, p. 4.

11. Gyanendra Pandey, *Routine Violence* (Stanford, Calif.: Stanford University Press, 2006), pp. 1-15.

12. Achille Mbembe refers here to all the police institutions, army, and administrators that actively maintain the socio-economic and daily order of a society. Achille Mbembe, *On the Postcolony* (Berkeley: University of California Press, 2001), pp. 174-75.

13. Arendt, *On Violence*, p. 56.

14. Dan Gillmor, *We the Media: Grassroots Journalism by the People, for the People* (Sebastopol, Calif.: O'Reilly, 2004), p. xix.

15. Thrift, "Immaculate Warfare?" p. 279.

16. Acille Mbembe, "Necropolitics," *Public Culture* 15, no. 1 (Winter 2003): 11-40.

17. Thrift, "Immaculate Warfare?" p. 282.

18. For further reading on temporality and time-space, see Anthony Giddens,

The Consequences of Modernity (Stanford, Calif.: Stanford University Press, 1990), pp. 10–16; Jon May and Nigel Thrift (eds.), *TimeSpace: Geographies of Temporality* (New York: Routledge, 2001), pp. 1–37.

19. Zigmund Bauman, *Community: Seeking Safety in an Insecure World* (Oxford: Polity Press, 2001), p 3.

20. Henri Lefebvre, "The Inventory (from *La Somme et Le Reste*, 1959)," in S. Elden, E. Lebas, and E. Kofman (eds.), *Henri Lefebvre: Key Writings* (New York and London: Continuum, 2003), pp. 166–177, esp. p. 173.

21. Richard Bauman, *Story, Performance, and Event* (Cambridge: Cambridge University Press, 1986), pp. 1–10; Victor W. Turner, *The Anthropology of Performance* (New York: PAJ Publications, 1985), pp. 72–98.

22. See, for example, the various perspectives on this issue in Judith Butler, *Precarious Life: The Power of Mourning and Violence* (London and New York: Verso, 2004), pp. 19–49; Cathy Carruth, *Unclaimed Experience: Trauma, Narrative and History* (Baltimore: Johns Hopkins University Press, 1996), pp. 10–24; Jennifer Radden, *The Nature of Melancholy: From Aristotle to Kristeva* (New York: Oxford University Press, 2000), pp. 335–344.

23. Sigmund Freud, "Mourning and Melancholia," *The Standard Edition of the Complete Psychological Works of Sigmund Freud* (London: Hogarth Press, 1957), pp. 243–258.

24. Jenny Edkins, *Trauma and the Memory of Politics* (Cambridge: Cambridge University Press, 2003), pp. 1–19.

25. LaCapra argues that the mythical belief in a past that has been lost may be combined with an apocalyptic, often blind Utopian quest to regain that lost wholeness or totality in a desired future. At times this occurs through violence directed against outsiders who have purportedly destroyed or contaminated the wholeness. Dominique LaCapra, *Writing History, Writing Trauma* (Baltimore: Johns Hopkins University Press, 2001), p. 195.

26. David Harvey, *Spaces of Hope* (California: University of California Press, 2000), pp. 131–180.

27. Traditionally the Utopian concept is identified with planning a system that is responsible for progressive spatial reform, advocating social justice and democracy. From an architectural-planning perspective, utopia is perceived as an organized place under a regulated regime with inflexible social and economic systems. The physical-architectural structure of a utopia is what defines and stabilizes a social process that is conceived as static and immutable. Among the best-known implemented utopias are Ebenezer Howard's Garden City and Le Corbusier's Ville Radieuse. Although they are different in their spatial organization, the idea common to both is that geometry defines time and that the implemented vision fosters social and historical change.

28. Oren Yiftachel, "Planning and Social Control: Exploring the Dark Side," *Journal of Planning Literature* 12, no. 4 (1998): 395–406.

29. Giddens, *The Consequences of Modernity*, p. 1.

CHAPTER 2

1. "How Will Malchei Israel Square Be Constructed?" *Yediot Iryat Tel Aviv* (1947): 1, Tel Aviv Municipal Archives.

2. Goldberg Moyshe (Director), *Hazira* [The Arena], Israel, Eran Riklis Productions Ltd. For further reading about Avraham Yaski, see Sharon Rothbard, *Avraham Yaski: Concrete Architecture* (Tel Aviv: Babel, 2007; in Hebrew), esp. pp. 91-93, 104-132.

3. City Spokesman, Malchei Israel Square, Tel Aviv Municipal Archives, 1966, file 25, folder 2532.

4. Yitzhak Arzi, to the Council Members, Tel Aviv Municipal Archives, 1977, file 25, folder 2532.

5. Dan Horowitz and Moshe Lissak, *Trouble in Utopia: The Overburdened Polity of Israel* (Tel Aviv: Am Oved, 1990; in Hebrew).

6. Ibid.

7. It is known as "the Protest of the 400,000" because of the estimated number of participants. Maya Michaeli, "The State Square," *Tel Aviv: Weekly Newspaper*, October 26, 2001, pp. 42-48.

8. On September 16, 1982, a group of Lebanese Christian Falangists entered the Palestinian refugee camps of Sabra and Shatila (near Beirut). They massacred between 800 (official Israeli figure) and 3,500 (according to the Israeli journalist Kapeliouk) people, including women and children. On the previous day, the Israeli army had entered this area of the city, sealed the camps from the outside world, and passively observed the events of September 16-18.

9. Irit Dekel, *The Enclave of Collectivity: Cultural Analysis of the Peace and Democracy Guardians, November 4, 1995, in Rabin Square* (Tel Aviv: Tel Aviv University Press, 2000; in Hebrew).

10. The Oslo Accords were agreements between the Israeli government and the Palestine Liberation Organization (the PLO) representing the Palestinians in 1993 as part of a peace process officially called the Declaration of Principles. The negotiations were undertaken in total secrecy, and breakthrough agreements were signed on August 20, 1993. A public ceremony was held in Washington, D.C., on September 13, 1993, with Yasser Arafat and Yitzhak Rabin. Despite the high hopes expressed in the Oslo Accords and in subsequent agreements, the problems have yet to be resolved.

11. Steve Basson, "'Oh Comrade, What Times Those Were!' History, Capital Punishment and the Urban Square," *Urban Studies* 7 (2006): 1147-1158.

12. Rob Krier, *Urban Space* (New York: Rizzoli, 1979), pp. 13-23; Aldo Rossi, *Architecture in the City* (Cambridge: MIT Press, 1982), pp. 20-27.

13. Jan Gehl, *Life between Buildings* (Berkshire: Van Nostrand Reinhold, 1987), pp. 7-32; Kevin Lynch, *The Image of the City* (Cambridge: MIT Press, 1960), pp. 1-13.

14. Neil Leach, *The Anaesthetics of Architecture* (Cambridge: MIT Press, 1999),

pp. 17–32; Susan Torre, "Claiming the Public Space: The Mothers of Plaza de Mayo," in Jane Rendell, Barbara Penner, and Iain Borden (eds.), *Gender, Space, Architecture* (London: Routledge, 2000), pp. 140–145; Lawrence J. Vale, *Architecture, Power and National Identity* (New Haven: Yale University Press, 1992), pp. 44–55.

15. See Emile Durkheim, *Elementary Forms of Religious Life* (New York: Free Press, 1965), pp. 3–24; Max Weber, *The Sociology of Religion* (New York: Beacon Press, 1963), pp. 1–19.

16. Sally Moore and Barbara Myerhoff, *Secular Ritual* (Assen: Van Gorcum, 1977), pp. 3–23.

17. Ibid.

18. Benedict Anderson, *Imagined Communities: Reflections on the Origins and Spread of Nationalism* (London: Verso, 1983), pp. 1–8.

19. Don Handelman, *Models and Mirrors: Towards an Anthropology of Public Events* (Cambridge: Cambridge University Press, 1990), pp. 10–21.

20. Victor W. Turner, *The Forest of Symbols* (New York: Cornell University Press, 1967), p. 19.

21. Richard Sennett, *The Spaces of Democracy* (New York: University of Michigan College of Ann Arbor, 1998), pp. 15–21. For further readings on the Agora and Greek architecture see G. E. M. de Ste. Croix, *The Origins of the Peloponnesian War* (London: Duckworth, 1972), pp. 267–284; Alexander Tzonis and Phoebe Giannisi, *Classical Greek Architecture* (Paris: Flammarion, 2004).

22. Leach, *The Anaesthetics of Architecture*, pp. 19–21.

23. James M. Jasper, *The Art of Moral Protest* (Chicago: University of Chicago Press, 1997), pp. 20–23.

24. Torre, "Claiming the Public Space."

25. Sarah Hellman and Tamar Rapport, "The Women in Black and the Challenge to the Social Order," *Theory and Criticism* 10 (1997): 175–192 (in Hebrew); Tova Benski, "Breaching Events and the Emotional Reactions of the Public: Women in Black in Israel," in Helena Flam and Debra King (eds.), *Emotions and Social Movements* (New York: Routledge, 2005), pp. 57–78.

26. Jeremy Bentham, *The Panopticon*, introduction by Miran Božovič (London and New York: Verso, 1995), pp. 29–95.

27. Michel Foucault, *The Order of Things: An Archaeology of the Human Sciences* (New York: Pantheon Books, 1970), pp. 51–78.

28. "The Decision of the Assembly in Tel Aviv," *Yediot Iryat Tel Aviv*, Tel Aviv Municipal Archives, 1954, p. 57; 1939, p. 196. Statement of British Palestine policy, issued May 17, 1939 (the MacDonald White Paper), which also outlined a five-year plan for the immigration of 75,000 (10,000 per annum plus 25,000) refugees. This "White Paper" should be understood in the context of escalated hostilities prior to the outbreak of World War II. It was evident to foreign policy experts that it was not in Britain's interests to offend the Arab and Muslim world. The White Paper remained in force until 1947.

29. Ibid.

30. On the role of the Geddes Plan in demarcating urban spatial order, see Hatuka and Forsyth, "Urban Design in the Context of Glocalization and Nationalism."

31. For further details of the Geddes Plan and its implementation, see Rachel Kallus, "Patrick Geddes and the Evolution of Housing Types in Tel-Aviv," *Planning Perspectives* 12, no. 3 (1997): 281–320.

32. In a contract that included a north-south division of the orchard, it was agreed that the southern part and the big pond would be given to the City Council, while the northern side, including the houses and wells, would be retained by the owner, who would supply water to the city. Documents from the early 1930s describe the Portalis orchard as owned and cultivated by the Jewish community. Despite good working relationships between the owner and the council, difficulties and suspicions continued. The partnership was terminated with the owner's initiative to sell his part to the City Council. Israel Rokach, "To Mr. San Salim Arafa," Tel Aviv Municipal Archives, 1934, file 1263a; Tel Aviv Council, "An Agreement," Tel Aviv Municipal Archives, 1925, file 1263a; Ebrahim Shuka Effendi Harbitali, "To the Mayor of Tel Aviv Council," Tel Aviv Municipal Archives, 1933, file 1263a.

33. Jaffa–Tel Aviv, *Town Planning Area*, Palestine Survey, 1945.

34. Lefebvre, *The Production of Space*, pp. 38–39. For discussion in the Israeli context see also Haim Yacobi, "Between Surveillance and Spatial Protest: Production of Space in the Mixed City of Lod," *Surveillance and Society* 2, no. 1 (2003): 55–77.

35. See, e.g., the protest on August 13, 1946, in Habima Square, "Tel Aviv in a Settlement Struggle," *Yediot Iryat Tel Aviv*, Tel Aviv Municipal Archives, 1946, pp. 46–47.

36. "The Day of Command in Tel Aviv," *Yediot Iryat Tel Aviv*, Tel Aviv Municipal Archives, 1939, p. 196.

37. According to Yatziv, a sector is a community or network of communities joined by their members' free will. Members usually agree about political, social, and cultural controversies; membership is active and usually indicates their views and beliefs. Gadi Yatziv, *The Sectorial Society* (Jerusalem: Bialik Institute, 1999; in Hebrew), p. 12.

38. Ibid., p. 8.

39. An attempt to reduce society to a homogeneous mass, orchestrated by Ben Gurion's *Mamlachtiut* (statehood) project, and intended to strengthen the political center and reinforce its authority over different groups and sectors of society. Horowitz and Lissak, *Trouble in Utopia*, pp. 40–66.

40. Tel Aviv Council, "5th Protocol of the Planning Committee," Tel Aviv Municipal Archives, 1945, file 4, folder 2615; Tel Aviv Council, "4th Protocol of the Planning Committee," Tel Aviv Municipal Archives, 1945, file 4, folder 2615.

41. "How Will Malchei Israel Square Be Constructed?" *Yediot Iryat Tel Aviv*, Tel Aviv Municipal Archives 1947, p. 1.

42. Ibid.

43. The council did not see the building as a single unit. M. Amiaz, "The Com-

mittee for New Council Buildings," Tel Aviv Municipal Archives, 1954, file 4, folder 1248.

44. Udo Kultermann, *Kenzo Tange: Architecture and Urban Design, 1946–1969* (London: Pall Mall Press, 1970), pp. 46–55.

45. Tel Aviv Council, "Proposed Regulations for Maintaining the Character of Malchei Israel Square," Tel Aviv Municipal Archives, 1966, file 13, folder 51.

46. Avi Melzer, "Malchei Israel Square," Tel Aviv Municipal Archives, 1970, file 25, folder 1531; Moshe Amiaz, "To the Mayor," Tel Aviv Municipal Archives, 1970, file 25, folder 2531.

47. Amiaz, "To the Mayor."

48. City Spokesman, "Competition for Design of the Monument," Tel Aviv Municipal Archives, 1970, file 25, folder 1347. The decision to erect the monument was made in 1970, but public debate began with the announcement of the competition in 1974. The council asked for proposals from ten sculptors and approved the jury's decision to accept Tumarkin's work in 1973.

49. Abba Kovner, "An Attempt to Define the Idea of the Monument," Tel Aviv Municipal Archives, 1971, file 25, folder 1348.

50. City Spokesman, "The Monument for the Holocaust and Revival in Malchei Israel Square," Tel Aviv Municipal Archives, 1973, file 25, folder 1350.

51. In 1973 a plea was presented to the Supreme Court to halt construction of the monument. Other delays were caused by the 1973 war and by local elections.

52. Aharon Papu, "A Demand to Cancel the Plan for Installing a Monument in Malchei Israel Square," Tel Aviv Municipal Archives, 1973, file 4, folder 1349, p. 2; Zvi Avi-Gai, "The Holocaust and Revival Monument," Tel Aviv Municipal Archives, 1974, file 25, folder 1350.

53. M. Savidor, "To Mr. Mayor," Tel Aviv Municipal Archives, 1972, file 25, folder 1347; Yehuda Shochat, "To the Mayor," Tel Aviv Municipal Archives, 1976, file 4, folder 1350.

54. Ombudsman, "Memorandum," Tel Aviv Municipal Archives, 1975, file 4, folder 150.

55. Yitzhak Arzi, "To the Council Members," Tel Aviv Municipal Archives, 1977, file 25, folder 2532.

56. Ilan Schori, "The Attack on the Voter," *Haaretz*, June 28, 1981.

57. Ilan Schori, "One Hundred Thirty Thousand Attend the Likud Congregation in Malchei Israel Square," *Haaretz*, 9/6/81, p. 1.

58. "The protest of the 400,000" refers to the (putative) number of participants; Maya Michaeli, "The State's Square," *Tel Aviv Weekly Newspaper* (2001): 42–48.

59. Michaeli, "The State's Square."

60. Benvenisti, *City of Stone*, pp. 1–4.

61. Gurevitch and Aran, "On the Place (Israeli Anthropology)."

62. Handelman, *Models and Mirrors*, p. 1.

63. Ibid., p. 1.

64. Speaker Yoram Meuhas (then Head of the Rabin Center). Israeli Knesset Interior and Environment Committee (2001), "Proposed Legislation for Rabin Square," *Hatach A-A*, Tel Aviv Historical Archive File, 14 Folder 263 pp. 12–16, p. 16.

65. LaCapra argues that the mythical belief in a past that has been lost may be combined with an apocalyptic, often blind utopian quest to regain that lost wholeness in a desired future. Sometimes this occurs through violence directed against outsiders who have purportedly destroyed or contaminated the wholeness. LaCapra, *Writing History, Writing Trauma*, p. 49.

66. For the role of symbolizing differences and conflict in cities, see Ruth Fincher and Jane Jacobs, *Cities of Difference* (New York: Guilford Press, 1998). For the discussion on the everyday practices, see Lefebvre, *The Production of Space*, pp. 352–400; Michel De Certeau, *The Practice of the Everyday Life* (Berkeley: University of California Press, 1984), pp. 91–110. For a discussion on contested public history of a place, see Dolores Hayden, *The Power of a Place: Urban Landscapes as Public History* (Cambridge: MIT Press, 1997).

67. LaCapra, *Writing History, Writing Trauma*, pp. 65–7.

68. Maoz Azaryahu, "The Spontaneous Formation of Memorial Space," *Area* 28, no. 4 (1996): 501–51.

69. Vered Vinizki-Sarusi, "Between Jerusalem and Tel Aviv: The perpetuation of Rabin and National Identity Discourse in Israel," in Lev Grinberg (ed.), *Contested Memory—Myth, Nation and Democracy: Thoughts after Rabin's Assassination* (Beer-Sheva: Humphrey Institute for Social Research, 2000; in Hebrew), pp. 19–38, esp. p. 27. See also Jo Ann Harrison, "School Ceremonies for Yitzhak Rabin," *Israel Studies* 6 (2002): 113–134.

70. Mira Engler, "A Living Memorial: Commemorating Yitzhak Rabin in the Tel Aviv Square," *Places* 12, no. 2 (1999): 4–11.

71. Eyal Dotan, "An End to the Trauma: Sterilization and Obliteration in Memory Representation," *Theory and Criticism* 17 (2000): 27–34 (in Hebrew).

72. Michel Foucault, "Of Other Spaces," *Diacritics* 16 (Spring 1986): 22–2.

73. Michel Feige, "Yitzhak Rabin: His Perpetuation and the Perpetuation of His Perpetuation," in Grinberg (ed.), *Contested Memory*, pp. 39–64; Yossi Yona, "Israel after Rabin's Assassination: Jewish State or All Citizens' State?" in Grinberg (ed.), *Contested Memory*, pp. 109–122.

74. Council Forum, Protocol 15, Tel Aviv Municipal Archives: March 3, 2002, p. 4.

75. This discursive change relates to post-modernist development and the corpus of urban design theory, developed after World War II and culminating in the 1960s. It opposes enlightened ideas in architecture and their implications for perceptions of time and space. The loss of a political, economic, social, and symbolic urban center due to physical disintegration of the urban fabric required challenging the positivist, modernist, functional worldview. This has led to a search for alternative modes of operation in the city, emphasizing the physical space, existing circumstances, and the local historical context.

76. Doron Zafrir, Interview with Author, May 28, 2000.

77. Council Forum, Protocol 15, Tel Aviv Municipal Archives: March 3, 2002, p. 5.

78. Doron Rosenblum, "A Modest Suggestion," *Haaretz*, November 5, 2000.

79. Engineers' and Architects' Association, "The Fight over Rabin Square," *Hatach A-A*, Tel Aviv Historical Archive File, 14 Folder 263, pp. 8–10. Tel Aviv Municipal Archives.

80. Israeli Knesset Interior and Environment Committee, "Proposed Legislation for Rabin Square," *Hatach A-A*, 2002: 12–16, esp. p. 12, Tel Aviv Municipal Archives.

81. Yoram Meuhas, Committee of the Interior and Environment, 2001:64, Tel Aviv Municipal Archives.

82. Council Forum, Protocol 15, Tel Aviv Municipal Archives: March 3, 2002, p. 5.

83. Ibid.

84. Ibid, p. 5.

85. Butler, *Precarious Life*, p. 1.

86. Henri Lefebvre, *Everyday Life in the Modern World* (London: Transaction Publishers, 1984), pp. 1–67.

87. De Certeau, *The Practice of the Everyday Life*, pp. 29–42.

88. Anthony Giddens, *Modernity and Self-Identity* (Cambridge: Cambridge University Press, 1991), pp. 144–180.

89. Edkins, *Trauma and the Memory of Politics*, p. 1.

90. Ibid.

CHAPTER 3

1. On the formal decision of April 8, 1921, see *Yediot Iryat Tel Aviv* (1921), Tel Aviv Municipal Archives.

2. For further reading about the mosque see Nimrod Luz, *The Arab Community of Jaffa and the Hassan Bey Mosque: Collective Identity and Empowerment of the Arabs in Israel via Holy Places* (Jerusalem: Floersheimer Institute, 2005; in Hebrew).

3. Eliezer Fougatch, Adv. Israel Perry, Board of Trustees for the Moslem Sanctuaries in Tel Aviv–Jaffa, Tel Aviv Municipal Archives, 1977, file 7-26-52.

4. David Fisher, "Hassan Bek Mosque: A Muslim-Jewish Cultural Center," Tel Aviv Municipal Archives, 1980, file 14, folder 84, p. 7.

5. "18 Were Killed in a Suicide Bombing in Tel Aviv; Israel Is Holding up an Attack in the Occupied Territories," *Haaretz*, June 3, 2001.

6. "Hundreds of Jew Rioters Lay Siege to Hassan Beq Mosque," *Haaretz*, June 3, 2001, page 1.

7. Charles Tilly, *The Politics of Collective Violence* (New York: Cambridge University Press, 2003), p. 55.

8. See for example the works of Dennis Rumley, *The Geography of Border Land-*

scapes (London: Routledge, 1991); David Storey, *Territory: The Claiming of Space* (England: Pearson Education Limited, 2001).

9. Peter Jackson and Jan Penrose (eds.), *Construction of Race, Place and Nation* (London: UCL Press, 1993), pp. 1–23.

10. Adriana Kemp, "Borders, Space and National Identity on Israel," *Theory and Criticism* 16 (2000): 13–40, p. 17.

11. Yasemin Nuhoglu Soysal, *The Limits of Citizenship* (Chicago and London: University of Chicago Press, 1994), pp. 1, 3.

12. Lefebvre, *The Production of Space*, p. 39.

13. Kevin Lynch, *The Image of the City* (Cambridge: MIT Press, 1960), pp. 14–45.

14. Ibid.

15. Nan Ellin, "Shelter from the Storm of Form Follows Fear and Vice Versa," in *Architecture of Fear*, ed. Nan Ellin and Edward James Blakely (New York: Princeton Architectural Press, 1997), pp. 13–45; Peter Marcuse and Ronald Van Kempen (eds.), *Of States and Cities: The Partitioning of Urban Space* (Oxford and New York: Oxford University Press, 2002), pp. 3–56; Sharon Zukin, *The Cultures of Cities* (Cambridge, Mass.: Blackwell, 1996), pp. 1–48.

16. Leonie Sandercock, *Towards Cosmopolis* (England: John Wiley and Sons, 1998), pp. 107–125; Young, *Justice and the Politics of Difference;* Fincher and Jacobs, *Cities of Difference*, pp. 1–24.

17. Iain Borden, "Thick Edge: Architectural Boundaries in the Postmodern Metropolis," in Iain Borden and Jain Rendell (eds.), *Intersection: Architectural Histories and Critical Theories* (London: Routledge, 2000), pp. 221–246.

18. Teresa P. R. Caldeira, *City of Walls: Crime, Segregation, and Citizenship in São Paulo* (Berkeley: University of California Press, 1999), pp. 1–16.

19. Mike Davis, *City of Quartz* (London: Verso New Left Books, 1990), pp. 3–17.

20. Lefebvre, *The Production of Space*, p. 38.

21. Rem Koolhaas, "Field Trip: (A) A Memoir: The Berlin Wall as Architecture," in *Small, Medium, Large, Extra-Large* (New York: Monacelli Press, 1995), pp. 212–233.

22. The conceptualization of the bridge and the door, as two typologies of borders, was originally defined by George Simmel. George Simmel, *Simmel on Culture: Selected Writings* (London: Sage Publications, 1997), pp. 170–173. His evocation of the bridge makes a provocative comparison with that of Heidegger in the essay "Building, Dwelling, Thinking," in *Poetry, Language, Thought* (New York: Harper Colophon Books, 1971).

23. Simmel, *Simmel on Culture*, p. 173.

24. Ibid., p. 172.

25. E. Mills (Chairman), "Rents Inquiry Committee Report, 14.2.38," *Public Record Office* 1934, file CO 733/262/5.

26. "Tel Aviv and Jaffa in the War of Independence," *Yediot Iryat Tel Aviv* 1–3 (1952): 47, Tel Aviv Municipal Archives.

27. Survey of Palestine, *Jaffa–Tel Aviv*, Scale, 1:1250, National Archives of Maps, 1924; Survey of Palestine, *Jaffa–Tel Aviv*, Scale, 1:2500, National Archives of Maps, 1938.

28. Goldman, "Tel Aviv: Transformation of a Suburb into a City, 1906–1935," pp. 16–23; Alona Nitzan-Shiftan, "Contested Zionism—Alternative Modernism: Erich Mendelson and the Tel Aviv Group in Mandate Palestine," *Architectural History* 39 (1996): 147–180.

29. Ron Fuchs, "The Palestinian Arab House and the Islamic Primitive Hut," *Muqarnas—An Annual for Islamic Art and Architecture* 15 (1998): 157–177.

30. Neal I. Payton, "The Machine in the Garden City: Patrick Geddes' Plan for Tel Aviv," *Planning Perspectives* 10 (1995): 359–381.

31. Orna Betser, *Apartment Houses in Tel Aviv in the Thirties—Their Development, Concept, and Design* (Haifa: Technion, unpublished M.A. thesis, 1984).

32. Kallus, "Patrick Geddes and the Evolution of Housing Types in Tel-Aviv."

33. "Menshiyeh Neighborhood," *Yediot Iryat Tel Aviv* (1936), Vol. 1–2:33, Tel Aviv Municipal Archives, p. 3.

34. Ibid.

35. Police, Report on the Origin and Beginning of the Jaffa Riots April, 1936, *Public Record Office*, 1936, CO 733/314/5.

36. Ibid.

37. Mills, 1934; Chief Secretary, "Questions of Relief and Compensation in Jaffa and Tel Aviv," *Public Record Office*, 11 August 1936, CO 733/313/7.

38. Palestine Post, "Jaffa's Jewish Quarter," 29.11.38, *Public Record Office* 1938, file CO 733/375/12; Palestine Post, "The Jews of Jaffa," 14.2.38, *Public Record Office* 1938, file CO 733/375/12.

39. "Tel Aviv in the Division Report," *Yediot Iryat Tel Aviv* (1937), vol. 4–3: 57–58, Tel Aviv Municipal Archives.

40. Ibid.

41. *Yediot Iryat Tel Aviv*, 1952.

42. Borden, "Thick Edge: Architectural Boundaries in the Postmodern Metropolis," p. 240.

43. The Planning Committee, "Menshiyeh, 1.8.6," Tel Aviv Municipal Archives, 1965, file 7(3), folder 251.

44. *Yediot Iryat Tel Aviv*, 1952.

45. Following the war Jaffa was "emptied" of its 95 percent Arab citizens and transformed from a thriving cultural and economic middle-class Arab center into a poor neighborhood of Jewish and Arab refugees. Benny Morris, *The Birth of the Palestinian Refugee Problem Revisited* (Cambridge and New York: Cambridge University Press, 2004), pp. 211–221.

46. Prime Minister David Ben Gurion demanded that all of Jaffa be annexed to

Tel Aviv. However, the city's mayor, Israel Rokach, supported only the annexation of the Jewish neighborhoods and resisted any additional territorial extensions without appropriate economic support from the government. The latter accepted these claims and decided to provide Tel Aviv with areas for expansion in return for providing municipal services to Jaffa. Arnon Golan, "The Demarcation of the Tel Aviv–Jaffa Municipal Boundaries following the 1948 War: Political Conflicts and Spatial Outcome," *Planning Perspectives* 10, no. 4 (1995): 383–398.

47. "The Formal Annexation of Jaffa to Tel Aviv," *Yediot Iryat Tel Aviv* 5–6 (1949): 73–74, Tel Aviv Municipal Archives.

48. Ibid., p. 74.

49. *Yediot Iryat Tel Aviv*, 1949.

50. Ibid.

51. For further reading, see "The History of Tel Aviv Boundaries," *Yediot Iryat Tel Aviv* 12 (1945): 156–157, Tel Aviv Municipal Archives; "The Formal Annexation of Jaffa to Tel Aviv," *Yediot Iryat Tel Aviv* 1–2 (1950): 4–7, Tel Aviv Municipal Archives.

52. Shalom Cohen, "A New Heart for Tel Aviv–Yafo," *Jerusalem Post*, 1.11.62.

53. Ibid.

54. Achuzot Hof, "Protocol of the Directorship, 30.5.63," Tel Aviv Municipal Archives, 1963, file 7(3), folder 251.

55. Ahuzot Hof, "Town Planning Competition for the Tel Aviv–Jaffa Central Area Redevelopment Project," Tel Aviv Municipal Archives, 1962.

56. Menshiyeh Neighborhood Committee, "To Mordechai Namir, 14.5.62," Tel Aviv Municipal Archives, 1962, file 4, folder 2685.

57. Yehoshua Rabinovitch, "To Mr. Shifman, 26.11.62," Tel Aviv Municipal Archives, 1962, file 4, folder 2684.

58. The council replied that "the goals are mutual . . . to implement the Menshiyeh development plans, and to create an environment that will bring prosperity, increase employment and education, and raise the social level." Pamphlet, "The Truth about the Menshiyeh Plan," Tel Aviv Municipal Archives, 1936, file 4, folder 2685.

59. Two prizes and six recommended awards were given by the jury, as announced in the final report. The Jury Report, "Town Planning Competition for the Tel Aviv–Jaffa Central Area Redevelopment Project, 1.9.63," Tel Aviv Municipal Archives, 1963, file 4, folder 2684.

60. Manfredo Tafuri, "Razionalismo critico nuovo utopismo, concorso per la ristrutturazione della zona centrale di Tel Aviv–Giaffa," *Casabella* 293 (1964): 18–42.

61. This is similar to other attempts to use architectural practices to promote national claims. See, for example, Sibel Bozdogan, *Modernism and Nation Building: Turkish Architectural Culture in the Early Republic* (Seattle: Washington University Press, 2001), pp. 2–15; Lawrence J. Vale, *Architecture, Power and National Identity* (New Haven: Yale University Press, 1992), pp. 44–55.

62. Consisting of W. Holford (Chairman), L. Kahn, P. Vage, B. Zevi, A. Sharon, M. Amiaz (City Engineer), Y. Perlestain, and Y. Dash.

63. Yaakov Ben Sira, "Menshiyeh," Tel Aviv Municipal Archives, 1965, file 4, folder 2618.

64. His objections to the proposed plan were based on three main points: (1) traffic and its intensity; (2) the idea that establishing a new commercial center would be a means of connecting Tel Aviv and Jaffa; and (3) the "concrete and modernistic" architectural language of the project.

65. Aharon Horovitz, "What will be the Identity of Tel Aviv-Jaffa in the Future," *Yediot Iryat Tel Aviv* 8-9 (1954): 2-8, Tel Aviv Municipal Archives.

66. Aharon Horovitz, "Gardens and Bathing—or Commerce along the Sea Shore of Tel Aviv-Jaffa, 9.3.62," Tel Aviv Municipal Archives, 1962, file 4, folder 2685.

67. Yaakov Ben Sira, "Urban Regeneration," Tel Aviv Municipal Archives, 1965, file 4, folder 2618.

68. Ben Sira, 1965:4.

69. Achuzot Hof, "Protocol of the Directorship, 12.5.66," Tel Aviv Municipal Archives, 1966, file 7 (3), folder 251.

70. Ibid.

71. The new Tel Aviv master plan, prepared in the 1980s by Adam Mazor, completely changed the conception, giving the city a new direction. Adam Mazor, *Master Plan of Tel Aviv and Jaffa: The Activities in the Business Center in Tel Aviv and Jaffa* (Ramat Gan: Urban Institute, 1983).

72. Peter Bogod and Unis Pigardo, *Jaffa Gate—Jaffa Promenade*, Tel Aviv Municipal Archives, 1992, 2343 (15) (in Hebrew).

73. See Kate Nesbitt, *Theorizing a New Agenda for Architecture: An Anthology of Architectural Theory, 1965-1995* (New York: Princeton Architectural Press, 1996), pp. 16-70.

74. Allan Colquhoun, "Twentieth-Century Concepts of Urban Space," in Allan Colquhoun (ed.), *Modernity and Classical Tradition: Architectural Essays 1980-1987* (Cambridge: MIT Press, 1991), pp. 223-233.

75. Kenneth Frampton, "Prospects for a Critical Regionalism," *Prospecta: Yale Architectural Journal* 20 (1983): 147-162; Alex Tzonis and Leonie Lefebvre, "The Grid and the Pathway," *Architecture in Greece* 15 (1981): 164-178.

76. Christopher Norberg-Schulz, *Genius Loci: Towards a Phenomenology of Architecture* (New York: Rizzoli, 1980).

77. Anthony Vidler, "The Third Typology," in *Rational Architecture: The Reconstruction of the European City* (Bruxelles: Archives d'Architecture Moderne, 1978), pp. 28-32.

78. Frederic Jameson, *Postmodernism: or, The Cultural Logic of Late Capitalism* (London: Verso, 1991), pp. 1-54.

79. See the Or Committee Report: www.or.barak.net.il/inside-index.htm, 2003.

80. Eyal Ziv and Eitan Eden, "The Exposure and Preservation of the Sea Wall of Old Jaffa," 5.7.98 *The Architects' Collection*.

81. However, due to differences in level between the wall and the land surface,

the plan could not be implemented. This has resulted in a metaphorical "wall" marked along the promenade. As one of the architects described it:

The natural state of the wall was weak . . . the stones had been damaged over the years by electricity cables and water pipes . . . it was impossible to expose the wall, though we wanted to very badly. But we did think it worthwhile to mark the wall . . . not to reconstruct the thing itself but to create an analogy. Eitan Eden, interview, January 22, 2002.

82. Bogod and Pigardo, *Jaffa Gate—Jaffa Promenade*, 8.

83. Lefebvre, *The Production of Space*, p. 39.

84. Ibid., esp. p. 384.

85. For further discussion see Leonardo Benevelo, *The Origins of Modern Town Planning* (London: Routledge, 1967); Francoise Choay, *The Modern City: Planning in the Nineteenth Century* (New York: George Braziller, 1967); David Harvey, *The Urbanization of Capital* (Oxford: Blackwell, 1985).

86. David Harvey, *The Condition of Postmodernity* (Oxford: Blackwell, 1989), pp. 121–199.

87. Ibid., 66–98.

88. Ibid.

89. On the idea of the state as a collective national space, see Anderson, *Imagined Communities*, pp. 37–46; Ernest Gellner, *Nations and Nationalism* (Ithaca, N.Y.: Cornell University Press, 1983), pp. 38–51; Eric Hobsbawm, "Introduction: Inventing Traditions," in Eric Hobsbawm and Terence Ranger (eds.), *The Invention of Tradition* (Cambridge: Cambridge University Press, 1983), pp. 1–14.

90. James Holston and Arjun Appadurai, "Cities and Citizenship." In James Holston (ed.), *Cities and Citizenship* (Durham: Duke University Press, 1999), pp. 1–18.

91. Peter Marcuse and Ronald Van Kempen, *Of States and Cities: The Partitioning of Urban Space* (Oxford and New York: Oxford University Press, 2002), p. 7.

92. Ibid.

93. For discussion about the differences between representations of space and representational spaces, see Lefebvre, *The Production of Space*, pp. 31–46.

94. Rachel Kallus and Hubert Law-Yone, "National Home/Personal Home: Public Housing and the Shaping of National Space," *European Planning Studies* 10, no. 6 (2002): 765–779.

95. For further discussion see Tamar Gozansky, *Formation of Capitalism in Palestine* (Haifa: Haifa University Press, 1986; in Hebrew); Amir Ben Porat, *Where Are Those Bourgeois? The Story of Israeli Bourgeoisie* (Jerusalem: Magnes, 1999; in Hebrew).

96. For further discussion see Zeev Sternhell, *Nation Building or a New State* (Tel Aviv: Am Oved, 1995; in Hebrew).

97. Geddes, *Town-Planning Report, Jaffa and Tel Aviv*.

98. Maoz Azaryahu, "Cultural Historical Outline of the Tel Aviv Seafront 1918–1948" (in Hebrew), *Horizons in Geography* 51 (2001): 95–112.

99. "The Amenities of Tel Aviv Beach, Central Zionist Archives," *Palestine Post*, file 103/201 [13.8.37].

100. Home, *Of Planting and Planning*, pp. 151–157; Schlör, *Tel Aviv, From Dream to City*, pp. 270–309.

101. Zvi Fogelson, "For the Mayor of Tel Aviv," Tel Aviv Municipal Archives, 1927, file 4, folder 2604a.

102. David Bloch, "Concession for the Sea Improvement within the Tel Aviv Boundaries," Tel Aviv Municipal Archives, 1927, file 4, folder 2604a.

103. Yacov Shifman, "Improvements in the City," *Yediot Iryat Tel Aviv* 3–4 (1935): 2, Tel Aviv Municipal Archives.

104. Tel Aviv Council, "Architectural Competition for Arrangement of the Seashore Improvement Plan," Tel Aviv Municipal Archives, 1934, file 4, folder 2672b.

105. "Towards the Fulfillment of the Gruenblatt Plan," *Yediot Iryat Tel Aviv* 7 (1936): 230–231, Tel Aviv Municipal Archives.

106. "Perfecting Tel Aviv, Problems and Suggestions," *Yediot Iryat Tel Aviv* 1–2 (1937–1938): 46–47, Tel Aviv Municipal Archives.

107. "Against the Gruenblatt Project," *Palestine Post*, Central Zionist Archives, file 103/201 [23.6.37].

108. "The Amenities of Tel Aviv Beach," *Palestine Post*, Central Zionist Archives, file 103/201 [13.8.37].

109. M. Roitman, "Concerning Tel Aviv Beach," *Yediot Iryat Tel Aviv* 1–2 (1937): 46–47, Tel Aviv Municipal Archives.

110. Ibid.

111. Yacov Shifman, "Planning for Seashore Improvements," *Yediot Iryat Tel Aviv* 6–7 (1938–1939): 150–151, Tel Aviv Municipal Archives.

112. "The Plan for Sea Improvement," *Yediot Iryat Tel Aviv* 7 (1939): 150–151, Tel Aviv Municipal Archives.

113. Shifman, "Planning for Seashore Improvements"; Yacov Shifman, "What Is Being Done with the Governmental Loans in Tel Aviv," *Yediot Iryat Tel Aviv* 7–9 1939–1940): 3–4, Tel Aviv Municipal Archives.

114. Atarim, "A New Beach for Tel Aviv," Tel Aviv: Atarim Archive, 1974, p. 13.

115. "The Annexation of Jaffa: Connection and Bridge between the Past and the Future," *Yediot Iryat Tel Aviv* 1–3 (1952): 2, Tel Aviv Municipal Archives.

116. Atarim, *Atarim, The Company for Developing Tourist Sites in Tel Aviv* (Tel Aviv: Atarim Archive, 1969).

117. Luigi Piccinato, "Professor Piccinato Lecture about Tel Aviv–Jaffa Beach Planning," Tel Aviv Municipal Archives, file 7 (13), folder 245 [8.5.63].

118. Tel Aviv Council, *The Year Book*, Tel Aviv Municipal Archives, 1970.

119. City spokesman, "Tel Aviv as a Tourist Center for Tourism," Tel Aviv Municipal Archives, file 13, folder 51, 1961.

120. Mizrahi Jews or Mizrahim, also referred to as Edot HaMizrach (Communities of the East), are Jews descended from the Jewish communities of the Middle

East, North Africa, central Asia, and the Caucasus. The term *Mizrahi* is used in Israel in the language of politics, media, and some social scientists for Jews from the Arab world and adjacent, primarily Muslim-majority, countries. This includes Jews from Iraq, Syria, Lebanon, Yemen, Iran, Afghanistan, Kurdistan, India, Pakistan, etc.

121. Department for Development and Property, "The Expropriation of Land for Development—Machlul Neighborhood," Tel Aviv Municipal Archives file 7(13), folder 246, 1960.

122. Treasury, "Machlul areas A, B, in Tel Aviv," Tel Aviv Municipal Archives, file 7(13), folder 246, 1960.

123. City spokesman, "A Tourist Center Will Be Established in Tel Aviv," Tel Aviv Municipal Archives, file 25, folder 3930, August 2, 1968.

124. City spokesman, "Mahlul Inhabitants Evacuating the Neighborhood," Tel Aviv Municipal Archives, file 7(13), folder 246, 1962.

125. Project Committee, "Protocol," Tel Aviv Municipal Archives, file 7(13), folder 246, 1962.

126. Luigi Piccinato, "Report Regarding Tel Aviv–Jaffa Beach Planning," Tel Aviv Municipal Archives, file 1-1962-1-22, 1964), pp. 6–7.

127. Luigi Piccinato, "Summary of Presentation," Tel Aviv Municipal Archives, file 7(13) folder 245, May 10, 1963.

128. Luigi Piccinato, "The Lecture of Professor Piccinato," Tel Aviv Municipal Archives, file 7(13), folder 245, May 7, 1963.

129. Moshe Amiaz, "The Visit of Professor Piccinato," Tel Aviv Municipal Archives, file 4, folder 3743, 1964.

130. Yehoshua Rabinovitch, "A Conversation with the City Engineer," Tel Aviv Municipal Archives, file 7(13), folder 245, 1965.

131. Atarim, "Atarim, A New Beach for Tel Aviv" (Tel Aviv: Atarim Archive, 1974).

132. Ibid., p. 15.

133. Laurence J. Silberstein, *The Postzionism Debates: Knowledge and Power in Israeli Culture* (London: Routledge, 1999), pp. 89–125; Lau Silberstien, "Problematizing Power: Israel's Postzionist Critics," *Israel-Palestine Journal* 2, no. 3 (2002): 97–107.

134. For further discussion about privatization and globalization increasing amid the ongoing Israeli-Palestinian dispute, see Uri Ram, *The Globalization of Israel: Mc-World in Tel Aviv, Jihad in Jerusalem* (New York: Routledge, 2008).

135. For a general overview see Tel Aviv Council, *The City Profile*, October 2002 (Tel Aviv: Tel Aviv Council Publications, 2002). For the complete data and documents see Tel Aviv City Council official website, http://www.tel-aviv.gov.il/Hebrew/Strategic/Index.asp.

136. Metropolitan Planning Team, *Tel Aviv Development Planning Policy*, Vol. A: 2, Israel: Office of Interior Affairs, 1996, esp. p. 11.

137. The Planning Committee, "The Plan to Develop the Dolphinarium Area 10/3/02," the Engineer Council Administration, 2002.

138. Ibid., p. 19.

139. Adi Ophir, "A Civil Society in Non-Stop City," in Yoav Peled and Adi Ophir (eds.), *Israel: From Mobilized to Civil Society?* (Tel Aviv and Jerusalem: Van Leer Institute and Hakibbutz Hameuchad, 2001; in Hebrew), pp. 113–180.

140. Ibid., p. 130.

141. Tel Aviv Council, *The City Profile*, p. 145.

142. Ronald Robertson, "Glocalization: Time-Space and Homogeneity-Heterogeneity," in Mike Featherstone, Scott Lash, and Ronald Robertson (eds.), *Global Modernities* (London and Newbury Park: Sage, 1995), pp. 25–44.

143. Tel Aviv Council, *The City Profile*, p. 144.

144. Jameson, *Postmodernism*, pp. 1–54.

145. UNESCO 2003, whc.unesco.org/sites/1096.htm

146. Harvey, *Spaces of Hope*, p. 58.

CHAPTER 4

1. "23 Died and about a Hundred People Injured in Two Suicide Bombings in South Tel Aviv," *Haaretz*, January 6, 2003, p. 1.

2. The band, "Shabak Samech," was active at the beginning of this century.

3. All of them regarded urbanization as a key feature of capitalist industrialization with ambivalence, seeing the city as both the product and the symbol of modernity with all its inherent conflicts. Durkheim saw urban life as a space for creativity and progress, and of moral decay and anomie. Weber viewed it as the cradle of industrial democracy, engendering instrumental reason and bureaucratic organization. Marx saw it as an indication of progress and productivity, but also as a site of poverty, indifference, and squalor. See Frank Dobbin (ed.), *The New Economic Sociology: A Reader* (Princeton, N.J.: Princeton University Press, 2004).

4. For further discussion see Manuel Castells, "The Class Struggle and Urban Contradictions: The Emergence of Urban Protest Movements in Advanced Industrial Societies," in John Cowely et al. (eds.), *Community or Class Struggle?* (London: Stage 1, 1977); David Harvey, *The Urbanization of Capital* (Oxford: Blackwell, 1985); David Harvey, *Social Justice and the City* (London: Edward Arnold, 1973).

5. Scott Lash and John Urry, *The End of Organized Capitalism* (Madison, Wis.: University of Wisconsin Press, 1987), pp. 1–16.

6. Saskia Sassen, *The Global City: New York, London, Tokyo* (Princeton: Princeton University Press, 1991), pp. 17–84.

7. Zukin, *Landscape of Power*, pp. 3–24; Zukin, *The Cultures of Cities*, pp. 1–48.

8. Jacobs, "Staging Difference," *Cities of Difference*, pp. 252–278; Iris Marion Young, *Global Challenges: War, Self Determination and Responsibility for Justice* (Cambridge, UK, and Malden, Mass.: Polity, 2007), pp. 159–186.

9. Harvey, *The Condition of Postmodernity*, pp. 66–98.

10. Lefebvre, *Writings on Cities* (Oxford, U.K.: Blackwell, 1996), pp. 65–85.

11. Lefebvre, *The Production of Space*, p. 373.

12. Gilles Deleuze and Felix Guattari, *A Thousand Plateaux: Capitalism and Schizophrenia* (Minneapolis: University of Minnesota Press, 1988), pp. 469–471.

13. Ibid.

14. See, for example, Paul Gilroy, *There Ain't No Black in the Union Jack* (London: Unwin, 1987); Bell Hooks, *Black Looks: Race and Representation* (London: Turnaround, 1992); Edward Said, *Covering Islam* (London and New York: Routledge, 1981); Homi K. Bhabha, *The Location of Culture* (London and New York: Routledge, 1994); Richard Dyer, *The Matter of Images: Essays on Representation* (London: Routledge, 1993).

15. For further discussion see Rosalyn Deutsche, *Evictions: Art and Spatial Politics* (Cambridge: MIT Press, 1998); David Sibley, *Geographies of Exclusion: Society and Difference in the West* (London: Routledge, 1995); Jennifer Wolch and Michael Dear, *Landscapes of Despair* (Cambridge: Polity Press, 1987).

16. It was bought by the Geula Company, directed by Meir Dizengoff, former head of the Tel Aviv City Council.

17. Yosef Tishler was born in Austria in 1887 and immigrated to Israel in 1920. He practiced urban planning and architecture until 1936.

18. Data gathered by the city council in 1937 state that there were 395 sheds inhabited by 2,215 persons. Ben Natan, "Population Density and Rents in Tel Aviv's Poor Neighborhoods," *Yediot Iryat Tel Aviv* 5–6 (1937): 119–125, Tel Aviv Municipal Archives.

19. The Jaffa riots lasted for several days of rioting and killing during the British Mandate of Palestine, May 1–May 7, 1921.

20. Keren Kayemeth LeIsrael—Jewish National Fund. "One of Israel's founding national institutions, established in 1901 at the 5th Zionist Congress in Basel, it spearheaded efforts to restore the Jewish People to its ancient homeland." http://www.kkl .org.il/kkl/kklmain_brown_eng.aspx

21. "About Conditions," *Yediot Iryat Tel Aviv* 3–6 (1921), Tel Aviv Municipal Archives; Arie Samsonov, "How Neve Shaanan Was Created," *Constructor and Builder* 140 (1967): 14–24, Tel Aviv Municipal Archives.

22. Yacov Perman, *The Notebook of Neve Shaanan in Jaffa–Tel Aviv*, Tel Aviv Municipal Archives, 1921, file 3–108, p. 6.

23. The British Mandate responded by freezing rents, but there were those who had no homes and were thus forced to pay any price.

24. Yacov Perman, *The Notebook of Neve Shaanan in Jaffa–Tel Aviv*, Tel Aviv Municipal Archives, 1921, file 3–108, pp. 5–6.

25. The Housing Construction Cooperative in Neve Shaanan, 1922.

26. Ibid., p. 12.

27. Ibid.

28. Protocol of the Neve Shaanan Cooperative, Tel Aviv Municipal Archives, File 4, folder 108, 1924; letter "To Dr. Ruppin," Tel Aviv Municipal Archives, file 4,

folder 108, 1924; interview with Chava Chernov, Tel Aviv Municipal Archives, 1997, file 30-1-25, p. 12. (Interviewer: Shula Vidrich.)

29. See map, Ben Nisim, "Tel Aviv Boundaries, Late 1924," Tel Aviv Municipal Archives, 1935E.

30. The Neve Shaanan Housing Construction Cooperative, protocol. Tel Aviv Municipal Archives, File 4, folder 108, 1922.

31. See map, Ben Nissim, "Tel Aviv Map C (Road Development)," Tel Aviv Municipal Archives, 1935C.

32. Levi Eshkol—Interview, Tel Aviv Municipal Archives, 1997, File 30-1-1, p. 6. (Interviewer: Shula Vidrich.)

33. Neve Shaanan Housing Construction Cooperative, "To Dr. Ruppin," Tel Aviv Municipal Archives, File 4, folder 108, 1924.

34. The Geula shareholders company was established in 1904 for sale of land with minimal profit. The company's founder and heads were Lev Goldberg, Zeev Gluskin, Menahem Ussishkin, and Meir Dizengoff. In 1905 the Jaffa-based company nominated Dizengoff as manager.

35. Zvi Belkovski, "Announcement," Tel Aviv Municipal Archives, File 6, folder 108, 1927.

36. Yacov Perman, "Protocol," Tel Aviv Municipal Archives, File 6, folder 108, 1927.

37. Ben Natan, "Density and Rents in the Poor Neighborhoods of Tel Aviv," *Yediot Iryat Tel Aviv* 5–6 (1936): 119–125, Tel Aviv Municipal Archives.

38. "Construction after WWII," *Yediot Iryat Tel Aviv* 10–12 (1948): 9–10, Tel Aviv Municipal Archives.

39. "The Central Bus Station, Tel Aviv-Jaffa," *Yediot Iryat Tel Aviv*, 8–9 (1934): 354, Tel Aviv Municipal Archives.

40. The development of the Palestine railway system is related to three key periods. In 1890 an unsupervised (and unprofitable) short track between Jerusalem and Jaffa was constructed by French capitalists to serve pilgrims. Then the Turkish Sultan Khalif proposed development of the Hedjas Lines, only partially completed due to the British invasion of Egypt. During the war the line was developed for strategic purposes. The north-south tracks were further developed during the British Mandate. A. F. Kirby, "Palestine Railways," in Middle East Centre, *St. Anthony's College Archive*, Kirby, File 1/5 Gb165-0172, 1948; B. K. Zipper, "Palestine Railways," in Middle East Centre, *St. Anthony's College Archive*, Kirby, File 1/5 Gb165-0172, 1938; Department of Ways and Works, "Railway in Palestine in 1914," in Middle East Centre, *St. Anthony's College Archive*, Scrivener: GB 165-0257 (1925a); Department of Ways and Works, "Railway Extensions Built by the Turks during the War," in Middle East Centre, *St. Anthony's College Archive*, Scrivener: GB 165-0257 (1925b); Department of Ways and Works, "Lines Built, Rebuilt or Converted by the British," in Middle East Centre," *St. Anthony's College Archive*, Scrivener: GB 165-0257 (1925c).

41. Regarding Lydda/Lod see Haim Yacobi, "The Architecture of Ethnic Logic:

Exploring the Meaning of the Built Environment in the 'Mixed' City of Lod—Israel," *Geographic Annual* 84B (3–4) (2002): 171–187.

42. Kirby, "Palestine Railways."

43. Zipper, "Palestine Railways."

44. Klein and Safir, "To Mr. Rokach," Tel Aviv Municipal Archives, File 4, folder 300a, 25.6.39.

45. The implemented plan is a hybrid of two different solutions by the architects Vitcover, Zelkind, and Luria.

46. The delays arose from the complexities of dealing with the British demand for a construction permit and approval of special funding from the regime; the private bus cooperative to be managed by the local council, and the architects who were not members of the city's engineering department. The Mayor, "The Central Bus Station," Tel Aviv Municipal Archives, file 4, folder 300a, 25.12.39; the City Engineer, "The Central Bus Station," Tel Aviv Municipal Archives, file 4, folder 300a, 8.3.40.

47. Petition to the Tel Aviv City Council, Tel Aviv Municipal Archives, file 4, folder 300a, 20.3.42.

48. "Construction after WWII," *Yediot Iryat Tel Aviv*, 10–12 (1948): 9–10. Tel Aviv Municipal Archives.

49. E. Perelson, "Railway Connections—Lydda–Tel Aviv–Jaffa," 10.2.48, in Middle East Centre, *St. Anthony's College Archive*, Kirby: 1/3 Gb165-0172.

50. "Poor Habitats in Tel Aviv–Jaffa: How and When They Would Be Destroyed," *Yediot Iryat Tel Aviv* 1–2 (1954): 22–23, Tel Aviv Municipal Archives.

51. The areas close to the sea, with greater economic and tourist value, were given precedence.

52. "Toward a New Transportation Center in Tel Aviv–Jaffa," *Yediot Iryat Tel Aviv* 6–7 (1953): 46–47, Tel Aviv Municipal Archives; Central Bus Station Committee Chairman, "The Central Bus Station," Tel Aviv Municipal Archives, File 4, Folder 304b, 22.11.57; A. Rudich, "The Problem of the Central Bus Station," Tel Aviv Municipal Archives, File 4, Folder 304b, 7.5.57.

53. S. Sushani, "The Problem of the Central Bus Station," Tel Aviv Municipal Archives, File 4, Folder 304b, 14.6.56.

54. The Mayor's Office announcement to the press, Tel Aviv Municipal Archives, File 4, Folder 302a, 9.2.53.

55. The City Council examined the alternative of building a new station on municipal land, in the area of Arlozorov Street (where it stands today). The intention was to create a combined railway and bus station. This plan was partially implemented in the 1990s. Moshe Amiaz, "The Central Station (Arlozorov), a Planning Survey," Tel Aviv Municipal Archives, File 4 Folder 304b, 28.8.53.

56. Kolin Zehavi, "The Southern Bus Depot," Tel Aviv Municipal Archives, File 23-2-1960-8, 1960; Kolin Zehavi, "The Northern Bus Depot," Tel Aviv Municipal Archives, File 23-2-1960-3, 1960.

57. Moshe Amiaz, "The New Bus Station," Tel Aviv Municipal Archives, File 25, Folder 2738, 23.3.75.

58. Ibid.

59. On September 18, 1962, a meeting took place between the landowners and the Council regarding use of the land and expansion of the bus station. In 1963 negotiations continued. The landowners were represented by Piltz, though there is no record of their asking Piltz to negotiate with the Council. In 1964, architect Vitkover was asked to present a revised plan, which was approved in June 1964. State Comptroller's Office, "The Central Bus Station in Tel Aviv," Tel Aviv Municipal Archives, File 25, Folder 2736, 8.3.66.

60. Ibid.

61. H. Ramot, "The Central Bus Station in Tel Aviv," Tel Aviv Municipal Archives, File 25, Folder 2736, 28.3.66.

62. Ibid.

63. Kikar Levinski (Levinsky Square), "The New Central Bus Station—A City under One Roof," Tel Aviv Municipal Archives, file 13, folder 40, 1967.

64. Haim Pikrash, "The Central Bus Station Constructed of Metal and Concrete," Tel Aviv Municipal Archives, File 13, Folder 39, 1968.

65. Alison Smithson, *Team 10 Primer* (Cambridge: MIT Press, 1968).

66. Kenneth Frampton, *Modern Architecture: A Critical History* (New York: Oxford University Press, 1980), esp. p. 273.

67. A. Rotem, "Half a Million Passengers Pass through the Central Bus Station," Tel Aviv Municipal Archives, File 13, Folder 39, 1968.

68. Planning Department, "The Construction of the Central Bus Station in Tel Aviv," Tel Aviv Municipal Archives, File 25, Folder 2738, 20.7.76; The Planning Department, "The Construction of the Central Bus Station in Tel Aviv," Tel Aviv Municipal Archives, File 25, Folder 2738, 11.1.76; David Shifman, "The Construction of the Central Bus Station in Tel Aviv," Tel Aviv Municipal Archives, File 25, Folder 2739, 2.11.75.

69. During this process the council found out that it was deceived and instead of enlarging the transport area the company increased commerce areas. During the process of planning it was agreed to allow a commercial space 12,000–13,000 meters square. The city engineer argued that this would make the project viable to the developer and would better serve the passengers. The council wished to invite a survey on this subject but due to budget limitations avoided it. Moshe Amiaz, "The New Bus Station"; Yehoshua Disenchuk, "The Central Bus Station," Tel Aviv Municipal Archives, File 25, Folder 2738, 31.5.78.

70. Health Ministry, "Air Pollution, and Noise," Tel Aviv Municipal Archives, File 25, Folder 2738, 15.5.74; Health Ministry, "Air Pollution Deriving from the Central Bus Station in Tel Aviv," Tel Aviv Municipal Archives, File 25, Folder 2737, 20.3.73.

71. Transport Ministry, "Conclusions of the Committee Concerning Alternative Appraisal of the Central Bus Station," Tel Aviv Municipal Archives, File 25, Folder 2739, 7.12.82.

72. A. Bukshpan, "Report of Alternative Appraisal of the Central Bus Station," Tel Aviv Municipal Archives, File 25, Folder 2739, 31.10.82.

73. Adriana Kemp and Rivka Rychman, "Migrant Labor in Israel," *Adva Report on Inequality*, July 2003.

74. Tel Aviv Council, *Strategic Plan for the Station Area* (Tel Aviv Council, 2004).

75. Mark Abrahamson, *Urban Enclaves, Identity and Place in America* (New York: St. Martin's Press, 1996).

76. Tel Aviv Council, *City Profile*, p. 116.

77. Ibid., p. 118.

78. Ibid., p. 4.

79. Tel Aviv Council, *Strategic Plan for the Station Area*, p. 9-13.

80. Ibid.

81. Ibid.

82. Ibid., pp. 14-23.

83. The research includes an analysis of the population in the area (Israelis and immigrant labors), a literature review, and an analysis of requirements based on advisory groups and assessments.

84. See, for example, David Harvey, *The Limits to Capital* (London and New York: Verso, 2006); David Harvey, *A Brief History of Neoliberalism* (New York: Oxford University Press, 2005).

Marcuse and van Kempen (eds.), *Of States and Cities;* Peter Marcuse and Ronald van Kempen (eds.), *Globalizing Cities: A New Spatial Order?* (Oxford and Malden, Mass.: Blackwell, 2000).

85. Marisa Carmona and Rod Burgess, *Strategic Planning and Urban Projects: Responses to Globalization from Fifteen Cities* (Delft, Netherlands: DUP Science, Delft University Press, 2001).

86. For further discussion see Amir Ben Porat, *Where Are Those Bourgeois? The Story of Israeli Bourgeoisie* (in Hebrew); Tamar Gozansky, *Formation of Capitalism in Palestine* (in Hebrew).

87. Foreign labor migration in Israel is a recent phenomenon. As a self-defined Jewish nation-state, Israel encourages migration of Jewish people worldwide. Following the 1967 war Israel gradually recruited Palestinians from Gaza and the West Bank to work in Israel. By 1987 they composed 7 percent of the labor force. The outbreak of the Intifada affected the labor force significantly, because the State prevented the Palestinians' entry to Israel. In 1993 Israel began recruiting labor immigrants. See Rebecca Raijman, Silvina Schammah-Gesser, and Adriana Kemp, "International Migration, Domestic Work, and Care Work: Undocumented Latina Migrants in Israel," *Gender and Society* 17, no. 5. (October 2003): 727-749.

88. In Israel, migrant workers are either "legal," recruited in their home countries for short-term contracts and then returned home, or "illegal," workers who reach Israel on their own as "tourists." "Legal" workers are concentrated in three sectors: agricultural workers from Thailand; construction workers from Romania, Bulgaria, China, and other places; and caregivers for the elderly and disabled, mainly from the Philippines. "Illegal" workers are employed in a variety of sectors but most prominently in

domestic work—housekeeping, childcare, and in restaurants (West Africans, South Americans, Eastern Europeans, and others). See Adriana Kemp and Rebecca Raijman, *Foreign Workers* (Israel: Adva Center, 2003), Report No. 13.

89. On August 18, 2002, Prime Minister Ariel Sharon declared that the government had decided to set up an immigration administration to reduce the number of illegal workers in Israel. As part of this strategy, the country was divided into 5 regions, each with a responsible immigration unit (north, south, and center, Jerusalem, Tel-Aviv) to allocate and/or deport illegal workers. On July 27, 2003, the newly commissioned official implemented the self-evacuation project. http://www.hagira.gov.il/ ImmigrationCMS/Messages/r60.htm

90. Tel Aviv Council, *City Profile*, p. 116.

91. Analysis of population characteristics is only partial. It does not include the immigrant workers population.

92. Tel Aviv Council, *City Profile*, October 2002.

93. Menashe Hadad and Michael Fadida, "Socio-economic Gaps between Districts in Tel Aviv," in David Nachmias and Gila Menahem (eds.), *Social Processes and Public Policy in Tel Aviv-Jaffa*, Volume II (Ramot: Tel Aviv University, 1997), pp. 61–82.

94. Naomi Carmon, "Urban Regeneration: Three Generations of Policy in Tel-Aviv," in David Nachmias and Gila Menahem (eds.), *Social Processes and Public Policy in Tel Aviv-Jaffa*, Volume II (Ramot: Tel Aviv University, 1997), pp. 105–137; p. 115 (in Hebrew).

95. Gila Menahem, "Urban Restructuring, Polarisation and Immigrants' Opportunities: The Case of Russian Immigrants in Tel-Aviv," Urban Studies 36, no. 9 (1999): 1551–1568.

96. Ibid.

97. This area was originally a focus for immigrants from Asian republics who followed relations who had settled here in the 1970s; ibid., p. 184.

98. Adriana Kemp and Rivka Ryman, "Migrant Labor in Israel," *Adva Report on Inequality*, p. 3.

99. Adriana Kemp and Rivka Ryman, "Non-state Actors and the New Politics of Labor Migration in Israel," *Israeli Sociology* 3, no. 1 (2001): 79–127. In Hebrew.

100. Zion Hashinshoni, "Areas of Rehabilitation in Tel Aviv-Jaffa," Report no. 20, Tel Aviv Municipal Archives, 1996, file 22-1-1966-3, p. 5.

101. Alona Nitzan Shiftan, "The City in White," *Theory and Criticism* 16 (2000): 227–232.

102. Rotbard, *White City, Black City*, pp. 97–282.

103. Izhak Schnell and Yoav Benjamini, "African Socio-Spatial Segregation Patterns in Tel-Aviv," *Israeli Sociology* c/1 (2001): 111–132 (in Hebrew).

104. Tovi Fenster and Haim Yacobi, "Whose Right to the City? On Urban Planning and Local Knowledge in Globalizing Tel Aviv-Jaffa," *Planning Theory and Practice* 6, no. 2 (2005): 191–211.

105. Lefebvre, *Writings on Cities*, p. 294.

106. See, for example, E. P. Thompson, *The Making of the English Working Class* (New York: Vintage, 1963).

107. Raymond Williams, *Culture and Society 1780-1950* (London: Chatto and Windus, 1958).

108. De Certeau, *The Practice of the Everyday Life*, pp. 34-39.

109. Giddens, *Modernity and Self-Identity;* Giddens, *The Constitution of Society.*

110. See, for example, Edward Krupat, *People in Cities* (Cambridge: Cambridge University Press, 1985), pp. 48-66; Torsten Hagerstrand, "The Domain of Human Geography," in R. J. Chorley (ed.), *Directions in Geography* (London: Methuen, 1973), pp. 67-88.

111. Toni Bennett, *Culture: A Reformer's Science* (St. Leonards, NSW: Allen and Unwin, 1998).

112. Steven Harris and Deborah Berke (eds.), *Architecture of the Everyday* (New York: Princeton Architectural Press, 1997), pp. 1-8.

113. Ibid., p. 3.

114. Andrea Palladio, *The Four Books on Architecture* (1570), translated by Robert Tavernor and Richard Schofield (Cambridge, Mass.: MIT Press, 2002).

115. Ann Cline, *A Hut of One's Own: Life outside the Circle of Architecture* (Cambridge: MIT Press, 1997).

116. Karen Franck and Quentin Stevens (eds.), *Loose Space: Possibility and Diversity in Urban Life* (London and New York: Routledge, 2007), p. 4.

117. For a fuller discussion about the everyday and the utopian, see Peggy Deamer, "The Everyday and the Utopian," in S. Harris and D. Berke (eds.), *Architecture of the Everyday* (New York: Princeton Architectural Press, 1997), pp. 195-216.

118. Rachel Kallus, "The Political Role of the Everyday," *City* 8, no. 3 (2004): 341-361.

119. Ananya Roy, "Urban Informality: Toward an Epistemology of Planning," *Journal of the American Planning Association* 71, no. 2 (2005): 147-158.

120. Bishwapriya Sanyal, "Planning as Anticipation of Resistance," *Planning Theory* 4 (2005): 225-245.

121. See, for example, Peter Marcuse, *Ethics of the Planning Profession: The Need for Role Differentiation* (Los Angeles: School of Architecture and Urban Planning, University of California, 1974); Leonie Sandercock, *Making the Invisible Visible* (Berkeley: University of California Press, 1998); Young, *Justice and the Politics of Difference.*

122. Paul Davidoff, "Advocacy and Pluralism in Planning," *JAIP* 31, no. 4 (November 1965): 331-337.

123. See, for example, Patsy Healy, "The Communicative Turn in Planning Theory and Its Implications for Spatial Strategy Formation," *Environment and Planning B: Planning and Design* 23 (1996): 217-234.

124. See, for example, the "Arab village" discourse and the process of rehabilitation of focal Arab cities such as Jaffa, Acco, and Jerusalem. See also Gil Eyal, "Between East and West: Discourse about the Arab Village in Israel," *Theory and Criticism* 3 (1993): 39-55 (in Hebrew); LeVine, *Overthrowing Geography*, pp. 215-248.

125. De Certeau, *The Practice of Everyday Life*, pp. 29–42.

126. Ibid., 36–37.

127. Ibid., 37.

128. Kallus, "The Political Role of the Everyday."

129. James Holston, "Spaces of Insurgent Citizenship," in Sandercock, *Making the Invisible Visible*, pp. 155–173, p. 167.

130. This analysis is based on participant observation and interviews. The author is also a local resident.

131. This is not urban but citizenship marginalization. The location of the immigrant workers in central Tel Aviv, their access to transport and resources, and recognition by the City Council increase their social status in the city.

132. Request for "self evacuation," see http://www.hagira.gov.il/ImmigrationCMS/zchuyot/English.aspx.

133. Labour immigrants were excluded, in part because the committee was not unanimous regarding their presence.

134. Each committee member had already been involved in struggle prior to the committee's establishment. However, the group was not united in their approach. Some were in favor of transforming the synagogue into a soup kitchen and shelter for the homeless. Others disagreed.

135. In particular with the local authority and council member Meital Zehavi.

136. According to the Ministry of Welfare, marginalized populations are characterized as social deviants and criminals. http://www.molsa.gov.il/MisradHarevacha/

137. Tel Aviv Council, *Strategic Plan for the Station Area*, Tel Aviv Council, 2004.

138. Ibid., p. 28.

139. Although one essential aspect of nation-building has been the dismantling of the primacy of urban citizenship and replacing it with the national, cities are still strategic arenas for the development of citizenship. Holston and Appadurai, "Cities and Citizenship," p. 2.

CONCLUSION

1. For further discussion about the separation discourse see Yacobi and Cohen (eds.), *Separation*.

2. Harvey, *Spaces of Hope*, p. 58.

3. Although one essential project of nation-building has been to dismantle the historic primacy of urban citizenship and replace it with national primacy, cities are still strategic arenas for the development of citizenship. Holston and Appadurai, "Cities and Citizenship," p. 2.

4. The conventional distinction is between formal and substantive aspects of citizenship. The formal refers to membership in a nation-state, the substantive to the civil, political, socio-economic, and cultural rights people possess and exercise. However, increasingly, formal membership in the nation-state is neither a necessary nor a sufficient condition for substantive citizenship. Ibid., p. 4.

5. Slavoj Žižek, *The Ticklish Subject: The Absent Centre of Political Ontology* (London and New York: Verso, 1999), pp. 171–244.

6. LaCapra, *Writing History, Writing Trauma*, p. 60.

7. The inflated global discourse on the memory of violent events and its use in ordering and stabilizing meanings is connected to the universal discourse about the Holocaust, what Andreas Huyssen calls a globalization paradox. The Holocaust has become emblematic of the failure of enlightenment. "It serves as a proof of Western civilization's failure to practice anamnesis, to reflect on its constitutive inability to live in peace with difference and otherness ... on the other hand, this totalizing dimension of Holocaust discourse so prevalent in much postmodern thought is accompanied by a dimension that particularizes and localizes. It is precisely the emergence of the Holocaust as a universal trophy that allows Holocaust memory to latch onto specific local situations that are historically distant and politically distinct from the original event" (p. 58). This global paradox is endemic to the Israeli situation, where the universal sovereignty of the memory of the Holocaust and the local Nakba, the Palestinians' version, exist simultaneously. Andreas Huyssen, *Present Pasts: Urban Palimpsests and the Politics of Memory* (Stanford, Calif.: Stanford University Press, 2003), p. 13.

8. See, for example, Judith E. Innes, "Information in Communicative Planning," *Journal of the American Planning Association* 64 (1998): 52–63; John Forester, *Planning in the Face of Power* (Berkeley: University of California Press, 1989); Patsy Healey, *Collaborative Planning: Shaping Places in Fragmented Societies* (London: Macmillan, 1997); Margo Huxley and Oren Yiftachel, "A New Paradigm of Old Mytopia? Unsettling the Communicative Turn in Planning Theory," *Journal of Planning Education and Research* 19, no. 4 (2000): 333–342.

9. Frederick Jameson, "The Politics of Utopia," *New Left Review* 25 (2004): 35–54.

10. John Friedman, "The Good City: In Defense of Utopian Thinking," *International Journal of Urban and Regional Research* 24, no. 2 (2000): 460–472.

11. Michel Foucault, *Power/Knowledge: Selected Interviews and Other Writings, 1972–1977* (New York: Pantheon Books, 1980); Stuart Hall, "The West and the Rest: Discourse and Power," in Stuart Hall and Bram Gieben (eds.), *Formations of Modernity* (London: Polity Press, 1992, 1993), 275–320; Edward W. Said, *Orientalism* (New York: Vintage Books, 1994).

12. Bernard Tschumi, "The Architectural Paradox" (1975), in Michael Hays (ed.), *Oppositions*, pp. 224–227.

13. See, for example, Bimkom, an organization established in May 1999 by (Israeli) planners and architects with the goal of strengthening the connection between human rights and spatial planning in Israel. http://www.bimkom.org

14. For further reading see the work of Antonio Gramsci and the work of Hubert Law-Yone about the role of the intellectual in the context of architecture and planning. Antonio Gramsci, *Selections from the Prison Notebooks*, edited and translated by Quentin Hoare and Geoffrey Nowell-Smith (London: Lawrence and Wishart, 1971); Hubert Law-Yone, "Artur Glikson: The Intellectual and the State," *Journal of Architectural and Planning Research* 21, no. 2 (2004): 102–111.

Selected Bibliography

ARCHIVES

Palestine Exploration Fund
Public Record Office (UK National Archives)
St. Anthony's, Middle East Center Archives
Tel Aviv Municipal Archives
The Israel Defense Forces Archives
Zionist Archive Jerusalem

Abrahamson, Mark. *Urban Enclaves: Identity and Place in America*. New York: St. Martin's Press, 1996.
Agamben, Giorgio. *Homo Sacer: Sovereign Power and Bare Life*. Trans. Daniel Heller-Roazen. Stanford, Calif.: Stanford University Press, 1998.
Anderson, Benedict. *Imagined Communities: Reflections on the Origins and Spread of Nationalism*. London: Verso, 1983.
Appadurai, Arjun. *Modernity at Large: Cultural Dimensions of Globalization*. Minneapolis, Minn.: University of Minnesota Press, 1996.
Arendt, Hannah. *On Violence*. New York: Harcourt, Brace and World, 1970.
Azaryahu, Maoz. *Tel Aviv: Mythography of a City*. Syracuse, N.Y.: Syracuse University Press, 2007.
———. "Hateva heenik lanu et hayam—mitvee lehistorya tarbutit shel Tel Aviv 1918–1948 [Cultural Historical Outline of the Tel Aviv Seafront 1918–1948]." *Horizons in Geography* 51 (2001): 95–112.
———. "The Spontaneous Formation of Memorial Space." *Area* 28, no. 4 (1996): 501–513.
Azoulay, Ariella. *Death's Showcase*. Cambridge: MIT Press, 2001.
Basson, Steve. "'Oh Comrade, What Times Those Were!' History, Capital Punishment and the Urban Square." *Urban Studies* 7 (2006): 1147–1158.

Baum, Matthew. *Soft News Goes to War*. Princeton, N.J.: Princeton University Press, 2003.

Bauman, Richard. *Story, Performance, and Event*. Cambridge: Cambridge University Press, 1986.

Bauman, Zigmund. *Community: Seeking Safety in an Insecure World*. Oxford: Polity Press, 2001.

Benevelo, Leonardo. *The Origins of Modern Town Planning*. London: Routledge, 1967.

Bennett, Toni. *Culture: A Reformer's Science*. St. Leonards, NSW: Allen and Unwin, 1998.

Benski, Tova. "Breaching Events and the Emotional Reactions of the Public: Women in Black in Israel," in Helena Flam and Debra King (eds.), *Emotions and Social Movements*. New York: Routledge, 2005.

Bentham, Jeremy. *The Panopticon*. Introduction by Miran Božovič. London and New York: Verso, 1995.

Benvenisti, Meron. *City of Stone*. Berkeley: University of California Press, 1996.

Berger, Tamar. *Diyonisus ba-senter* [Dionysus at Dizengoff Center]. Tel Aviv: Hakibbutz HaMeuhad, 1998.

Bhabha, Homi K. *The Location of Culture*. London and New York: Routledge, 1994.

Bishara, Azmi. "Reflections on October 2000: A Landmark in Jewish-Arab Relations in Israel." *Journal of Palestine Studies* 30, no. 3 (2001): 54–67.

Bollens, Scott A. "City and Soul: Sarajevo, Johannesburg, Jerusalem, Nicosia." *City* 5, no. 2 (2001): 87–169.

Booth, Kim, and Tim Dunne. *Worlds in Collision: Terror and the Future of Global Order*. New York: Palgrave Macmillan, 2002.

Borden, Iain, and David Dunster. *Architecture and the Sites of History: Interpretations of Buildings and Cities*. Oxford: Butterworth Architecture, 1995.

Bozdogan, Sibel. *Modernism and Nation Building: Turkish Architectural Culture in the Early Republic*. Seattle: Washington University Press, 2001.

Broadbent, George. *Emerging Concepts in Urban Space Design*. London: Van Nostrand Reinhold, 1990.

Buder, Stanley. *Visionaries and Planners: The Garden City Movement and the Modern Community*. New York: Oxford University Press, 1990, pp. 133–156.

Bufacchi, Vittorio. "Violence." In Iain McLean and Alistair McMillan (eds.), *The Concise Oxford Dictionary of Politics*. Oxford: Oxford University Press, 2003.

Butler, Judith. *Precarious Life: The Power of Mourning and Violence*. London and New York: Verso, 2004.

Calhoun, Craig, Paul Price, and Ashley Timmer (eds.). *Understanding September 11*. New York: New Press, 2002.

Carmon, Naomi. "Urban Regeneration: Three Generations of Policy in Tel-Aviv." In David Nachmias and Gila Menahem (eds.), *Mehkere Tel-Aviv-Yafo: tahalikhim hevratiyim u-mediniyut tsiburit [Social Processes and Public Policy in Tel Aviv-Jaffa]*, Volume II. Ramot: Tel Aviv University Press, 1997, pp. 105–137.

Carmona, Marisa, and Rod Burgess. *Strategic Planning and Urban Projects: Responses to Globalization from Fifteen Cities.* Delft, Netherlands: DUP Science, Delft University Press, 2001.

Carruth, Cathy. *Unclaimed Experience: Trauma, Narrative and History.* Baltimore: Johns Hopkins University Press, 1996.

Celik, Zeynep. *Urban Forms and Colonial Confrontations: Algiers under French Rule.* Berkeley: University of California Press, 1997.

Benevelo, Leonardo. *The Origins of Modern Town Planning.* London: Routledge, 1967.

Coleman, Alice. *Utopia on Trial: Vision and Reality in Planned Housing.* London: H. Shipman, 1990.

Coleman, Roy. *Reclaiming the Streets: Surveillance, Social Control and the City.* Cullompton, Devon: Willan, 2004.

Colquhoun, Allan. "Twentieth-Century Concepts of Urban Space." In Allan Colquhoun (ed.), *Modernity and Classical Tradition: Architectural Essays 1980–1987.* Cambridge: MIT Press, 1991.

Cowely, John, et al. (eds.). *Community or Class Struggle?* London: Stage 1, 1977.

Davidoff, Paul. "Advocacy and Pluralism in Planning." *JAIP* 31, no. 4 (November 1965): 331–337.

Davis, Mike. *Ecology of Fear: Los Angeles and the Imagination of Disaster.* New York: Metropolitan Books, 1998.

Deamer, Peggy. "The Everyday and the Utopian." In S. Harris and D. Berke (eds.), *Architecture of the Everyday.* New York: Princeton Architectural Press, 1997.

De Certeau, Michel. *The Practice of the Everyday Life.* Berkeley: University of California Press, 1984.

Dekel, Irit. *Muvla'at hareut, nitua'ach tarbuti shel 'mifgashei mishmarot hashalom ve-Hademocratya 4.11.95' be-kikar Rabin* [The Enclave of Collectivity: Cultural Analysis of the Peace and Democracy Guardians, November 4, 1995, in Rabin Square]. Tel Aviv: Tel Aviv University Press, 2000.

Deleuze, Gilles, and Felix Guattari. *A Thousand Plateaux: Capitalism and Schizophrenia.* Minneapolis: University of Minnesota Press, 1988, pp. 469–471.

de Ste. Croix, G. E. M. *The Origins of the Peloponnesian War.* London: Duckworth, 1972.

Deutsche, Rosalyn. *Evictions: Art and Spatial Politics.* Cambridge: MIT Press, 1998.

Dobbin, Frank (ed.). *The New Economic Sociology: A Reader.* Princeton, N.J.: Princeton University Press, 2004.

Dotan, Eyal. "An End to the Trauma: Sterilization and Obliteration in Memory Representation." *Te'oryah u-vikoret* [Theory and Criticism] 17 (2000): 27–34.

Durkheim, Emile. *Elementary Forms of Religious Life.* New York: Free Press, 1965.

Dyer, Richard. *The Matter of Images: Essays on Representation.* London: Routledge, 1993.

Edkins, Jenny. *Trauma and the Memory of Politics.* Cambridge: Cambridge University Press, 2003.

Eide, Kjell. "Note on Galtung's Concept of 'Violence.'" *Journal of Peace Research* 8, no. 1 (1971): 71.

Engler, Mira. "A Living Memorial: Commemorating Yitzhak Rabin in the Tel Aviv Square." *Places* 12, no. 2 (1999): 4–11.

Eyal, Gil. "Between East and West: Discourse about the Arab Village in Israel." *Te'oryah u-vikoret* [Theory and Criticism] 3 (1993): 39–55.

Fanon, Frantz. *The Wretched of the Earth* (commentary by Jean-Paul Sartre and Homi K. Bhabha). New York: Grove Press, 2004.

Featherstone, Mike, Scott Lash, and Ronald Robertson (eds.). *Global Modernities.* London and Newbury Park: Sage, 1995.

Feige, Michel. "Yitzhak Rabin: His Perpetuation and the Perpetuation of His Perpetuation." In Lev Grinberg (ed.), *Zikaron be-mahaloket: mitos, le'umiyut ve-demokratyah: Iiyunim be-ikvot retsah Rabin* [Contested Memory—Myth, Nation and Democracy: Thoughts after Rabin's Assassination]. Beer-Sheva: Humphrey Institute for Social Research, 2000, pp. 39–64.

Fenster, Tovi, and Haim Yacobi. "Whose Right to the City? On Urban Planning and Local Knowledge in Globalizing Tel Aviv-Jaffa." *Planning Theory and Practice* 6, no. 2 (2005): 191–211.

Fincher, Ruth, and Jane M. Jacobs (eds.). *Cities of Difference.* New York: Guilford Press, 1998.

Forester, John. *Planning in the Face of Power.* Berkeley: University of California Press, 1989.

Foucault, Michel. *"Society Must Be Defended": Lectures at the Collège de France, 1975–1976,* edited by Mauro Bertani and Alessandro Fontana. New York: Picador, 2003.

———. "Of Other Spaces." *Diacritics* 16 (Spring 1986): 22–27.

———. *Power/Knowledge: Selected Interviews and Other Writings, 1972–1977.* New York: Pantheon Books, 1980.

———. *The Order of Things: An Archaeology of the Human Sciences.* New York: Pantheon Books, 1970.

Frances, Kuo E., and William C. Sullivan. "Aggression and Violence in the Inner City: Effects of Environment via Mental Fatigue." *Environment and Behavior 7,* vol. 33 (2001): 543–571.

Frampton, Kenneth. "Prospects for a Critical Regionalism." In *Prospecta: Yale Architectural Journal* 20 (1983): 147–162.

———. *Modern Architecture: A Critical History.* New York: Oxford University Press, 1980.

Franck, Karen, and Quentin Stevens (eds.). *Loose Space: Possibility and Diversity in Urban Life.* London and New York: Routledge, 2007.

Freud, Sigmund. "Mourning and Melancholia." *The Standard Edition of the Complete Psychological Works of Sigmund Freud.* London: Hogarth Press, 1957, pp. 243–58.

Friedmann, John. "City of Fear or Open City?" *Journal of the American Planning Association* 68 (2002): 237–243.

Friedmann, John. "The Good City: In Defense of Utopian Thinking." *International Journal of Urban and Regional Research* 24, no. 2 (2000): 460–472.

Galtung, Johan. "Violence, Peace, and Peace Research." *Journal of Peace Research* 6, no. 3 (1969): 167–191.

———. "A Structural Theory of Aggression." *Journal of Peace Research* 1, no. 2 (1964): 95–119.

Garfinkel, Harold. *Studies in Ethnomethodology.* Englewood, N.J.: Prentice Hall, 1967.

Gehl, Jan. *Life between Buildings.* Berkshire: Van Nostrand Reinhold, 1987.

Gellner, Ernest. *Nations and Nationalism.* Ithaca, N.Y.: Cornell University Press, 1983.

Giddens, Anthony. *Modernity and Self-Identity.* Cambridge: Cambridge University Press, 1991.

———. *The Consequences of Modernity.* Stanford, Calif.: Stanford University Press, 1990.

———. *The Nation-State and Violence.* Berkeley: University of California Press, 1985.

Giles, Wenona, and Jennifer Hyndman (eds.). *Sites of Violence: Gender and Conflict Zones.* Berkeley: University of California Press, 2004.

Gillmor, Dan. *We the Media: Grassroots Journalism by the People, for the People.* Sebastopol, Calif.: O'Reilly, 2004.

Gilroy, Paul. *There Ain't No Black in the Union Jack.* London: Unwin, 1987.

Golan, Arnon. "The Demarcation of the Tel Aviv–Jaffa Municipal Boundaries following the 1948 War: Political Conflicts and Spatial Outcome." *Planning Perspectives* 10, no. 4 (1995): 383–398.

Gozansky, Tamar. *Hitpathut ha-capitalizm be-Palestinah* [Formation of Capitalism in Palestine]. Haifa: Haifa University Press, 1986.

Graham, Stephen. *Cities, War, and Terrorism: Towards an Urban Geopolitics.* Cambridge, Mass.: Blackwell, 2004.

Gramsci, Antonio. *Selections from the Prison Notebooks.* Edited and translated by Quentin Hoare and Geoffrey Nowell-Smith. London: Lawrence and Wishart, 1971.

Grinberg, Lev. *Shalom medumyan, śiah milhamah: keshel ha-manhigut, ha-politikah veha-demokratyah be-Yiśra'el 1992–2006* [Imagined Peace, Discourse of War: The Failure of Leadership, Politics and Democracy in Israel 1992–2006]. Tel Aviv: Resling, 2007.

Hadad, Menashe, and Michael Fadida. "Socio-economic Gaps between Districts in Tel Aviv." In David Nachmias and Gila Menahem (eds.), *Mehkere Tel-Aviv-Yafo: tahalikhim hevratiyim u-mediniyut tsiburit* [Social Processes and Public Policy in Tel Aviv-Jaffa], Volume II. Ramot: Tel Aviv University Press, 1997, pp. 61–82.

Hagerstrand, Torsten. "The Domain of Human Geography." In R. J. Chorley (ed.), *Directions in Geography.* London: Methuen, 1973.

Hall, Peter. *Cities Tomorrow: A Peaceful Path to Real Reform.* Later published as *Garden Cities of Tomorrow.* Oxford: Blackwell, 2002, pp. 87–141.

Hall, Stuart. "The West and the Rest: Discourse and Power." In Stuart Hall and Bram Gieben (eds.), *Formations of Modernity*. London: Polity Press, 1992, 1993, pp. 275–320.

Handelman, Don. *Models and Mirrors: Towards an Anthropology of Public Events*. Cambridge: Cambridge University Press, 1990.

Harris, Steven, and Deborah Berke (eds.). *Architecture of the Everyday*. New York: Princeton Architectural Press, 1997.

Harrison, Jo Ann. "School Ceremonies for Yitzhak Rabin." *Israel Studies* 6 (2002): 113–134.

Harvey, David. *The Limits to Capital*. London and New York: Verso, 2006.

———. *A Brief History of Neoliberalism*. New York: Oxford University Press, 2005.

———. *Spaces of Hope*. California: University of California Press, 2000.

———. *The Condition of Postmodernity*. Oxford: Blackwell, 1989.

———. *The Urbanization of Capital*. Oxford: Blackwell, 1985.

———. *Social Justice and the City*. London: Edward Arnold, 1973.

Hatuka, Tali, and Leslie Forsyth. "Urban Design in the Context of Glocalization and Nationalism: Rothschild Boulevard, Tel Aviv." *Urban Design International* 10, vol. 2 (June 2005): 69–86.

Hayden, Dolores. *The Power of a Place: Urban Landscapes as Public History*. Cambridge: MIT Press, 1997.

Healey, Patsy. *Collaborative Planning: Shaping Places in Fragmented Societies*. London: Macmillan, 1997.

———. "The Communicative Turn in Planning Theory and Its Implications for Spatial Strategy Formation." *Environment and Planning B: Planning and Design* 23 (1996): 217–234.

Hellman, Sarah, and Tamar Rapport. "The Women in Black and the Challenge to the Social Order." *Theory and Criticism* 10 (1997): 175–192 (in Hebrew).

Hobsbawm, Eric. "Introduction: Inventing Traditions." In Eric Hobsbawm and Terence Ranger (eds.), *The Invention of Tradition*. Cambridge: Cambridge University Press, 1983.

Holston, James. "Spaces of Insurgent Citizenship." In Leonie Sandercock, *Making the Invisible Visible*. Berkeley: University of California Press, 1998. pp. 155–173.

Holston, James, and Arjun Appadurai. "Cities and Citizenship." In James Holston (ed.), *Cities and Citizenship*. Durham: Duke University Press, 1999.

Home, Robert. *Of Planting and Planning: The Making of British Colonial Cities*. London: E. and F. N. Spon, 1997.

Hooks, Bell. *Black Looks: Race and Representation*. London: Turnaround, 1992.

Horowitz, Dan, and Moshe Lissak. *Metsukot ba-utopyah: Yiśra'el—hevrah be-omes yeter* [Trouble in Utopia: The Overburdened Polity of Israel]. Tel Aviv: Am Oved, 1990.

Huxley, Margo, and Oren Yiftachel. "A New Paradigm of Old Mytopia? Unsettling the Communicative Turn in Planning Theory." *Journal of Planning Education and Research* 19, no. 4 (2000): 333–342.

Huyssen, Andreas. *Present Pasts: Urban Palimpsests and the Politics of Memory.* Stanford, Calif.: Stanford University Press, 2003.

Innes, Judith E. "Information in Communicative Planning." *Journal of the American Planning Association* 64 (1998): 52–63.

Iyengar, Shanto. *Is Anyone Responsible? How Television Frames Political Issues.* Chicago: University of Chicago Press, 1991.

Jacobs, Jane M. *Edge of Empire: Post-Colonialism and the City.* London: Routledge, 1996.

Jameson, Frederick. "The Politics of Utopia." *New Left Review* 25 (2004): 35–54.

————. *Postmodernism: or, The Cultural Logic of Late Capitalism.* London: Verso, 1991.

Jasper, James M. *The Art of Moral Protest.* Chicago: University of Chicago Press, 1997.

Kaldor, Mary. *New and Old Wars: Organized Violence in a Global Era.* Stanford, Calif.: Stanford University Press, 1999.

Kallus, Rachel. "The Political Role of the Everyday." *City* 8, no. 3 (2004): 341–361.

————. "Patrick Geddes and the Evolution of Housing Types in Tel-Aviv." *Planning Perspectives* 12, no. 3 (1997): 281–320.

Kallus, Rachel, and Hubert Law-Yone. "National Home/Personal Home: Public Housing and the Shaping of National Space." *European Planning Studies* 10, no. 6 (2002): 765–779.

Kalyvas, Stathis N. *The Logic of Violence in Civil War.* Cambridge: Cambridge University Press, 2006.

Kemp, Adriana, and Rebecca Raijman. *"Ovdim zarim" be-Yiśra'el [Foreign Workers in Israel].* Israel: Adva Center, 2003, Report No. 13.

Kemp, Adriana, and Rivka Ryman. "Non-state Actors and the New Politics of Labor Migration in Israel." *Sotsyologyah Yiśre'elit* [Israeli Sociology] 3, no. 1 (2001): 79–127.

King, Anthony. *Colonial Urban Development: Culture, Social Power and Environment.* London: Routledge, 1976.

Krier, Rob. *Urban Space.* New York: Rizzoli, 1979.

Krupat, Edward. *People in Cities.* Cambridge: Cambridge University Press, 1985.

Kultermann, Udo. *Kenzo Tange: Architecture and Urban Design, 1946–1969.* London: Pall Mall Press, 1970.

LaCapra, Dominique. *Writing History, Writing Trauma.* Baltimore: Johns Hopkins University Press, 2001.

Lash, Scott, and John Urry. *The End of Organized Capitalism.* Madison, Wis.: University of Wisconsin Press, 1987.

Law-Yone, Hubert. "Artur Glikson: The Intellectual and the State." *Journal of Architectural and Planning Research* 21, no. 2 (2004): 102–111.

Leach, Neil. *The Anaesthetics of Architecture.* Cambridge: MIT Press, 1999.

Lefebvre, Henri. "The Inventory (from *La Somme et Le Reste,* 1959)." In S. Elden,

E. Lebas, and E. Kofman (eds.), *Henri Lefebvre: Key Writings*. New York and London: Continuum, 2003, pp. 166–177.

———. *The Production of Space*. Oxford, U.K.: Blackwell, 1991.

———. *Everyday Life in the Modern World*. London: Transaction Publishers, 1984.

Lequeux, Emmanuelle. "Reinventer: les Formes de la Cite." *Beaux Arts Magazine* 260 (February 2006): 76–83.

LeVine, Mark. *Overthrowing Geography: Jaffa, Tel Aviv, and the Struggle for Palestine, 1880–1948*. Berkeley: University of California Press, 2005.

Luz, Nimrod. *Kehilat Yafo haaravit ve-misgad haasan beq: gibush zehut kollektivit, ha'atsama a'tsmit ve-hitangdut* [The Arab Community of Jaffa and the Hassan Bey Mosque: Collective Identity and Empowerment of the Arabs in Israel via Holy Places]. Jerusalem: Floersheimer Institute, 2005.

Lynch, Kevin. *The Image of the City*. Cambridge: MIT Press, 1960.

Lyon, David. *Theorizing Surveillance: The Panopticon and Beyond*. Cullompton, Devon: Willan, 2006.

Makdisi, Usama, and Paul A. Silverstein. *Memory and Violence in the Middle East and North Africa*. Bloomington: Indiana University Press, 2006.

Mann, Barbara E. *A Place in History: Modernism, Tel Aviv, and the Creation of Jewish Urban Space*. Stanford, Calif.: Stanford University Press, 2006.

Marcuse, Peter. *Ethics of the Planning Profession: The Need for Role Differentiation*. Los Angeles: School of Architecture and Urban Planning, University of California, 1974.

Marcuse, Peter, and Ronald van Kempen (eds.). *Of States and Cities: The Partitioning of Urban Space*. Oxford and New York: Oxford University Press, 2002.

———. *Globalizing Cities: A New Spatial Order?* Oxford and Malden, Mass.: Blackwell, 2000.

Massey, Doreen. *For Space*. London: Sage, 2005.

May, Jon, and Nigel Thrift (eds.). *TimeSpace: Geographies of Temporality*. New York: Routledge, 2001.

Mbembe, Achille. "Necropolitics." *Public Culture* 15, no. 1 (Winter 2003): 11–40.

———. *On the Postcolony*. Berkeley: University of California Press, 2001.

Menahem, Gila. "Urban Restructuring, Polarisation and Immigrants' Opportunities: The Case of Russian Immigrants in Tel-Aviv." *Urban Studies* 36, no. 9 (1999): 1551–1568.

Moore, Sally, and Barbara Myerhoff. *Secular Ritual*. Assen: Van Gorcum, 1977.

Nesbitt, Kate. *Theorizing a New Agenda for Architecture: An Anthology of Architectural Theory, 1965–1995*. New York: Princeton Architectural Press, 1996.

Newman, Oscar. *Defensible Space: Crime Prevention through Urban Design*. New York: Collier Books, 1973.

Nitzan Shiftan, Alona. "The City in White." *Te'oryah u-vikoret* [Theory and Criticism] 16 (2000): 227–232.

Norberg-Schulz, Christopher. *Genius Loci: Towards a Phenomenology of Architecture*. New York: Rizzoli, 1980.

Norris, Pippa, Montague Kern, and Marion Just (eds.). *Framing Terrorism: The News Media, the Government, and the Public.* New York: Routledge, 2003.

Or, Theodore. "The Report by the State Commission of Inquiry into the Events of October 2000." *Israel Studies* 11, no. 2 (2006): 25–53.

Palladio, Andrea. *The Four Books on Architecture* (1570), translated by Robert Tavernor and Richard Schofield. Cambridge, Mass.: MIT Press, 2002.

Pandey, Gyanendra. *Routine Violence.* Stanford, Calif.: Stanford University Press, 2006.

Parent, Claude. "Claude Parent: La citta ribelle/Claude Parent: The Rebel City." *Domus* 887 (November 2005): 68–71.

Peled, Yoav, and Adi Ophir (eds.). *Yiśra'el, me-Hevrah Meguyeset le-Hevrah Ezrahit?* [Israel: From Mobilized to Civil Society?]. Tel Aviv and Jerusalem: Van Leer Institute and Hakibbutz Hameuchad, 2001.

Porat, Amir Ben. *Hekhan hem ha-burganim ha-hem?: Toldot Ha-Burganut Ha-Yiśre'elit* [Where Are Those Bourgeois? The Story of Israeli Bourgeoisie]. Jerusalem: Magnes, 1999.

Portugali, Yuval. *Implicit Relations: Society and Space in the Israeli-Palestinian Conflict.* Dordrecht and Boston: Kluwer Academic, 1993.

Poyner, Barry. *Design against Crime: Beyond Defensible Space.* London and Boston: Butterworths, 1983.

Radden, Jennifer. *The Nature of Melancholy: From Aristotle to Kristeva.* New York: Oxford University Press, 2000.

Raijman, Rebecca, Silvina Schammah-Gesser, and Adriana Kemp. "International Migration, Domestic Work, and Care Work: Undocumented Latina Migrants in Israel." *Gender and Society* 17, no. 5. (October 2003): 727–749.

Ram, Uri. *The Globalization of Israel: McWorld in Tel Aviv, Jihad in Jerusalem.* New York: Routledge, 2008.

Refuerzo, Ben J., and Stephen Verderber. "Effects of Personal Status and Patterns of Use on Residential Satisfaction in Shelters for Victims of Domestic Violence." *Environment and Behavior* 7, vol. 21 (1989): 413–434.

Riches, David (ed.). *The Anthropology of Violence.* Oxford, UK, and New York: Blackwell, 1986.

Rossi, Aldo. *Architecture in the City.* Cambridge: MIT Press, 1982.

Rotbard, Sharon. *Avrahan Yaski: adrikhalut concretit* [Avraham Yaski: Concrete Architecture]. Tel Aviv: Babel, 2007.

———. *Ir levanah, Ir shehorah* [White City, Black City]. Tel Aviv: Babel, 2005.

Roy, Ananya. "Urban Informality: Toward an Epistemology of Planning." *Journal of the American Planning Association* 71, no. 2 (2005): 147–158.

Said, Edward W. *Orientalism.* New York: Vintage Books, 1994.

———. *Covering Islam.* London and New York: Routledge, 1981.

Sandercock, Leonie. *Making the Invisible Visible.* Berkeley: University of California Press, 1998.

Sanyal, Bishwapriya. "Planning as Anticipation of Resistance." *Planning Theory* 4 (2005): 225–245.

Sassen, Saskia. "Governance Hotspots: Challenges We Must Confront in the Post September 11th World." In Kim Booth and Tim Dunne (eds.), *Worlds in Collision: Terror and the Future of Global Order.* New York: Palgrave Macmillan, 2002.

———. *The Global City: New York, London, Tokyo.* Princeton: Princeton University Press, 1991.

Scarry, Elaine. *The Body in Pain: The Making and Unmaking of the World.* New York: Oxford University Press, 1985.

Schlör, Joachim. *Tel Aviv, from Dream to City.* London: Reatkin Books, 1999.

Schmidt, Bettina E., and Ingo W. Schröder (eds.). *Anthropology of Violence and Conflict.* London and New York: Routledge, 2001.

Schnell, Izhak, and Yoav Benjamini. "African Socio-Spatial Segregation Patterns in Tel-Aviv." *Sotsyologyah Yiśre'elit* [Israeli Sociology], c/1 (2001): 111–132.

Segal, Rafi, and Eyal Weizman. *A Civilian Occupation: The Politics of Israeli Architecture.* London and New York: Verso; Tel Aviv: Babel, 2003.

Segev, Tom. *One Palestine Complete: Jews and Arabs under the British Mandate.* U.K.: Little, Brown and Company, 1999.

Sen, Amartya. *Identity and Violence: The Illusion of Destiny.* New York: W. W. Norton and Co., 2006.

Sennett, Richard. *The Spaces of Democracy.* New York: University of Michigan College of Ann Arbor, 1998.

Shavit, Yacob, and Gideon Biger. *ha-Historyah shel Tel-Aviv* [History of Tel Aviv (1909–1939)]. Ramot: Tel Aviv University Press, 2001.

Sibley, David. *Geographies of Exclusion: Society and Difference in the West.* London: Routledge, 1995.

Smithson, Alison. *Team 10 Primer.* Cambridge: MIT Press, 1968.

Sternhell, Zeev. *Binyan umah o tikun hevrah?* [Nation Building or a New State]. Tel Aviv: Am Oved, 1995.

Tel Aviv Council. *Profil ha-ʿir: October 2002* [The City Profile: October 2002]. Tel Aviv: Tel Aviv Council Publications, 2002.

Thompson, E. P. *The Making of the English Working Class.* New York: Vintage, 1963.

Thrift, Nigel. "Immaculate Warfare? The Spatial Politics of Extreme Violence." In Derek Gregory and Allan Pred (eds.), *Violent Geographies: Fear, Terror, and Political Violence.* New York: Routledge, 2007, pp. 273–294.

Tilly, Charles. *Regimes and Repertoires.* Chicago: University of Chicago Press, 2006.

———. *The Politics of Collective Violence.* New York: Cambridge University Press, 2003.

Torre, Susan. "Claiming the Public Space: The Mothers of Plaza de Mayo." In Jane Rendell, Barbara Penner, and Iain Borden, eds., *Gender, Space, Architecture.* London: Routledge, 2000, pp. 140–145.

Tschumi, Bernard. "The Architectural Paradox" (1975). In K. Michael Hayes (ed.),

Oppositions Reader: Selected Readings from a Journal for Ideas and Criticism in Architecture, 1973–1984. New York: Princeton Architectural Press, 1998, pp. 224–227.

Turner, Victor W. *The Anthropology of Performance.* New York: PAJ Publications, 1985.

———. *The Forest of Symbols.* New York: Cornell University Press, 1967.

Tzonis, Alexander, and Phoebe Giannisi. *Classical Greek Architecture.* Paris: Flammarion, 2004.

Tzonis, Alex, and Leonie Lefebvre. "The Grid and the Pathway," *Architecture in Greece* 15 (1981): 164–178.

Vale, Lawrence J. *Architecture, Power and National Identity.* New Haven: Yale University Press, 1992.

Vidler, Anthony. "The Third Typology." In *Rational Architecture: The Reconstruction of the European City.* Bruxelles: Archives d'Architecture Moderne, 1978.

Vinizki-Sarusi, Vered. "Between Jerusalem and Tel Aviv: The Perpetuation of Rabin and National Identity Discourse in Israel." In Lev Grinberg (ed.), *Zikaron be-mahaloket: mitos, le'umiyut ve-demokratyah: Iiyunim be-ikvot retsah Rabin* [Contested Memory—Myth, Nation and Democracy: Thoughts after Rabin's Assassination]. Beer-Sheva: Humphrey Institute for Social Research, 2000, pp. 19–38.

Virilio, Paul. *Speed and Politics.* Cambridge: MIT Press, 2007.

Weber, Max. "The Profession and Vocation of Politics." In *Weber: Political Writings*, edited by Peter Lassman and Ronald Speirs. Cambridge: Cambridge University Press, 1994.

———. *The Sociology of Religion.* New York: Beacon Press, 1963.

Wigley, Mark. "Editorial." *Assemblage* 20 (Violence, Space), (1993): 6–7.

Williams, Raymond. *Culture and Society 1780–1950.* London: Chatto and Windus, 1958.

Wolch, Jennifer, and Michael Dear. *Landscapes of Despair.* Cambridge: Polity Press, 1987.

Yacobi, Haim. "Between Surveillance and Spatial Protest: Production of Space in the Mixed City of Lod." *Surveillance and Society* 2, no. 1 (2003): 55–77.

———. "The Architecture of Ethnic Logic: Exploring the Meaning of the Built Environment in the 'Mixed' City of Lod—Israel." *Geographic Annual* 84B (3–4) (2002): 171–187.

Yacobi, Haim, and Shelly Cohen (eds.). *Hafradah: ha-politikah shel ha-merhav be-Yisra'el* [Separation: The Politics of Space in Israel]. Tel Aviv: Xargol and Am Oved Publishers, 2006.

Yatziv, Gadi. *Ha-hevrah ha-sektoryalit* [The Sectorial Society]. Jerusalem: Bialik Institute, 1999.

Yiftachel, Oren. "Planning and Social Control: Exploring the Dark Side." *Journal of Planning Literature* 12, no. 4 (1998): 395–406.

Yona, Yossi. "Israel after Rabin's Assassination: Jewish State or All Citizens' State?" In Lev Grinberg (ed.), *Zikaron be-mahaloket: mitos, le'umiyut ve-demokratyah: Iiyunim be-ikvot retsah Rabin* [Contested Memory—Myth, Nation and Democracy: Thoughts after Rabin's Assassination]. Beer-Sheva: Humphrey Institute for Social Research, 2000, pp. 109–122.

Young, Iris Marion. *Global Challenges: War, Self Determination and Responsibility for Justice*. Cambridge, UK, and Malden, Mass.: Polity, 2007.

———. *Justice and the Politics of Difference*. Princeton: Princeton University Press, 1990.

Žižek, Slavoj. *Welcome to the Desert of the Real! Five Essays on September 11 and Related Dates*. London and New York: Verso, 2002.

———. *The Ticklish Subject: The Absent Centre of Political Ontology*. London and New York: Verso, 1999.

Zukin, Sharon. *The Cultures of Cities*. Cambridge, Mass.: Blackwell, 1996.

———. *Landscape of Power: From Detroit to Disneyworld*. Berkeley: University of California Press, 1991.

Index

Note: Numbers in italics refer to illustrations; the letter *t* following a page number denotes a table.

Milton Keynes UK
Ingram Content Group UK Ltd.
UKHW011948090524
442389UK00012B/143